A PEOPLE'S HISTORY OF ENVIRONMENTALISM IN THE UNITED STATES

A People's History of Environmentalism in the United States

Chad Montrie

continuum

Continuum International Publishing Group

The Tower Building, 11 York Road, London SE1 7NX

80 Maiden Lane, Suite 704, New York, NY 10038

www.continuumbooks.com

First published 2011

British Library Cataloguing-in-Publication Data
A catalogue record for this book is available from the British Library.

ISBN   HB: 978-1-4411-1672-7
       PB: 978-1-4411-9868-6

Typeset by Newgen Imaging Systems Pvt Ltd, Chennai, India
Printed and bound in India

For John Cumbler

Contents

Preface

This book is meant to offer a fresh look at the history of environmentalism in the United States, exploring the movement's origins and development with an emphasis on the experience and contributions of working people and their families. In that manner, *A People's History of Environmentalism* challenges the traditional, prevailing version of events, which tends to focus on the thoughts and deeds of a few elite individuals and—like looking through the wrong end of a telescope—unwittingly narrows our perspective and leads us to errors of interpretation. By examining environmental activism's ripening with the mass of common people in mind, doing history "from the bottom up," a different and arguably more accurate rendering of the past emerges, one that not only incorporates a full range of historical actors but also addresses certain fault lines in how we tell their story.

While the new account is something that will interest professional historians and other academics, the primary audience for *A People's History* is students in undergraduate and graduate courses as well as environmentalists. Toward this end, the book relies on selected parts of primary sources, supplemented by insights from the existing secondary literature, to make various observations about key moments in time. The point is to be readable and accessible rather than dense and exhaustive, tracing the contours of a coherent revisionist narrative that will be filled in during decades to come. A number of other historians have already begun to examine long-neglected aspects of Americans' relationship with nature, however, writing detailed studies on specific topics that allow me to make particular generalizations. Readers interested in this work should refer to the Bibliographic Essay following the Conclusion.

Chad Montrie
Lowell, Massachusetts

Acknowledgments

Because it's taken me so long to actually write this book, I've accumulated more than the usual debts and reasons for gratitude. Most importantly, *A People's History of Environmentalism in the United States* would not have been possible without the mentoring hand of John Cumbler. He has been a role model for me as a scholar and activist, and our countless hours of conversation over the years have been full of invaluable, critical guidance.

At the University of Massachusetts Lowell various people have gone to great lengths to aid my research and writing, including my department chair, Joseph Lipchitz, and the college dean, Nina Coppens. Also, Jannette Marquez and Alice DaSilva were all too ready with answers to questions about mind-warping forms and bureaucratic mazes. At the library, Rose Paton and Deborah Friedman oversaw my many odd Interlibrary Loan requests, and at the university's Center for Lowell History, Martha Mayo, Janet Pohl, and Janine Whitcomb assisted early archival work.

Lastly, there were many ordinary and extraordinary ways that various friends and family supported my engagement with the past. This time around Christoph Strobel, Sheila Kirschbaum, Maryann Zujewski, and Sandra Garcia Mangado, in particular, each had a large part in helping me figure out what I wanted to say and how to say it. And, as always, my mother, stepfather, sisters, and daughter kept me grounded. I hope the printed pages to follow show at least some measure of what that meant.

Introduction: Shaking Up What, When, and Why

On a clear, sunny day in 1841, a young woman we know only as Ella took a break from her duties as a weaver in one of the many textile mills in Lowell, Massachusetts. Writing about the moment later, she explained how she gazed through a window at the "blue vault" of sky, feeling her heart flutter "like a prisoned bird," longing painfully "for an unchecked flight amidst the beautiful creation around me." Shut up in the "crowded, clattering mill," Ella studied "the still and lovely scenes" beyond, which "sent their pure and elevating influence with a thrilling sweep across the strings of the spirit-harp." Such woeful sentiments, she well knew, were quite common among the other thousands of Lowell operatives also desperately struggling with the transition to an urban industrial landscape, and they provoked various forms of individual coping and collective resistance.[1]

Sometimes the operatives sought escape from the mills in their limited free time, with a short walk to the city's outskirts, like another young woman who wrote under the pen name V.C.N. As she strolled along the Merrimack River, V.C.N. gazed "upon the glories and beauties of the waters, the woods, the fields, and the sweet, blue heavens that with tinseled clouds and gorgeous drapery, enclosed the scene" while pondering "the Creator of them all." A few went even farther, returning for a stretch of days, weeks, or even permanently to the pastoral homesteads where they had spent most of their early lives. "Friends," one J.R. consoled in a letter to those she left behind, "think not while surrounded by the green fields, feasting my mind with their beauties, that I do not cast a sympathizing thought to the many shut up in the mills, constantly toiling, without time to look upon the broad face of nature, and 'view the glorious handworks of the Creator.'"[2]

After migrating from farms scattered about New England's hills and valleys, mill hands like Ella, V.C.N., and J.R. experienced a change in the manner and setting of their work, and this had profound implications for their thinking about nature. Back home, labor varied, characterized by different tasks during a day or week or year, making direct use of the land and its resources, indoors as well as outdoors, often with opportunities for socializing with siblings, parents, and neighbors. "In the forenoon I did housework," recorded Tryphena Eli White in her diary on June 24, 1805, and while she was out "picking greens," a friend "hallo'd" to her "to come and help kill a rattlesnake."[3] In this and other writing done by farm-dwelling girls and women there was little of the flowery, "literary romantic" vocabulary or style that so heavily marked the stories, poems, and correspondence of industrial operatives later. That particular turn seems to have been a product of working within the confines of brick mills, at rows of machines, under close supervision, hour after hour, day after day. Suffering those conditions, the workers began to see nature as something else, something "out there," a place to flee from labor, where they could take needed leisure and where they could be provoked to philosophical musing about God, beauty, and time.

A century after the "mill girls" first went through the wrenching impact of migration and industrialization, men and women working in the new auto plants of the upper Midwest had a strikingly similar experience. Many moved from the countryside and exchanged self-directed farmwork for regimented labor at machines (by now the assembly line had been introduced). In response, some of the men took up hunting and fishing or resumed those familiar activities but on different terms. "Of course, your first thought is to be that of downing game," wrote Carl Hubert in the *The Bowhunter*, a journal associated with one of the numerous county-level, working-class sportsmen's clubs. "However, equally as important is the God-given opportunity to get away from teeming cities and the rush of everyday living and plant your feet on the good soil of a quiet backwoods trail."[4]

In fact, the new urban industrial environment affected all the members of autoworkers' families and provoked a reaction from them too. This is eloquently portrayed by Harriet Arnow Simpson in *The Dollmaker*, which follows members of the Nevel family from their Appalachian homestead to Detroit during World War II. At one point, Gertie, the strong and reliable mother, peers from her kitchen door at the "ugly-voiced and dirty" brown sparrows taking up space on the coal-shed roof, reminding her of two red birds she had seen once back home. "If she shut out the alley," Gertie considers, "she could smell cold creek water and cedar, the cedar smell strong and clean, like on a still, misty morning."[5]

Yet this new wave of folks who moved from country to city, from farm to factory, were not content simply to seek out a haven in the woods or a natural landscape in their imagination. Sportsmen's clubs were initially concerned with fish and game conservation, but it wasn't long before they began to tackle air and water pollution. They hosted speakers to learn more, lobbied legislators and governors, supported control legislation, and effectively put environmental issues on the public agenda by the 1940s. "Pollution was the top topic of discussion at the December [Michigan United Conservation Clubs] directors meeting in Detroit," reported *The Genesee Sportsmen* in 1949. "The directors heard Governor-elect G. Mennen Williams state that anti-pollution legislation is among 'first priority matters' of his legislative program."[6]

Autoworkers and their families also organized through their union, the United Auto Workers (UAW), which sent representatives to testify at hearings, mobilized voters, supported neighborhood groups, and aided in pickets at public meetings. This was all done toward the end of enhancing outdoor recreational opportunities, protecting area waterways, and improving air quality. The point, UAW president Walter Reuther insisted, was to work with local, state, and federal governments "to come to grips with the problems of neglect, with the problems of indifference which are destroying not only our natural resources but which are corrupting and corroding the very environmental atmosphere that we breath and live in each day of our lives."[7] The International and locals even established their own summer camps for autoworkers' children, which combined play in "nature" with civics lessons. Or, as the UAW recreational director Olga Madar put it, to "teach them how democracy works—in the down-to-earth way that living with others in the out-of-doors can provide."[8]

Some of my own extended family attended a UAW summer camp outside Toledo, Ohio, since my grandfather worked for Dana Auto Parts and belonged to Local 12. This was lore I had in my mind years ago, when I was writing another book, *Making a Living*, and did some research at the Walter P. Reuther Library of Labor and Urban Affairs, on Wayne State University's Detroit campus. There, I sifted through a vast array of union memos, letters, and reports, trying to piece together the connection between people's experience with industrial work and their relationship to nature. I was and probably still am the only historian to use the Reuther archives for that purpose, however, which speaks to reasons for fundamental flaws in the current, prevailing explanation for the origins and development of environmentalism.

According to the most widely held version of events-—among scholars, activists, and the engaged general public-—the U.S. environmental movement was a phenomenon brought into being by publication of Rachel Carson's *Silent Spring* in 1962. The book's impact, so the story goes, was largely due to improvements in economic well-being and increased leisure time experienced by people living in suburbs after World War II. This meant they could care more about quality of life and, as they witnessed events like a televised oil spill near Santa Barbara, California, many became members of mainstream environmental groups led by far-sighted people such as the Sierra Club's David Brower.

In the 1970s, following on the heels of the first Earth Day, a growing environmental constituency supported legislation establishing regulatory controls, pushed through Congress by certain dedicated members of the House and Senate. Those controls helped to lessen air and water pollution and to mitigate other adverse effects of the new consumer society. Then, during the late 1970s and the early 1980s, two groups of "radicals," one at Love Canal and the other in Warren County, North Carolina, also pioneered confrontational grassroots environmentalism. This started what we call the "environmental justice" movement, which began to address toxics and "environmental racism."[9]

This is, more or less, the narrative that you encounter everywhere. "Environmental values were based not on one's role as a producer of goods and services," argues the historian Samuel Hays in *Beauty, Health, and Permanence*, "but on consumption, the quality of home and leisure." Filling in the details, another historian, Ted Steinberg, explains in *Down to Earth* that "[Rachel] Carson's eloquent book combined with an extraordinary dry spell, a super-heated political climate, a series of made-for-TV ecological disasters, plus an arresting image of earth as seen from outer space all dramatized the elemental interdependence of life on the planet." These events helped reveal the ecological underpinnings of "modern consumer society," he notes, and that laid the groundwork for the environmental movement.[10]

Recently, in marking the fortieth anniversary of Earth Day, the *New York Times* also developed an online timeline highlighting the most significant environmental changes since World War II. First among major events was passage of the Bald and Golden Eagle Protection Act (1940), followed by deadly smog in Donora, Pennsylvania (1948), California's pioneering auto-emission standards (1960), publication of *Silent Spring* (1962), congressional action on air pollution and wilderness protection (1963 and 1964), the Santa Barbara oil spill (1969), and the first Earth Day (1970). With that watershed, according to the *Times*, there was more congressional action on environmental issues, besides growing concern with toxic waste after Niagara Falls (Love Canal) residents discovered toxic sludge leaking into their homes near the end of the decade.[11]

Still, the academic accounts, as well as numerous popular books, documentary films, internet web pages, and newspapers and magazines, are generally off the mark. They repeat a mythology not borne out by my own research at the Reuther archives and similar collections or by the latest research of several other environmental historians. Dipping into the stream of publications that draws on those efforts, it is possible to see a different interpretation taking shape, a revisionist account that acknowledges the critical role working people played in shaping the environmental movement. This new history challenges the traditional version of events in several respects, particularly in terms of when things happened, how they happened, and why they happened.

First, the revisionist account alters the standard "periodization," the approach historians take to dividing the past into meaningful chunks (which varies depending on the field). Part of what led folks to identify *Silent Spring* as the beginning of it all, and what keeps them repeating this claim over and over, is that it serves as an all-too-easy way to understand history. Carson's book is a good bookend. Marking the period that followed by the Santa Barbara oil spill, the first picture of Earth from space, and the first Earth Day also tidies things up. But writing workers into the story moves the origins of environmentalism back in time and requires recognition of otherwise unrecognized or underacknowledged moments and experiences as key points of change, complicating the story we tell.

As the comparison of antebellum Lowell mill girls and twentieth-century autoworkers suggests, environmental consciousness and activism predated Rachel Carson. To be sure, those workers did not call themselves environmentalists, and we should be wary of examining the past by anything other than its own terms. At the very least, however, the efforts of working-class sportsmen's clubs and the United Auto Workers in the 1940s and 1950s compels us to throw out 1962 or any later dates as the environmental movement's start. And they suggest that we might not have an entirely accurate chronology of the most meaningful events in subsequent decades. In the fall of 1965, for example, the United Auto Workers hosted more than one thousand participants in a "Clean Water Conference," the largest such meeting on that issue up to that point, although not a single American environmental history textbook or course reader mentions it.

Second (and this is related to the first point), the new narrative expands the list of important historical actors to include a whole host of additional leaders. Rachel Carson, Stewart Udall, David Brower, Gaylord Nelson, and Lois Gibbs certainly should continue to figure in environmentalism's telling. Each had a high profile that facilitated raising consciousness and turning ideas into policy. Yet any complete register of key figures should also include the likes of Massachusetts public health activist Henry Ingersoll Bowditch, Civilian Conservation Corps director Robert Fechner, and Oil, Chemical and Atomic Workers union leader Tony Mazzocchi.

Similarly, broadening whom we identify as subjects in the past requires that we see the problems with a top-down version of history. To peg most if not all of the responsibility for the rise and growth and impact of the environmental movement on any one author, Sierra Club director, senator, or union official is to grossly misstate how change happened. In redrafting our narrative, we need to incorporate the millions of ordinary Americans who engaged in various activities to address health hazards in their workplaces and a range of environmental problems in their communities. Quite often, they were responsible for pushing "leaders" to act, rather than the other way around.

Third, and perhaps most importantly, the revisionist interpretation points to new factors and forces to explain what caused change over time. In place of suburbanization, the new narrative concentrates on urbanization, the demographic shift that preceded it, and industrialization, what was drawing people to cities in the first place. When the fictional Nevels moved from a rural homestead in Appalachia to a dirty, grey block in Detroit so that the father could join the ranks of assembly line workers in a nearby factory, the family played out a story actually experienced by millions of people over two centuries. This move from the country to the city and the subsequent transformation of work set the stage for a modern environmental movement.

Living in the cities and laboring in mills and factories, migrants and immigrants confronted a range of threats to their health, from disease pathogens harbored in sewage-tainted drinking water to toxic chemicals that polluted the air of workplaces and neighborhoods. They lost direct contact with nature through their labor as well, which farming and other rural occupations had allowed and required. Corralled to run looms in textile mills or to fit bolts on wheels in auto plants, the new wage workers missed the countryside they had left behind and the practical way they had engaged it. Together, the exposure to pollution and the experience of alienation (or separation) from nature are what led workers and their families to develop a new environmental sensibility, to link that sensibility to local and (eventually) national problems, and to act on that sensibility in all manner of ways.

There is, however, one very important qualification to make to this last observation. Industrialization was never entirely restricted to urban areas and environmental activism certainly happened in the countryside. In fact, as the final chapter of this book shows, some of the most militant environmental protest of the twentieth century occurred in remote Appalachian hills and hollows as well as southern California fields and orchards. In these and other rural places industrial capitalism dramatically transformed both labor and landscape, much as it did in the cities, and this transformation prompted common people there to respond in kind. Although they did not suffer all of the draw-backs of life in the concrete jungle, they knew routinized, dangerous work and relentless corporate greed, as well as poisoned water and barren soil, and that was enough to provoke.

Before going any further to elaborate on this interpretation, I also have to note several caveats, or warnings, about perspective. These are especially directed to the academics reading over our shoulders, some of whom will undoubtedly raise objections about the approach taken here. To start with, when we search for the working-class roots of environmentalism in the United States, we are necessarily drawn to the East and Midwest as much or more than to the West, a region that, somewhat understandably, has long held a privileged place in reckonings made by environmental historians. The Industrial Revolution was initially centered in the Northeast and, generally speaking, swept westward. *A People's History of Environmentalism* reflects that fact in the content and organization of its chapters, with case studies and examples that tend to focus (though not exclusively) on the people and places within the area delimited by the Mississippi and Ohio rivers.

In addition, the book attends to class more than race and gender. This does not mean it ignores these important aspects of personal identity and social structure—both show up again and again, if only because they are inextricably entangled with class in people's real lives—but it does not treat them as the main concern. I tell the story this way for various reasons. Key among them is the analytical clarity that can come from isolating or emphasizing a particular historical factor, something I learned from my training in American women's history (in that case, focusing exclusively on women, and more recently wom-en's gender, helps correct for the traditional male-centered view of the past). Another reason is that, within the so-called trinity, class does seem to be the central element in common people's relationship with nature over time (e.g., even much of the way racial slavery conditioned African American slaves' and their white masters' experience with the land was really about class).

Lastly, it is difficult to grasp developments in the post–World War II era simply by starting in those years and moving forward. Fully understanding the origins and ripening of the movement requires a long view that encom-passes the past couple of centuries. There were many significant precedents for modern disputes over natural resource use, advocacy for pollution control, and protests against environmental injustice. Massachusetts enacted its first law to regulate waste disposal in rivers and streams as early as 1878, for example, and even that followed on the heels of decades of lawsuits and direct action by farmers and others angered by industrial use of waterways. On the other hand, there initially was considerable popular resistance to nineteenth-century park creation as well as to fish and game laws, what Karl Jacoby calls "environmental banditry." A sound account of environmentalism also needs to explain how and why this resistance had dissipated by the 1930s and 1940s, opening the way for working people to play a central role in the environmental movement.

The first chapter of *A People's History*, "Puritan to Yankee Redux: Farming, Fishing, and Our Very Own Dark, Satanic Mills," begins with a brief survey of New England settlers' pre- and post-Revolutionary farming as well as their use of area streams and rivers for subsistence and commercial fishing and for small mills to grind grain, saw timber, and card wool. The chapter then sketches the expansion of industrial manufacturing and increased rural-to-urban migration, examines opposition by farmers and fisherman to mill dams that flooded upstream land and blocked migratory fish, links factory work in swelling cities to romantic literary expression by mill girls, and details early campaigns to advance legislation aimed at pollution control.

Following the various trends, I point out that while people succeeded in prompting New England states to establish fish commissions, giving the government responsibility for natural resources, those agencies quickly morphed into something that tended to the interests of elites. They went from protecting fish as a food source to managing fish and game for sport, then largely a leisure activity for (actual and aspiring) aristocrats. Likewise, courts increasingly ruled in favor of factories and mills in riparian disputes, claiming that industry made a better public use of waterways than farmers and others. The progressive voices demanding that something be done to control industrial waste disposal were marginalized or silenced as well, and many rivers and streams inevitably degenerated into virtual "sewer basins" during the following decades.

Chapter 2 picks up the story in the late nineteenth century. The title, "Why Game Wardens Carry Guns and Interpretive Rangers Dress like Soldiers: Class Conflict in Forests and Parks," speaks to the disenchantment of common people with conservation laws as well as state and national park management. State and federal laws regulating hunting and fishing and the wholesale prohibition of nonrecreational land use within park boundaries disregarded traditional community ethics, a "moral ecology" fashioned by locals over time, one that allowed certain uses of the natural world according to established customs and rules. They also drove many into permanent wage labor.

For a time, local people resisted, willfully but covertly violating laws and ignoring park boundaries, thwarting the ostensibly good intentions of scientists and bureaucrats. But game wardens and park rangers (assisted in some cases by the U.S. Army) ultimately imposed a new order on the land. This was a process in which class and ethnicity were sometimes if not often conflated, since conservation and park proponents frequently identified Native Americans (in the West), Italian immigrants (in the Northeast) and African Americans (in the South) as among the worst offenders. What is interesting is that common people eventually did become an important constituency supporting government regulation of hunting and fishing as well as rules covering access and use in public parks. That change is linked to several other changes in the lives of many workers and their families, namely rural-to-urban migration and the shift from work on the land to labor in mills and factories.

Chapter 3, "Missionaries Find the Urban Jungle: Sanitation and Worker Health and Safety," follows working people to the cities and their new workplaces. First, it examines the environmental crisis that accompanied urbanization and industrialization and recounts various efforts to respond. This section of the book focuses on the experience of ordinary urban dwellers, particularly working-class immigrants, overwhelmed by ubiquitous pollution, foul odors, and chronic disease in densely packed wards and districts. Additionally, it concentrates on working people's complicated role in elite-led sanitation reform, including what impact these efforts made on their environmental consciousness. The reform was mostly a matter of change being imposed from the top (once again) but also included community mobilization, and in that respect it has a certain germane significance to the development of working-class environmentalism.

The chapter chronicles the rise of "industrial hygiene" as well. This new field involved some of the same Progressive reformers engaged in sanitation and public health movements and dealt directly with the dangerous circumstances faced daily by workers on the job. It broke through disbelief and skepticism, as well as outright corporate intransigence, to establish the reality of various occupational hazards and to associate those hazards with unregulated working conditions. In time, worker health and safety experts helped generate recognition of hazards beyond factories and mills—following noxious waste products from manufacturing into surrounding communities—which created the context for legislative action on a broader scale. And all of this was later aided by at least some elements of organized labor, including unions (the United Steel Workers, United Auto Workers, and the like) typically viewed as antipathetic to controlling or preventing air and water pollution.

Working-class environmental consciousness and activism was also nudged along by work relief programs during the 1930s, the subject of Chapter 4. "Green Relief and Recovery: By Which Working People and Nature Get a New Deal" recounts the federal government's response to the Depression. It looks specifically at the more innovative initiatives meant to address economic and environmental problems simultaneously. As waves of Americans began losing their jobs, President Franklin Delano Roosevelt drew on his interests in conservation to create federal agencies that employed those in need to repair the country's long-abused natural resources. The general success of these efforts left an important legacy, demonstrating the practical value of ecological thinking to millions (both participants and observers alike) and making parks and forests much more accessible for outdoor recreation.

Perhaps the best-known and most comprehensive attempt to blend relief for the unemployed with nature's mending was the Civilian Conservation Corps (CCC), which Chapter 4 gives primary consideration. The CCC was established in 1933 and, over the course of nearly ten years, enrolled nearly 3 million young men to plant trees, prevent forest fires, control soil erosion, build protective dunes, as well as construct trails, roads, and shelters in state and national parks. This work experience certainly had an impact on the young men, helping them and their families to survive (they were required to send most of their wages back home) and infusing them with a new or renewed appreciation for nature. The CCC projects also made an impression on people in surrounding communities, who received various benefits from the work, such as improved soil fertility and increased tourism. In fact, the corps played a very important part in enabling the steep rise in working-class visitation at state and national parks during the 1930s and in the decades to follow.

Chapter 5, "A Popular Crusade: Organized Labor Takes the Lead against Pollution," builds on the preceding chapters and begins to address the more immediate origins and development of environmentalism. Focusing particularly on the years after World War II, this section of the book looks at campaigns by working-class sportsmen's clubs, local and international unions, as well as dissident movements (opposition forces within established unions) to enact, strengthen, and enforce pollution-control laws. From Pittsburgh, Pennsylvania, to Gary, Indiana, and many other places in between and beyond, ordinary people adopted ecological attitudes and advanced initiatives to address environmental problems. Among the factors prompting their organized efforts was a sense of alienation from labor and nature, a product of rural-to-urban migration and exchanging farmwork for factory work.

On the one hand, having lost direct contact with the natural world through labor and in their living space, many workers sought alternative means for encountering forests, streams, and wildlife, including auto camping and sport hunting and fishing. That leisure experience became the basis for thinking about ways of protecting the environment closer to home. On the other hand, workers and their families simply had no choice but to concern themselves with environmental hazards, potent threats to their health in their workplaces and communities. By transforming their sportsmen's clubs into organizational advocates for regulatory legislation and, just as importantly, by infusing their unions and labor councils with such broader social concerns (beyond wages and hours), they pioneered a larger, mainstream movement to deal with pollution. This was helped by a set of receptive union leaders with a progressive vision (e.g., Walter Reuther, president of the UAW) as well as a resurgence of liberal ideals.

For some segments of the working class, however, it became apparent that enacting regulatory legislation was not enough to get redress. Consequently, they began to adopt a more radical agenda, demanding community empowerment, blending economic and environmental concerns, and often rejecting any kind of compromise. To achieve their goals, they started using militant tactics, preferring direct action over lobbying or lawsuits, sometimes willfully but nonviolently breaking the law, and in a few cases, using property destruction or even violence. I examine the variation in tactics and goals in Chapter 6, "To Stir Up Dissension and Create Turmoil: Inventing Environmental Justice," delving into examples of working people's confrontational activism and, at the same time, coming back around to the countryside, acknowledging the way twentieth-century industrial capitalism affected that part of the United States too.

This section of the book starts by revisiting events at Love Canal and Warren County (which historians usually identify as the beginning of the "environmental justice" movement), drawing on interpretations that cast those campaigns in a new light, particularly by revealing their social dimensions. The chapter then turns to a chronicle of the United Farm Workers' earlier fight to organize mostly Mexican and Mexican American field hands in southern California, in part to protect them from exposure to pesticides. This is followed by a look at insurgent efforts in the mountains and hollows of central Appalachia, where underground coal miners, small farmers, and others employed nonviolent civil disobedience as well as industrial sabotage to stop strip mining. Together, the UFW campaign and the revolt in the coalfields demonstrate that an alternative brand of environmentalism was already in the making by the 1960s.

The Conclusion highlights once again why we need to put working people into our narrative about the origins and development of modern environmentalism, and how that perspective changes the story we tell. It also considers the contemporary significance of the interpretation, suggesting that rethinking the history of environmental activism has a bearing on the ways we define environmental activism in the present. One clear example of this is the jobs versus environment problem, the supposedly mutually exclusive choice that often divides workers and environmentalists (as if people can't be both). The problem is premised on the assumptions that the choice has always been an issue for workers, and rarely if ever have workers picked environmental quality over economic security (as if they had to). Looking back in time, we see that none of these assumptions is entirely true, a fact that opens options for avoiding the quandary as well as building a stronger, broader movement for change in the future.

1

Puritan to Yankee Redux: Farming, Fishing, and Our Very Own Dark, Satanic Mills

On his trip down the Concord River with his brother in August 1839, Henry David Thoreau was especially eager to avoid Lowell, Massachusetts, already the center of the country's Industrial Revolution. Before they had the city in sight, in fact, the siblings left the Concord for the Middlesex Canal, a 6-mile-long, northwestward arc through the woods, which put them on the Merrimack River. That circuitous route allowed the pair to skirt mills, boardinghouses, shops, and streets, an urban-industrial landscape not in keeping with what the two wanted to see, hear, or ponder on their journey. Even on the canal, Thoreau wrote in his deadpan style, "we did not care to loiter in this part of our voyage."[1]

Among his many objections, the infamous transcendentalist blamed "the factories at Lowell," as well as the dams that provided them with power, for the decline of once-abundant migratory fish. Shad and eel were still taken from the Concord River, but only as far as the Middlesex Dam, all the way downstream, near the confluence with the Merrimack. Farther upstream they were gone, unable to use poorly constructed fishways to make their ancient run. "Perchance, after a few thousands of years," Thoreau hoped, "if the fishes will be patient, and pass their summers elsewhere, meanwhile nature will have leveled the Billerica dam, and the Lowell factories, and the Grass-ground River run clear again, to be explored by new migratory shoals."[2]

Less than two years later, in June 1841, the Reverend Amos Blanchard, pastor of the First Congregational Church in Lowell, delivered an address to consecrate the new Lowell Cemetery. This "garden cemetery," like others of its kind, was intended for both eternal rest of the dead and pleasant leisure for the living, and it was situated on the banks of the Concord, near the Lawrence Street Bridge, 2 miles from the Merrimack. Blanchard claimed that put it "far from the marts of business" as well as "the spreading abodes" of city residents. He also praised the sequestered cemetery's mix of natural forest and "ornaments of artificial cultivation," which declared the divine presence and elicited "perpetual worship."[3]

Yet Blanchard was being somewhat disingenuous. In the audience for the consecration that day were Oliver Whipple and many others responsible for the canals, manufactories, and burgeoning clusters of housing appearing not just along the Merrimack but even more so along the Concord. Whipple had donated the land for the cemetery and served as president of the proprietors for the next few years, but he was quite aware of (and probably uneasy about) the quick-paced, far-reaching transformation of Lowell, some quite nearby. Like the Mt. Auburn Cemetery in Boston, established by the upper-class members of the Massachusetts Horticultural Society, the burial ground in Lowell had a particular purpose. A garden cemetery's beautiful landscape, explains Tamara Plakins Thornton, "its gravestones' inspiring inscriptions, and its infusion with the promise of a life hereafter would impress visitors with just how ultimately meaningless are the material rewards of this world by comparison with the transcendent beauty of nature, the legacy of a virtuous life, and the glory of reunion with one's Maker."[4]

Had Thoreau and his brother continued their journey on the Concord River, they would have encountered an impediment on the other side of the Lawrence Street Bridge at Wamesit Falls, a location within sight of the cemetery, where a dam channeled water to a power canal for Whipple's powder mills. Beyond that, they would have found a dam at Massic Falls, where another canal supplied waterpower to a flannel mill. Then, north of the Church Street Bridge, the two would have met yet another dam, where the collected force of water turned the turbines of the Middlesex Mills. All of these establishments, besides others set back from the river banks, drew workers who lived in surrounding tenements and homes.

What was happening in antebellum Lowell (and elsewhere), the different though similar observations suggest, was a struggle between competing ways of regarding and inhabiting the natural world. In fact, the various competing views were inextricably linked. The urge, will, and ever-expanding ability to control nature for profit is what provoked the era's flood of paeans to nature's intrinsic value, beauty, harmony, and holiness as well as strident defense of traditional land use. But the divergent perspectives could not be reconciled, even when "captains of industry" tried to intervene. Just as they sacrificed their paternalist labor arrangements (company housing, good wages, etc.) in the face of corporate competition, they eventually gave up on efforts to create a bucolic urban landscape (parks and promenades, flower gardens, etc.) when it clashed with an overriding commitment to market-driven industrial production.

One great fear among common people and elites alike was that manufacturing in Lowell and other cities in New England would become the equivalent of Britain's "dark satanic mills." Not surprisingly, as it edged in that direction, American industry inspired a good amount of protest, much of it centered on disagreements about the right relationship to the environment. When the shift to manufacturing was in its early stages, with factory waste polluting waterways and ever-higher mill dams continuously flooding upstream meadows and fields as well as blocking migratory fish runs, farmers and fishermen saw that as an unacceptable encroachment on their traditional way of life. In response to the specter of change, a few individuals took crowbars in hand and pulled the offending dams down when planting or fishing seasons required (acting within the law, at least for a while). Others circulated petitions, worked through local and state governments, and filed lawsuits. Initially, rulings in court cases went in their favor, disallowing permanent upstream flooding, and state after state in New England established fish commissions to oversee the construction of fishways around dams. Over time, though, court rulings on riparian (river) law aided the interests of mills and factories at everyone else's expense, and the fish commissions became consumed by the task of propagating fish for elite sport anglers.

With the power of mill investors and managers growing, the young women who came from distant farms to be the first mill operatives also wasted little time before starting to register complaints against industrial manufacturing, eloquently stating their position in correspondence, prose, and poetry. Some of the complaints were inspired by basic economic concerns, such as wage reductions and boardinghouse rate hikes, but they spoke to a sense of separation from nature too. Before migrating to Lowell, the "mill girls" knew only subsistence-oriented farming as part of a family production unit, which often involved varied, self-directed work indoors and outdoors. Consequently, operatives sometimes described the brick buildings where they labored as prisons, and they bemoaned regimentation of their days by factory bells. These conditions provided a new point of comparison, prompting them to think of the natural world as a refuge, a place for escape "out there." The new conditions provoked action as well, including "turnouts," or strikes, and "turnover," temporarily or permanently leaving the mills for rural homesteads. "I think less of the factory," declared a popular labor song of the time, "than of my native dell."

As the verses built toward their end, the singer finally announced, "I'm going to leave the factory / And return to my native land."[5]

After the Civil War, when waves of immigrants and other migrants began replacing the native-born young women as factory hands, environmental conditions in Lowell, Chicopee, Holyhoke, and other manufacturing cities throughout New England only worsened. Rivers and brooks, in particular, were filthy, smelly, and unhealthy. To address the problem, in 1878 Henry Bowditch and other radical public health activists convinced the Massachusetts General Court to pass a law prohibiting industrial and municipal discharge of refuse or any polluting substances into any stream or public pond in the state.[6] The legislature bowed to corporate pressure, however, and exempted the Connecticut and Merrimack rivers as well as the lower Concord. Five years later, Lowell's city physician described the lower Concord as "a sewer basin" that "undoubtedly exerts an unhealthful influence on those living upon its banks."[7] In the decades that followed, board of health statistics suggested that Lower Belvidere and other working-class neighborhoods along the Concord were among the most deadly places to live in the city. Nevertheless, an important precedent had been established, one that advanced the legitimacy of state intervention to protect the environment and people's health from industry.

Reasonable Use

Prior to the onset of industrialization in New England and even many decades after, the predominant way of making a living in the region was farming, mostly subsistence based. Methods and crops varied across the region according to soil type, available land, local climate, and other factors, but eighteenth- and early-nineteenth-century farm families tended to be need—rather than profit—oriented. There was little effort to produce a surplus for market and, when families did have more corn, apples, eggs, or flax than they could consume themselves, the exchange they made was usually in kind (bartering one item for another) or simply recorded in a store ledger as a credit. Labor was dealt with in a similar way, not hired for actual cash wages but something reciprocated by one person and another within the community.

Along the Charles, Concord, Nashua, and Merrimack rivers in Massachusetts, the areas that eventually saw the first fully integrated mills and factories and also happened to be among the longest-settled areas in New England, inhabitants practiced a variation of "mixed-husbandry" land use. This was a traditional way of farming brought over by the Puritans from England. Its essence was summed up by a local, common saying, "No grass; no cattle; no cattle, no manure; no manure, no crops." Meadows were annually fertilized during spring freshets (floods), when rich silt settled out of the water, and this sustained seasonal production of grass. Farmers cut the meadow grass and fed it to their cattle, and the cattle, in turn, produced manure that farmers used to maintain soil fertility for crops. The animals, as historian Brian Donohue points out, essentially served as a means to transfer nutrients from one part of the landscape to the other.[8]

Well aware of the important role meadows played, farmers managed them intensively. Yet they did this with an eye on long-term family and community persistence, carefully conserving rather than thoughtlessly abusing the resource. Certainly, at times, New England farmers could and did use the natural world in ways that showed lack of foresight and undermined their ability to live off the land, but mixed husbandry proved to be fairly sustainable. Many generations came and went before its demise. When that did finally happen, one problem was population growth. Eventually, there was no longer enough arable land available for every child to follow in the footsteps of their parents. Another problem was the way increasingly larger mills and factories began to affect brooks and rivers, with ever-higher dams permanently flooding upstream meadows and, incidentally, blocking migratory fish runs.[9]

As Thoreau put it, the main attraction of the Concord River for the first English settlers had been "its grassy meadows and its fish," though by the time he made the boat trip with his brother in 1839, that era was quickly passing away. "Salmon, Shad, and Alewives were formerly abundant here, and taken in weirs by the Indians, who taught this method to the whites," he wrote, "by whom they were used as food and as manure, until the dam [at Billerica], and afterward the canal at Billerica, and the factories at Lowell, put an end to their migrations hitherward." Similarly, he observed how farmers on one of the Concord's tributaries recently waited for the water there to subside so that they could drive their teams afield (into the meadows) as usual. The water remained high and "speedy emissaries revealed the unnatural secret, in the new float-board, wholly a foot in width, added to their already too high privileges by the dam proprietors."[10]

Of course, dams were not some new innovation in waterway management that suddenly appeared on the scene with factory production. During the seventeenth and eighteenth centuries, grinding grain, carding wool, and sawing lumber were all done at mills powered by water. The thirty-year diary of a New Hampshire farmer Matthew Patten, for example, records his reliance on a mill owner, Samuel Moor. When Patten carried sacks of wheat and cut timber to

Moor's mills, as he regularly did until his death in 1795. He thereby saved his family the many hours it would take to do the work of grinding and sawing by hand. An underthrow wheel, turned by sending dammed water through a race, was much more efficient.[11]

The early dams did sometimes cause problems for upstream farmers and local fishermen, but usually there was an effective means of redress. In 1721, after the dam at Billerica Falls mentioned by Thoreau was first raised higher, complaints followed in a flurry, as backed-up waters covered upstream meadows. The commission of sewers, with the power to regulate river flow, delayed action, so a special committee appointed by the Governor's Council interceded. Subsequently, the dam was lowered "and no further protests were heard from the upstream towns through the course of the eighteenth century."[12] In similar cases, courts were willing to intervene on the side of suing plaintiffs, following prevailing language of riparian law, at least to recognize that harm was done and to award damages or force a remedy. When two mill owners, Edmond Baker and Daniel Vose, balked at constructing a fishway despite the fact that they were running their mills at full capacity during migration, they found little sympathy from the presiding judge. In the 1808 case, the court ruled that the right to build a dam implied limitations, namely "to protect the rights of the public to the fishery."[13]

Although interpretations varied and changed over time, common law also allowed dam breaking by the aggrieved. Even in a state such as Massachusetts (which passed mill acts in the early nineteenth century that threw all disputes over to the courts) there was widespread acknowledgment that direct action had some legitimacy.[14] For instance, after Joseph Ruggles raised his dam on the Housatonic another ten inches in 1796 and caused a nearby marsh to fill with stagnant water, Elijah Boardman and other inhabitants of New Milford destroyed part of the structure. They claimed that the water was responsible for the "bilious remitting fever" and "fever and ague" that had raged in the village for four years and thereby the dam was a public nuisance. In the end, the jury ruled for Ruggles on the grounds that the stagnant water was not conclusively proven to be responsible for all the sickness. Had the medical experts called to testify established this link more convincingly, the ruling might have gone the other way and the dam breaking accepted as a necessary response.[15]

Actually, though, most preindustrial dams were tolerable obstructions because the mills they served made a direct contribution to the lives of local residents—in this sense they were public rather than private—and, just as importantly, they operated seasonally. After farmers harvested their wheat, corn, and rye and sheered their sheep of wool in the fall, they carried much of the grain to a mill for grinding and sent the wool to a mill for carding. With fewer demands on their time after the harvest, they cut timber from their woodlots in the winter and hauled it to a mill for sawing. In late spring, the mills could lift the gates on the mill dams to allow migratory fish runs, to let freshets through, and to leave upstream meadows dry for summer cutting.[16]

Yet this all began to change in the opening decade of the nineteenth century. By that point, New England's rivers were dotted with spinning mills that used overshot waterwheels to power carding machines as well as drawing and spinning frames, requiring higher dams and permanent ponds. One such operation on the Chicopee River, started in 1810 by William Levi, and Joseph Chapin, employed eight to ten workers turning raw wool into yarn, which was then put out to local women to weave. The Chapins' mill and others like it saw hard times when war with Britain ended in 1815 and higher-quality imports once again flooded the American market, but the more highly capitalized operations survived and new ventures started.[17]

Only a year after peace was made, a group of investors known as the Boston Associates built a large, multistory cotton mill at Waltham, an enormously important step in the development of a full-fledged American textile industry. The Waltham mill used waterpower to perform every part of cotton cloth production under one roof, from carding to weaving, a feat made possible by Francis Cabot Lowell's successful theft of plans for power looms from his visits to several British mills. As it became clear that the Charles River was insufficient to increase production to meet demand, the associates bought up land near the Merrimack River's Pawtucket Falls and built a series of mills to turn out textiles. Shortly afterward, they began textile manufacturing in other cities, including Nashua and Manchester, New Hampshire, all of which used the Merrimack in a similar fashion.[18]

In fact, the region's waterways were affected by a wide range of industrial production. At Chicopee, in the shadow of four huge textile mills, the sons of Nathan Ames continued their father's shovel, hoe, and edge-tool business, which he had begun on the Concord River in 1790. Nathan Ames, in particular, helped turn the town into one of New England's centers for ironworks and, eventually, machine production. Similarly, Hartford, Connecticut, had thriving iron and brass works, while Enfield, Massachusetts, cast its lot with carpet making and Springfield, Massachusetts, initiated a long history of producing guns and ammunition, each town and its various industries drawing power from the Connecticut River.[19] Tanning evolved as well, with firms like the White Brothers transforming raw hides into finished leather on the banks of the Concord in Lowell.

Individually and as a group, the new mills and factories had a qualitatively different impact on New England's waterways than established, older users. Prior to hosting the celebrated Waltham textile mill, the site on the Charles was used by John Boies for making paper. The dam he built for that purpose in 1738 created only a small millpond and generated no protest. After Patrick Tracy Jackson purchased the mill from Boise for the Boston Manufacturing Company, however, the new owners raised the height of the dam, and water flooded hundreds of acres in Waltham, Watertown, Newton, and Weston. Likewise, soon after the Boston Associates turned their attention to Lowell, they met an ever-increasing need for more waterpower by adding 2 feet of granite to the existing Pawtucket dam, creating a 1,100 acre millpond and deadening the river's current for 18 miles.[20]

As dams proliferated and increased in size, farmers and fishermen and even small mill owners (who had to deal with high water flooding their wheels) responded as they often had in the past. They petitioned state legislatures, initiated lawsuits, and (in a few cases) took matters into their own hands with assaults on offending obstructions. A break with tradition was in the works, though, as a complementary redefinition of riparian law accompanied the advance of industrial capitalism across the land. This did not happen all at once, yet it shifted the balance of power from common people to elites and undermined the resistance, ultimately putting control over nature more firmly in the hands of manufacturers.

In New Hampshire, like other states, courts initially tended to endorse the age-old "natural-flow" rule, an assumption that water ought to flow as it has customarily flowed. This rule sanctioned a range of water use but held anything that was not directly needed to sustain the life of people or animals (such as a millpond) as outside those bounds and an injury to others' property. In the 1830s, however, New Hampshire courts began to assess disputes over water according to a rule of "reasonable use," and they recognized manufacturing as one among a number of reasonable uses. In time, the courts also started to distinguish manufacturing as a comparably better use, contributing more to a certain kind of (favored) economic development, limiting the rights of other users to seek damages for flooded fields, absent fish, or disease-breeding stagnant waters.[21]

As late as the second half of the nineteenth century, though, mill owners and other industrial-minded water users in New Hampshire had to be mindful that people there still had a common law right to tear down or alter a dam determined to be a public nuisance. When a group of men attacked a dam at Lake Winnipesaukee in September 1859, the leaders and followers assumed their action was both legitimate and lawful, and they made no effort to be covert or secretive. Their attack was part of a long-simmering conflict, pitting farmers (who cut hay from lake and river meadows) against the Lake Company (which built dams to supply water to downstream Massachusetts factories by way of the Merrimack River). Several years earlier, after the company began implementing development plans at Newfound Lake and Lake Wentworth, "a number of persons, principally irresponsible men" (as the company agent described them), demolished a coffer dam (a temporary structure built to hold back water during excavation). At the end of the decade, tensions intensified and locals organized a second assault. In response to this and other dam breaking, the New Hampshire legislature passed a mill act constraining aggrieved parties to submit complaints to a committee appointed by the state's Supreme Judicial Court.[22]

Massachusetts had annulled dam breaking as a common law right just before the end of the eighteenth century, and an amended mill act capped the sum of damages for flooding at four pounds per year. Within a few decades, the state supreme court went even farther. As Chief Justice Lemuel Shaw noted in one particular ruling, "In consideration of the advantage to the public to be derived from the establishment and maintenance of mills, the owner of the land shall not have an action for their necessary consequential damage against the mill owner, to compel him to prostrate his dam; and thus destroy or reduce his head of water."[23]

The powers of corporations to use Massachusetts waterways at will were expanded yet again, with the Supreme Judicial Court's decision in *Hazen v. Essex Company*. The owner of a small mill upstream from the newly finished dam in Lawrence had sued for damages caused by the Essex Company's millpond waters flooding his waterwheel. But company lawyers claimed Essex rightfully exercised the power of eminent domain, which allowed taking private property for public purposes, and owed nothing. The court agreed, dismissed the case because the mill owner did not seek relief for a matter of property harmed accordingly, and thereby equated economic development of the sort at Lawrence (large textile mills) with a higher public use. In effect, this justified the sacrifice of certain property rights for others. "By the latter part of the nineteenth century," Ted Steinberg explains, "it was commonly assumed, even expected, that water should be tapped, controlled, and dominated in the name of progress—a view clearly reflected in the law."[24]

To Sap the Life Blood from Young Veins

River valley farmers, fishermen, and small mill owners were not the only ones who had to confront the social and environmental changes ushered in by manufacturing. "No group felt the impact of early industrialization more," argues

Thomas Dublin, "than young women in the New England countryside." They were the primary component of the first labor force in the new mills, and by 1860 something like 60,000 of them were employed in the region's cotton textile industry alone.[25] These operatives were single, usually in their late teens, and hailed from southern Vermont, southern New Hampshire, western Massachusetts, as well as parts of Maine, Connecticut, and upstate New York. They were recruited (or rather, their families let them leave somewhat isolated rural homesteads) with the promise of relatively good wages and residence in a boardinghouse, where their moral character would be closely supervised by a boardinghouse keeper.

On the farm, the young women had an intimate relationship with the natural world through their work, which varied through the course of a day and the seasons of the year. This engagement with the environment sustained a way of thinking about nature that was primarily utilitarian, focused on use. After migrating to work in urban mills, however, the operatives' lives were dramatically different. They were confined to hot, noisy workrooms for hours on end, tending machines under close supervision, regimented according to a strict timetable announced by clanging bells. Under those conditions, the women felt separated from the natural world, which was no longer a place where work was done but a thing apart from labor and much more important for its aesthetic and spiritual dimensions.[26] "A strong feeling for the beauties of nature, as displayed in the solitudes the writers have left at home," Charles Dickens wrote after visiting Lowell and reading one of the mill girls' famed literary journals, "breathes through its pages like wholesome village air."[27]

Provoked by industrial capitalism, the operatives started to think of the natural world as a place for casual leisure, mental reflection, and, particularly when there was a chance to return home, temporary or permanent escape "to enjoy a short season of freedom."[28] The young women also began to draw on what they observed beyond the mill gates, as well as what they remembered about or experienced in a visit to their old rural homesteads, as a foil to indict the economic order that threatened to make them slaves to industrial tyrants. The grumbling, strikes, and turnover (leaving the mills) that began so soon after the young women's arrival in Lowell, Chicopee, Nashua, and other mill towns were not only about wage cuts, increased boardinghouse rates, and machine speed-ups. The disillusionment and protest came from the mill workers' sense of estrangement from nature as well.[29]

Of course, New England transcendentalists like Ralph Waldo Emerson and Henry David Thoreau earned fame by their own criticism of industrial capitalism. Often in an ornate and ostentatious style, they wrote about the links between nature's intrinsic and symbolic value and the dubious exchange of freedom for material goods. What made the mill girls different (besides the fact that they were women) is that their attitudes and observations were firmly rooted in actual experience as industrial wage workers. When a young woman named Mary penned a poem for the radical *Voice of Industry* in 1846, for example, she employed plenty of flowery rhetoric and hyperbole, but she knew what she was talking about. "I stand and gaze from my prison walls," Mary wrote in reference to the mill where she worked, looking out "on yonder flowing river." In this meditative hour (as Emerson might describe it) she wondered if the river was made by God "to add to the miser's gold" or "to cheer and bless or race," recognizing that, for now, "its sparkling waters roll, with grandeur pride and grace, to seek their mighty ocean bed, their final resting place, an emblem of Purity and Truth, made from thy aim to turn, to sap the life-blood from young veins, and fill the funeral Urn!"[30]

Before their confinement within "pent-up walls" of a "noisy mill," young women lived on family farms, making measurable and acknowledged contributions to meeting basic needs and wants.[31] A woman's sphere encompassed many different tasks, including feeding poultry, milking cows, making butter and cheese, tending the garden, gathering berries and other wild edibles, preserving and pickling, shucking corn, paring apples, making cider and applesauce, cooking, washing, tidying the house, making soap and candles, preparing flax, cleaning fleece, spinning, knitting, weaving, and dyeing cloth, as well as bearing and caring for children. This diverse activity was done alone, in pairs, and as parts of larger groups, and it frequently blurred the line between labor and leisure. Just as importantly, it put women in direct contact with soil and water, plants and animals, as well as weather and climate.[32]

Although they did not understand the experience in modern terms, female members of farm households gained a wealth of firsthand knowledge about ecological relationships by cultivating vegetables, herbs, and flowers. In a record she kept interleaved among the pages of agricultural almanacs between 1819 and 1821, Anna Howell frequently noted the damage done by storms, frosts, and pests, as well as possible remedies. In one entry for June 1821, she noted that planting cucumbers between peas would shield them from the cold while planting an onion in each hill would keep "the yellow winged bug" at bay.[33] When these and other methods were successful, women's gardens produced a bountiful harvest that rightly filled them with pride. Visiting her neighbor, Mrs. Hopkins, in the summer of 1805, Tryphena Ely White was treated to a garden tour and returned to her own home laden with "a posy of pinks," a handful of young onions, and a cucumber, "which was the only one big enough to pick."[34]

Girls and women also witnessed the bounty and beauty of fields and forests on trips to gather wild herbs and pick berries. Sometimes they went to find pyrola, or wintergreen, to make a tea to soothe an elder's rheumatism (hence its alternate name, rheumatism weed). In other cases they went looking for strawberries, currants, raspberries, blueberries, and blackberries to eat fresh or make into preserves or to use for medicinal purposes. In her popular domestic economy manual, *The American Frugal Housewife*, Lydia Maria Child recommended both tea and syrup prepared from blackberry leaves to treat dysentery. Likewise, she counseled use of a chickweed poultice for toothache and "black cherry-tree bark, barberry bark, mustard-seed, petty morel-root, and horseradish, well steeped in cider," for jaundice.[35]

The production of household goods by rural farm families was yet another part of their close relationship with nature, demanding a familiarity with its many facets. They made soap for laundry by leaching wood ashes in a barrel and boiling the lye in a great pot outdoors, but doing this required a good, plentiful water supply too. Tryphena Ely White recorded that the kettle of boiling soap "does not seem to do well" because, suffering through a string of weeks without rain, "we were obliged to make it of river water," which had too many minerals in it.[36] Similarly, women relied on the natural world to make candles, using beeswax, deer suet, moose fat, bear grease, mutton tallow, or berries from the bayberry bush.[37] More frequently, almost every day, they made butter and cheese from cow's milk. Maintaining a herd of cows for this required "paying attention to what the cows were eating and the quality of water they were drinking, the characteristic habits and behavior of the individual milk cows, and the passing of the seasons that brought warmer or cooler temperatures and necessitated different milking techniques."[38]

To produce textiles, women used flax and wool from their family's own flax fields and sheep. After male members of the household pulled flax plants and removed the seeds, mothers and their daughters put the fibers on a spinning wheel, bleached the thread with water and ashes, wove it on a loom, and bleached the linen again in the sun. Wool had to be picked over and carded, combed and greased, and spun into skeins on a wheel, knitted or woven on a loom, and then sent to the local fulling mill. To add color, there were a variety of natural dyes at hand, derived from the bark of oak, hickory, sassafras, and birch trees as well as from boiled pokeberry, onion skins, pressed goldenrod, and black walnut hulls.[39]

In the early nineteenth century, however, all of this was changed for young women who migrated to labor in textile mills. They left their rural homesteads and severed the direct relationship they had with the natural world through work. Textile production still started with raw cotton and wool, and the mills were (initially) part of what might be most accurately described as "semiru-ral" landscapes, nestled beside rivers, surrounded by farms and pastures and woodlands, but daily life for operatives was not the same as it was back home. Probably the most common objection was about the routine confinement. After only a brief stint in a Lowell weave room, Susan Brown complained to her diary about being "immured within the massey walls of a hateful factory" and vowed to return to her family in Epsom, New Hampshire. "Sixteen weeks today!" she wrote, "But it will not be sixteen weeks longer here."[40]

To be sure, not every operative felt so averse toward their new situation. Sally Rice left Somerset, Vermont, at the age of 17 and eventually made her way to a textile mill in Thompson, Connecticut, glad to be away from a rocky farm "in the wilderness" and eager for independence. "I can never be happy there," she wrote her parents. "I feel as though I have worn out shoes and strength enough riding and walking over the mountains."[41] Others who never gave in to the temptation to roam, however, seemed perfectly satisfied. Sarah Bennett tried to get her cousin Olive Sawyer to leave rural New Hampshire and join her at a mill in Haverhill, Massachusetts, but Olive married and happily played her part in establishing a new farm instead. "I live in the woods among the stumps and owls," she wrote Sarah, betrothed to "one of the kindest husbands that ever a woman had," with "enough of every thing to eat and drink." Although, she admitted, "I don't live in the style and fashions of the gay and noble."[42]

Immured within the mills from five in the morning until seven in the evening, with a half hour each for lunch and dinner, doing the same thing over and over, most operatives tended to find millwork exhausting and monoto-nous. It could be dangerous and unhealthy too. Machines caught fingers, limbs, and hair (women were scalped in a few cases), and the air was a mix of heavy smoke from oil lamps and bits of cotton or wool fibers. Not surprisingly, mill girls frequently fell ill from working under these conditions and left their posi-tions for days, weeks, and even months to recuperate. Not long after coming to Lowell from Rochester, New Hampshire, in the 1830s, Permielia Dame wrote to her brother about becoming sick and taking an absence. She had intended to answer his last letter earlier, Permielia explained, but "my health being very bad and my eyes very weak that I was obliged to leave the Factory for a short time." A trip to Boston did not seem to help, so she "went to New Hampshire and there visited all our friends and connections."[43]

The common occurrence of injury and illness was at the heart of growing agitation and organizing in the years to follow. "We are perfectly certain, from personal observation," wrote one Massachusetts trade unionist, "that these long hours of labor in confined rooms, are very injurious to health, and we doubt whether it would be using too harsh terms to say, that the whole system is one of slow and legal assassination."[44] Immediate measures must be taken, another worker from New Hampshire wrote, to aid "those who are shut up within the 'Prison walls of a Factory,' where we are continually inhaling cotton-dust, lamp smoke, and away from wholesome pure air."[45]

The new working conditions and the way they compared with the rural agrarian experience young women knew while growing up also explain operatives' new attitude about nature. They shifted from a utilitarian to a romantic view, one in which use and material values were supplanted by symbolism and spiritual transcendence. This is vividly captured in the mill girls' writing, particularly the poems, stories, and essays they published in literary journals, quite common in rural New England but even more popular among the many thousands of workers living together in the tight-knit communities created by urban mills. Some of these journals were criticized by labor advocates for being corporate mouthpieces or too much influenced by the conservative ministers who often helped oversee their publication. Yet the *Lowell Offering*, the *Olive Leaf and Factory Girls' Repository*, and others were filled with contributions that marshaled observations about nature to express reservations about the new, emerging order. There was need for retreat "from the haunts of selfish men," one operative wrote, "to learn thy Maker's ways" in the "purest of society, with brook and bird, and flowers and tree."[46] Similarly, young women's correspondence with friends and family and their articles and letters to the editor in newspapers, as well as the memoirs and autobiographies written later, often employed descriptions of beauty and harmony in the natural world as a foil.

At the start of industrialization, escape to nature was still possible just outside the mills. In Lowell, the areas around buildings were planted with flowers, and the Boston Manufacturing Company's first agent, Kirk Boott, made a point of establishing a line of elms along the main thoroughfare to make a shaded promenade, which operative Maria Currier called a "delightful retreat." By the mid-1840s, the promenade was flanked by two city-owned parks, the North and South Commons. Prominent citizens (among the leading industrial lights) also established the garden cemetery consecrated by Reverend Amos Blanchard. Its forty-five wooded acres included winding paths and a small lake.[47] Mill worker Lydia Sarah Hall described the place in verse as "That forest wild ... like a spot enchanted," where the "tearful eye of nature glistened" to look on the dead gathered in the ground.[48]

Mill owners and managers were primarily concerned with production, however, and that interest did not always complement operatives' interest in taking regular leisure outdoors. "You don't realize how unpleasant it is for females to be confined in a factory month after month," one Exeter, New Hampshire, worker wrote in the *Factory Girls Album*, "with no time to enjoy the sunshine and flowers—the blue sky and the green grass." If they were allowed to go away for an hour or two, she explained, they would be happy and work better.[49] Even when they did escape, the mills and the city could rudely disrupt attempts at communing with nature in gleeful reverie. As V.C.N. walked along the banks of the Merrimack River one morning, she felt a serene calm until "roused by the peeling tones of the bell which told me that I was wanted, when I arose and walked into the city where, as usual, all was noise and bustle."[50]

To get farther away, operatives used hard-earned wages to take short trips by stagecoach or train. Some deliberately sought out "the wild" to encounter the divine. Writing from the Mount Washington House in New Hampshire, Sarah Bagley wished her friends had come along "to enjoy with us the wild, romantic, mountain scenery around." The view, she said, was "grand and sublime … beyond the power of words to describe," and it prompted a soul "to sit still and commune with its Maker."[51] Others waxed eloquently about pastoral scenes. After an excursion to Lebanon Springs, on the other side of Worcester, E.C.T. wrote a brief account of this kind. "Those who have for any length of time been pent up in a cotton mill and factory boarding-house," she explained, "can appreciate the pleasures of a journey through the country, when the earth is dressed in her richest roves of green, bedecked with flowers, and all smiling with sunlight." What she saw was not wilderness, but "farmhouses, gardens and orchards, barns, grass-lands, fields of corn and grain, potatoe plants, wood-lots, pasture-lands, with herds of neat cattle, flocks of sheep, &c., all beautifully interspersed." The trip confirmed for her the notion "that man had made the town, but God made the country."[52]

In fact, operatives' most trenchant criticism of industrial capitalism centered on the rural landscapes of their old homesteads, which they frequently recalled in flights of imagination (albeit with considerable embellishment). In a story titled "Cure for Discontent," one young woman claimed that thinking about her native village while "doing her duty" in the mill was what made the labor tolerable.[53] Similarly, E.D. took solace in a "waking dream," returning to "the green hills of my childhood" in her mind, picturing her home amid vines and flowers, with the garden blooming, "the orchard laden with its golden fruit, and a silver stream meandering through the field." She was forced back to reality by the factory bell, which reminded her that she was "still a wanderer far from home and those I love."[54]

Although mill girls' memories were not entirely fabricated, they crafted them in a manner to make the most striking comparison with the urban-industrial environment. Betsey Chamberlain, for example, recalled a paradisiacal childhood in Wolfeboro, New Hampshire, before going to New Market, New Hampshire, and later Lowell. She "waded the pond for lilies, and the brooks for minnows ... roamed the fields for berries, and the meadows for flowers ... wandered the woods for ivy-plums, and picked ising-glass from the rocks ... watched the robins that built for many years their nest in the chest-nut tree ... and nursed, with truly motherly care, the early lambs and chickens." There was some work-being done in this recollection, but very little by the standards of actual expectations, even for a young girl, and the work seems almost secondary to more passive delight in nature.[55]

Sometimes operatives actually returned home, but in their letters to friends left behind they still filtered their observations (and criticism of industrialization) through literary romantic stylistic techniques. Once she was in Cabot, New Hampshire, Huldah J. Stone wrote an open letter to the *Voice of Industry*, particularly advising those in Lowell to commence study of the beautiful, "the sublime, volume of Nature, if we would learn God aright."[56] Another operative reported on the progress of her journey for members of the Female Labor Reform Association (FLRA) of Manchester, New Hampshire, feeding their desire for virtual escape. "Here I shall remain a few weeks, in the retirement of a country residence," J.R. wrote, "to enjoy a short season of freedom.... And amid this pleasant repast I do not forget you." She was taking time to wander along the river, watching "its course as it wends its way to meet the beautiful Merrimack, listening to merry songs of birds, sending forth their joyful notes." Yet she was often awakened from the "pleasing revery" and "led to think of the evils growing up in the present state of society, which must undermine all glorious scenes with 'her thousand votaries of art.'"[57]

By the 1830s and 1840s, working conditions in New England textile mills were generating a good amount of protest, starting with several unsuccessful, loosely coordinated "turnouts" (or strikes) and maturing with the creation of lasting organizations, such as the FLRA. In these efforts, female operatives very much identified as daughters of propertied rural farmers, and they folded their sense of separation from the natural world into their more decidedly economic grievances. "The graceful form, the bright and sparking eye, the blushing cheek and the elastic motions of 'Industry's Angel daughters,'" declared one factory critic, did not belong "to Lowell Cotton Mills, but to New England's country

Homes," where "the fair cheek, kissed by the sunlight and the breeze, grew fresh and healthful."[58] Wage cuts were an insult to workers' dignity and threatened their economic independence, while long hours threatened to steal their health and well-being. "To the hardy independent yeomanry and mechanics, among the Granite Hills of New Hampshire, the woody forests of Maine, the cloud capped mountains of Vermont, and the busy, bustling towns of the old Bay State," operative Amelia Sargent appealed, "ye! who have daughters and sisters toiling in these sickly prison-houses which are scattered far and wide over each of these States, we appeal to you for aid in this matter."[59]

In the end, though, rural Yankee women dealt with the disagreeable circumstances of urban industrial life by simply leaving (or never going to) the mills. Subsequently, managers increasingly filled their place in the industrial economy with other migrant and immigrant labor, particularly Irish and French Canadians, which they deemed more suitable for unchecked exploitation, or at least without any pretense at paternalism.[60] As manufacturing expanded, textile mills and other factories also more brazenly polluted the waterways of towns and cities where the changing labor force lived. Disregarding romantic sentiments about nature as beautiful and sublime, they used local rivers and brooks "for readily disposing of waste liquors and other refuse," as the Massachusetts Board of Health put it in 1872, and thereby compounded the various other public health threats to workers living in cramped housing nearby.[61] Additionally, and not incidentally, rising levels of pollution introduced a new threat to migrating fish populations, which were already in decline because dams blocked their spawning runs. All of this, in turn, provoked a multifaceted reform campaign, linked to the earlier battles over riparian law and just as thoroughly permeated by class conflict as those confrontations.

A Legitimate Right to Nature's Gifts

Taking a stand shortly after the Civil War, radicals on the Massachusetts and New Hampshire state boards of health rejected the idea that clean water and pure air were a privilege, and they invoked natural rights philosophy to argue for pollution controls that would protect all people. "We believe that all citizens have an inherent right to the enjoyment of pure and uncontaminated air, and water, and soil," the Massachusetts board members declared, "and that no one should be allowed to trespass upon it by his carelessness, or his avarice, or even his ignorance."[62] Suggesting the influence of their Bay State colleagues, the New Hampshire board stated that "every person has a legitimate right to nature's gifts—pure water, air, and soil—a right belonging to every individual, and every community upon which no one should be allowed to trespass through carelessness, ignorance, or other cause." A decade later, the Connecticut board embraced "the duty of government to protect the weak from oppression of the strong," particularly the poor, who suffered most from "unwholesome surroundings and other unsanitary conditions." It was only a matter of time, the members declared, before each state "must provide some official means to protect the public at large."[63]

Among the worst polluters of New England waterways in the nineteenth century were paper mills and woolen textile mills, though cotton mills, metalworks, tanneries, and other manufacturing contributed a considerable share of chemical and material residue as well. Every day in Lowell, River Meadow Brook received millions of gallons of waste "liquors" from washing, bleaching, and dyeing cloth at the Lowell Bleachery, 60,000 gallons of oil-heavy wash water from shell production at U.S. Cartridge, and 300,000 gallons of wastewater from scouring wool, washing cloth, and dyeing stock at U.S. Bunting. Not surprisingly, in 1883 the local board of health described the stream as "one of the most serious public nuisances that has ever existed in the city," noting its "intolerable stench" and the many complaints by residents along its banks.[64] Yet River Meadow Brook carried its filth only a short distance to the Concord River, which received millions of gallons of other noxious trade waste from the Waterhead, Bay State, Belvidere, and Sterling (textile) mills as well as the White Brothers tannery. This then flowed into the Merrimack River, which collected still more industrial pollutants as it passed Lawrence, Haverhill, Amesbury, and Newburyport on the way to the sea.[65]

In addition to production waste, the region's mills and factories were a significant source of human sewage. To serve hundreds of employees, companies usually built large privies, or water closets, which emptied into the nearest stream by means of a ditch or, less often, enclosed piping. In Chicopee, Massachusetts, the nearly 100 manufacturing establishments there disposed of their workers' wastes in either the Chicopee River or Connecticut River, creating what the Massachusetts state board of health called a "very offensive stench." Similarly, the iron, brass, hardware, wool, and cotton firms in New Britain, Connecticut, dumped their workers' effluent (2,500 pounds of feces and 3,500 gallons of urine each day) directly into Piper's Brook. According to farmers living downstream, this gave the brook's water a "very disagreeable" stench, rendered it "wholly unfit for the use of cattle," killed what fish it once accommodated, and spread "typho-malarial fever."[66]

During the nineteenth century, the perceived threat that industrial pollution and human sewage posed to peoples' health was amplified by the way they understood disease. At least until the 1880s, even doctors knew nothing of the germ theory (the idea that microbes caused sickness). Instead they tended to accept some version of the miasmatic theory, which traced illness back to miasmas (effluvia from decomposing waste matter), such as the filth in Piper's Brook. There was also a sense that cramped living conditions caused and communicated zymotic (or contagious) diseases. When he reported on the sanitary conditions of Lowell in 1849, Dr. Josiah Curtis pointed out "the many lanes and alleys" without proper drainage, which left "house-slops and other refuse" to rot in place and indicated to him "where zymotic diseases prevail." Likewise, he was disturbed by the rapid influx of new residents, "especially of foreign population," which filled "every habitable tenement to an unhealthfully dense degree."[67] "The local unsanitary conditions of many of the tenements and the absence of proper sewers," as the city board of health put it decades later, "have a proportionately unfavorable effect on the health of the inhabitants."[68]

With New England waterways noticeably fouled by the 1860s and 1870s, more and more lawsuits addressed water quality rather than water quantity. Citizens took their complaints to local and state governments as well, describing the problem and calling for action.[69] Speaking before the Agricultural Board of Connecticut, a farmer named James Olcott encouraged the common people to "agitate" in order to "cleanse" the state of the "social evil" of pollution "by sewage from families and factories." No person "ignorant of the insane conditions which have changed our New England climate from one of the most salubrious to one of the worst in the world," he continued, should be sent to the legislature or entrusted with any official position.[70] In Massachusetts, in 1869, the state responded to the increased public concern by establishing a state board of health, the first in the nation. Dr. Henry Ingersoll Bowditch, who had been a militant abolitionist and who continued to participate in struggles for women's rights as well as housing reform, chaired the board, and he focused much of its attention on municipal sewage and industrial wastes in rivers and streams.

In 1878, following on the heels of a statewide investigation, the Massachusetts State Board of Health (MSBH) recommended control legislation, which the legislature passed. The law prohibited the discharge of human waste, refuse, and other pollutants into any water within 20 miles of a public waterway, the historian Ted Steinberg explains, but it exempted the Connecticut and Merrimack rivers as well as the Concord River's last stretch, the part coursing through Lowell.[71] Even with these important exceptions, however, industrial interests immediately began lobbying against the legislation. They also attacked the MSBH, an action that prompted the governor to merge the board with the board of lunacy and the board of charity and to install Charles Francis Donnelly, a corporate lawyer with family connections to textile manufacturers, as chair. The new merged board "fell into the hands of self-seeking capitalists," Bowditch claimed, "afraid of the millstreams being cleaned from the pollutants poured into them by the mills."[72] Still, the law had established the legitimacy of state intervention to address environmental problems, and the principle behind it could not be suppressed.

When the Supreme Judicial Court decided *Brookline v. Mackintosh* (1882), it ruled in favor of the defendant, who had dumped arsenic and other wastes into the Charles River. But the decision also noted that "however useful and necessary" or longstanding, the practice of polluting water could be restricted if the state felt that polluting was "incompatible with the health, safety, and welfare of the community." Four years later, the legislature passed a stronger water purity act, as John Cumbler notes, "specifically designed to protect the streams and ponds used for drinking." Meanwhile, the governor had reestablished the board of health and appointed two reformers and two members associated with manufacturers to fill it out. One of the latter, Hiram Mills, the chief engineer for the Essex Company in Lawrence, worked with Ellen Swallow Richards and William Sedgwick to develop water-quality standards as well as to establish the Lawrence Experiment Station, a pioneering water-treatment facility. Although this effectively reduced industrial and municipal water pollution to a problem for engineers and chemists to solve with filtration and additives, it also demonstrated the lasting legacy of earlier efforts by Bowditch and others.[73]

Something very similar happened, in fact, with renewed efforts to revive the declining stock of New England's migratory fish. "Salmon had disappeared from the upper Connecticut River after construction of a dam near the Connecticut-Massachusetts border in 1798," Richard Judd observes, "and shad had been stopped by a higher dam built in South Hadley in 1849." Likewise, the 30-foot high dam at Lawrence, finished in 1847, ended fish runs on the upper part of the Merrimack. Leading up to the middle of the century, dams on tributary streams and brooks and the increasing amount of waste that poisoned waters, lowered dissolved oxygen, and covered spawning grounds had taken a toll as well. In response to citizen pleas demanding restoration of what once was an important source of food, in 1866 Massachusetts and Connecticut established fish commissions, and New Hampshire, Vermont, and Maine did the same the following year. Recognizing the need to coordinate their efforts and work out a regional approach, these states created the New England Commission of

River Fisheries. Additionally, Massachusetts and other states began to establish state fish hatcheries with the hopes of scientifically propagating their way out of the problem, and sidestepping the issue of obstructing dams and pernicious pollution.[74]

By the end of the nineteenth century, with increased interest in sport fishing among privileged elites, the region's fish commissions (which became fish and game commissions) changed their focus. They turned pisciculture programs away from the original purpose of stocking fish for food, concentrated on raising fingerling species that served the interests of leisure-minded anglers, and imposed new restrictions on access, redefining the fish as property of the state governed by strict rules. Stocking trout and salmon (rather than shad and pickerel) narrowed the beneficiaries of conservation, and establishing open seasons, prohibiting certain equipment or techniques, and limiting the catch all spoke to a different use of the natural resource.[75] "Sometimes it has been charged by those who have not given the subject careful consideration," the Connecticut Commission for Fish and Game defensively stated, "that this commission is largely engaged in propagating game fishes for the few at the expense of the many."[76]

To gain compliance, the state agencies relied on local sheriffs, constables, and wardens appointed by select boards or town councils. Those officials were reluctant to prosecute neighbors for violating unpopular laws, however, and justices were often predisposed against convictions, especially when the accused were too poor to pay fines. In the community at large, citizens who brought complaints risked retaliation, and many tended to follow a code that made it a disgrace to inform on violators.[77] Much like the allowance for dam breaking decades earlier, there was a persistent sense, especially in smaller, rural towns, that local, common people knew best (rightly or wrongly) how the land and waters around them should be used.

With conservation polarized along class lines and the state managing nature for the sake of the elite, it was increasingly common for working people to be branded as environmental outlaws while those with wealth, power, and privilege described themselves as the most enlightened and sensible. This is doubly ironic because the same people who were taking such a great interest in sport fishing (as well as recreational hunting) also were from the segment of society with the greatest responsibility for the environmental degradation caused by capitalism. One of the ways they resolved this was by setting aside certain areas where different rules applied, both conservation of fish and game and preservation of so-called wilderness. This left the rest of the landscape open to the ravages of extractive industry and manufacturing. At the same time, at least for a few more decades, working people willfully ignored the new arrangement, continuing traditional practices that had since been transformed into crimes—poaching, stealing timber, and so on. As industrialization took many from the woods and fields to the factory floor, however, they acquired their own reasons to adopt a corresponding, modern "love for the outdoors."

2

Why "Game Wardens" Carry Guns and Interpretive Rangers Dress like Soldiers: Class Conflict in Forests and Parks

After serving as a game warden in Vermont for more than a decade, starting just before the opening of the twentieth century, New Englander Henry Chase had a good sense of the challenges and dangers that came with the job. "We need laws framed by unselfish men who have made a scientific study of the conditions," he wrote, "and then we must have these laws enforced by equally unselfish men who are in sympathy with the cause, and who possess sufficient courage and intelligence to do their work honestly and thoroughly." Practically speaking, a game warden also needed to have "familiarity with the country in which he is working." That could be aided by a reliable, local guide, though there was always the risk of treachery and betrayal. "Natives of a given community" Chase noted, "are loath to act as informers against their neighbors."[1]

In some instances, despite the supposed scientific soundness of conservation, the "unselfish men" executing the law had to be ready to use force, to catch and hold violators or simply to defend themselves. Outlining the powers of game wardens, Chase made a point to quote the Vermont attorney general's 1908 statement on the matter, to answer any doubt or reason for hesitation. If resisted while making a lawful arrest, the legal opinion explained, an armed officer "may use such force as is necessary to overcome the resistance, even to the taking of life." In that case, "if the person resisting is killed by the officer it is justifiable homicide; if the officer is killed, it is murder." To prepare for the possibility of a violent confrontation, Chase advised, wardens should carry the very best weapons, since "his very life may depend upon the excellence of his gun."[2]

Out West, in the country's first national parks, protecting natural resources and preserving wilderness also carried the potential for dangerous conflict, since establishing acts and administration ran up against many local peoples' traditional use of the land. After Yosemite was established in 1890, the secretary of the interior asked for U.S. troops to patrol the area, "to prevent timber cutting, sheep herding, trespassing, or spoliation in particular." Toward that end, Captain A.E. Wood was made the first acting superintendent and Troops I and K of the Fourth Cavalry—fresh from chasing Geronimo and his Apache band around Arizona and just before they were sent to the Philippines to put down a popular insurrection there—were set to work in the park. Different troops cycled in and out during the years to follow, but the army was not permanently withdrawn until 1914, once nearby residents were deemed sufficiently pacified. A force of "civilian rangers," as H. Duane Hampton puts it, took the soldiers' place.[3] Two years later, when the federal government created the National Park Service to oversee the growing park system, it was no coincidence that its rangers were uniformed in a military-style outfit, including a soft-brim "army campaign" Stetson.

By one telling, the recommendations of Henry Chase and the record of U.S. troops' policing Yosemite both demonstrate the hard-fought battle to finally end centuries of rapacious destruction. As dispassionate technicians and modern mystics attempted to advance badly needed new ideas and policies, the standard rendering goes, they met a firestorm of stubborn, backward-looking opposition. Those who stayed the course and risked their lives were visionaries and heroes. Yet there were social elements and implications to these efforts, missing in the traditional interpretation, that better explain the resistance encountered. Conservation and preservation advocates disregarded the existing relationship common people had with nature through work, ignored the strains of appreciation and the capacity for collective restraint those same people exhibited, and concentrated decision making in the hands of a few supposedly enlightened individuals with recourse to the state's coercive authority.

Well into the late nineteenth century, most Americans were rural dwellers and made a living, in some manner or form, from the land. In that work, they were often guided by what Karl Jacoby calls a moral ecology, a set of written and unwritten (but usually environmentally sound) rules that had accumulated, so to speak, over a long period of time. They were shared by most if not every member of a community and enforced without any formalized structure, often simply by ostracizing an offender. But laws restricting fishing and hunting, regulations governing logging, and enactments creating state and national parks that prohibited any use besides recreation conflicted with these preexisting values and customs. In addition, they came from outside the community, crafted by a largely unaccountable bureaucracy and imposed through agents who sometimes used despotic (and not entirely lawful) methods. That is what provoked malice and various acts of environmental banditry, including all manner of efforts to continue age-old practices despite their prohibition.[4]

During the antebellum period of American history, before the Civil War, there had been some commonly understood recognition that farmers, fishermen and others could effectively regulate their own use of nature. On January 7, 1840, for example, Goldsborough, Maine, residents petitioned for a law allowing creation of a local fish committee that would meet annually to confer about removing dams or other obstructions and "take such Steps & measures as well in their judgment" that would best promote fish passage up Harbor Stream and into Forbes Pond. This was in no way odd or unprecedented, merely an extension of what people were already doing. "Fishers and other rural petty producers," Richard Judd points out, had "learned to manage their resources in a variety of local contexts to preserve stability and equity." In Goldsborough, as elsewhere, "regulatory mechanisms varied from internalized norms and subtle social pressures to elaborate written codes." Within this context, a recognized history of community governance, only 11 days after the town residents sent the petition, the Maine legislature granted their request.[5]

In the years after the Civil War, however, decision making about New England waterways gravitated to state and regional bodies with an increasing amount of contempt for local knowledge and practice. To be sure, the new role of the state originated partly with efforts by radicals to protect working peoples' health, threatened by industrial and municipal waste. And fish commissions were initially established to restore migratory fish that once served as an important food source, fish that disappeared as ever-higher dams blocked their runs and pollution poisoned their spawning grounds. Yet those motivations were quickly corrupted, and by the 1890s the point of state intervention (through fish commissions and otherwise) was to defend and extend the interests of manufacturing interests, on the one hand, and the concerns of wealthy sport anglers, on the other.

Likewise, local timber management in the region was steadily displaced by state and eventually national oversight (the federal Bureau of Forestry was created in the 1870s, a Forest Reserve Act was passed in 1891, and the U.S. Forest Service was established in 1905). The forest-conservation movement, born out of popular concern, focused on a host of problems associated with forest abuse by large logging operations and paper mills, including soil erosion, failing farms, out-migration, flooding, and the survival of small-scale timber operations. Yet the new regulatory framework greatly interfered with local use, and some legislation, such as the Weeks Act, passed in 1911, definitively put forest policy at the service of profit-driven corporations. That law enabled the federal government to purchase huge tracts of land and created a system of federal and state cooperation to protect the nation's timber from fires. Numerous smaller private holdings were consolidated into national forests and their integrity was maintained with the understanding that the areas would be leased to big logging companies.

To be sure, in the public discussion about prohibiting common peoples' customary use of the natural world and putting oversight and management in the hands of the state, proponents quite frequently identified those with criminal instincts by their race or ethnicity. "The people of all the New England States," New York Zoological Society President Henry Fairfield Osborn wrote, "are poorer when the ignorant whites, foreigners, or negroes of our southern states destroy the robins and other song birds of the North for a mess of pottage."[6] Additionally, within many communities there were usually tensions between ethnic and racial groups (e.g., whites and blacks in the South, native-born and immigrants in the East, etc.), expressed through less than equitable application of the rules embedded in a dominant group's "moral ecology." The common characteristic that seemed to make all the ethnic and racial groups deficient in the eyes of elites, however, and the attribute that also set the smug critics apart, was class. "The alien [foreign] hunter is usually employed as a laborer on some large construction work, lives in a camp with a horde of his fellows," *Forest and Stream* explained, "and hunts the robin, the chippie or the blue bird solely as food."[7] Likewise, many of the poor whites and blacks in question were sharecroppers or, in the northeastern and western states, small farmers and trappers.[8]

What complicates this story further is that common peoples' resistance to resource conservation and wilderness protection was not absolute, and it dissipated over time, at least by the 1920s and 1930s. The shift was due primarily to the dual experience of migration and industrialization. Like the mill girls in the 1830s and 1840s, when other rural dwellers left the countryside for cities and farms for factories their relationship with nature was transformed. It became less a thing to know and engage through labor and more of a thing to escape to or dream about. "We ask you to sympathize with us in our attempt to furnish some sort of outdoor recreation for the factory girl and the factory man," implored Ethelbert Stewart, the commissioner of labor statistics, at the 1926 National Conference on Outdoor Recreation, "the vamp matcher in a shoe factory who must handle 720 pairs of shoes an hour ... the toe-cutter in the sheep-killing beds in our slaughter houses who must handle 400 sheep an hour." This, he said, is "whom we would like to save from the insanity that follows industrial fatigue."[9] That new attitude was ground for workers' reconciliation with fish and game laws, timber management, and the like, but especially for the expansion of state and national park systems.

Adirondack Pirates and Allegheny Aliens

Although there were many contentious disputes over control of natural resources in New England at the close of the nineteenth century, that kind of conflict was certainly not a uniquely regional affair. Other parts of the country witnessed similar discord for much the same reason, including large swaths of the Northeast, particularly whole sections of New York and Pennsylvania. In upstate New York, creation of an Adirondack reserve and imposition of new, strict conservation laws challenged homesteaders living within its boundaries (lawfully and not) who were used to regarding the woods, streams, and ponds as a commons. At the same time, in various Pennsylvania counties, southeastern European immigrant laborers (Italians, Hungarians, etc.) repeatedly clashed with game wardens, judges, and others over when, what, where, and why to hunt.

The original inspiration and motivation for closing off the Adirondack area came from George Perkins Marsh's book *Man and Nature*, published in 1864, with a telling subtitle, "Or, Physical Geography As Modified by Human Action." Predicting drastic ecological consequences from rural peoples' unwise use of the land, Marsh called for removing resources from local control and putting them in the hands of scientists and government technicians. Sportsmen seeking a permanent hunting ground and industrialists worried about the effects of deforestation on adequate water flow needed to run mills followed in step, and they made a proposal to the state legislature. In the report accompanying an initial enabling bill, the drafting committee made a certain emphasis. The legislators hoped that the "fashionable young men of the period" would "replace the vicious enervating, debasing pleasures of the cities" with "boating, tramping, hunting, and fishing expeditions," and that required "some measure to preserve the game, and the forest which affords it shelter."[10]

By 1885, the state of New York had created the Adirondack forest preserve overseen by a forest commission, and in 1892, it combined the preserve as well as adjoining private lands into a 3-million acre park. Subsequently, the assembly also enacted more restrictive fish and game laws, which limited the number of deer any one hunter could kill to three (and later two) per year, prohibited traditional hunting practices such as "jacking" (blinding deer with lights) and "hounding" (hunting with dogs), and outlawed the use of nets by fishermen. To enforce the new rules, they also created a "forest police," which could (without a warrant) arrest anyone violating those provisions or others adopted by the commission. The first patrols reported both gross infractions and frequent hostility, situations the *New York Times* headlined with "Pirates of the Forest" and "Stealing Is Their Trade."[11]

Of course, the Adirondacks were not and did not suddenly become a lawless land. Guided by the notion that they had a natural right to subsistence, locals regarded undeveloped lands as open to hunting and foraging, without worrying that neighbors would accuse them of trespassing. The "rights of the woods," however, were circumscribed. Game blinds, fish weirs, and traplines, like homesteads and improved areas in general, notes Karl Jacoby, were "exclusive property" and off limits to anyone else's use but their owner's. Similarly, even those parts of the woods theoretically open to all were governed by certain conventions. While there was considerable anger about laws restricting hunting to summer and early fall (to accommodate vacationing sport hunters), residents recognized the need for confining their hunting to certain times of the year. "There was a universal code," Franklin County resident David Merrill recalled, "that deer should not be disturbed while 'yarding,' or in the breeding season, and this applied to birds as well." Taking a few cords of stove wood or cutting timber to build a house or barn, although in violation of new rules that made the entire forest state property, also had social legitimacy, as long as they were appropriated for subsistence rather than commercial sale.[12]

Frustrated with the new regulatory regime, locals used their superior knowledge of the landscape and the reliability of community cohesion to thwart objectionable enforcement whenever and wherever possible. While the forest commission still struggled to map state holdings, residents were less than helpful with surveyors attempting to establish property lines, and they sometimes burned, cut down, or otherwise destroyed trees blazed to mark boundaries. Game wardens faced obstacles as well, especially if they were from the area they oversaw, hired because they had knowledge of the land and what people were doing there. They risked social exclusion or even violent retribution for trying to do their job, and this made them a little hesitant. "The game wardens are prompt against a stranger," the *Forest Quarterly* reported in 1902, "but the local offenders who go unpunished are numberless." When the wardens were outsiders, or less inclined to extend partiality to friends and kin, their movements were closely tracked and reported, making it difficult for them to actually encounter thieves and poachers.[13]

Those caught stealing timber or poaching game, in fact, were often never convicted. While it remained lawful to cut trees as well as farm on private lands within the park, if boundary lines between public and private land were in dispute (helped by destruction of survey markers), violators could claim they didn't know they were doing wrong. Additionally, locals who witnessed a violation tended to claim they were unable to recognize their neighbors or their draft animals, and sympathetic courts refused to punish them. Of the seven people that one fish and game warden prosecuted in 1894, "three were acquitted, one never showed up to trial, and one, having pled guilty to killing a deer out of season, received only a suspended sentence." Only two suffered any penalty, small fines for illegal fishing, which they settled by serving a few days in jail rather than paying.[14]

Yet the most intense and violent reaction was directed at wealthy absentee landowners, who had bought up large tracts, established private parks there, and attempted to protect their property for exclusive use. "The poor, as well as the men of moderate means," a New York Assembly investigative committee reported in 1899, "are complaining that our forest lands are rapidly being bought up by private clubs, and are closely watched by alert game keepers, and thus, as they claim, and not without some reason, our [woods] are all being monopolized by the rich; that we are apeing [sic] the English plan of barring the poor man from the hunt." The tensions this created came to a head with the murder of an estate owner named Orrando Dexter, who had tangled with locals several times and had initiated numerous lawsuits against them. "Dexter's murder illustrates and must intensify the bitterness felt by the small farmers and woodsmen in the Adirondacks, and by those who have been long accustomed to hunt and fish where they wished," the New York World editorialized, "against the rich men who have established great estates in the forest, fenced them with wire and dotted them with signs: 'No trespassing,' 'No poaching.'" Other private park owners as well as the forest commission responded by hiring additional guards and foresters, while residents felt even more emboldened to rip down signs, cut fences, shoot at guards, and set fire to the woods. In a way, this resistance worked, prompting owners of some of the largest private parks to sell land to the state, the result being a significant increase in the size of the forest preserve.[15]

In fact, while local people demonstrated considerable resentment toward the new order being imposed on the woods and waters around them, they also started to rely on state conservation in place of community-based regulation. When forester John Hunkins and his assistants first traveled to St. Lawrence County, they were "unable to obtain a boat or any accommodations from these people for any consideration," and they believed that their lives were "in constant jeopardy, either from those we had prosecuted or from those who feared being called to account for their many misdeeds." Over time, however, residents adopted Hunkins and his staff as allies in the fight against outsiders. "While conservationists might depict rural folk as ignorant and environmentally destructive," Karl Jacoby argues, "residents pointed out that many violators in the Adirondacks were in fact drawn from the ranks of ostensibly enlightened sports hunters."[16]

One state over, in Pennsylvania, the line between local violators of conservation laws and the people engaged to enforce them was, at least for a while, more sharply drawn, in part because ethnic prejudice assumed a greater role in the conflict. Game law advocates and the wardens who implemented the law tended to single out Italians, Hungarians, and other southern and eastern Europeans as especially brazen offenders. Still, there was a clear class dimension. "The scourge of lumber-camps in big-game territory, the mining camps and the railroad-builders is a long story," William Homaday, the New York Zoological Society director, complained. "It is a common thing for 'the boss' to hire a hunter to kill big game, to supply the hungry outfit, and save beef and pork."[17] When Pennsylvania State Game Commissioner Joseph Kalbfus tried to get a law passed banning aliens from hunting and possessing firearms, his proposal was initially sidelined by representatives in the statehouse beholden to organized labor. They insisted "that the measure originated with corporations," he complained, "whose sole purpose was to take from the poor man the power to defend himself and his family from oppression." The tables, so to speak, were temporarily turned on him. Kalbfus was labeled an "agent of corporations" while "the alien, particularly the Italian, who, from his actions, seemed to think that the word 'Liberty' on our escutcheon meant license to do as one pleased, was lauded to the skies."[18]

Game conservation in Pennsylvania was first promoted by rural landowners, small farmers concerned about the increasing number of urban and out-of-state hunters (carried to the countryside by new railroads) making tracks across their fields and pastures. The first laws, passed in the late nineteenth century, established bag limits and closed seasons, prohibited Sunday hunting and killing of all but a few species of game birds, and limited hunters to hunting only with a gun. After initially relying on local constables for enforcement, additional legislation created several game warden positions and deputy game protectors for each county (the latter, ominously, paid through half the fines assessed violators). In at least some areas, immigrants who had come to work rural quarries and mills as well as other local residents willfully disregarded the conservation restrictions, and farmers made no objection, as long as no property was damaged and poachers were discreet. "A sort of tacit agreement between farmers and hunters emerged," the historian Louis Warren writes, "allowing local men access to hunting grounds, in violation of state law but in keeping with local understandings." This effectively "defined the boundaries of a new local commons, embedded within the state commons and operating parallel to it."[19]

Perhaps because the number of immigrants steadily increased, however, latent mistrust surfaced and tensions intensified. Cultural differences and language barriers kept native-born farmers and foreign-born laborers apart, and immigrant hunting practices did not always fit neatly with existing local customs. They usually did not ask permission to shoot game on private property and they went after groundhogs, songbirds, and other strange quarry to supplement what food they could buy with their meager wages. Consequently, there was growing support for a nonresident license law, which the state legislature passed in 1903, defining nonnaturalized immigrants as nonresidents and requiring them to pay a $10 annual fee to hunt (residents did not have to pay a fee until 1912).

Yet the new law only exacerbated ill feeling and violations of game laws continued. After a farmer let an officer use his telephone to aid the arrest of an Italian poacher, the *New Castle News* reported in 1907, he found one of his cows shot dead the next day and a note reading, "This is for assisting the police." In another instance, after a farmer called authorities on Italian hunters for trespassing, dozens of fellow immigrants showed up in the area asking for his whereabouts. To some extent, they really had no other choice but to act this way, boxed in as they were by laws that criminalized what once had been a routine part of how they made a living. "By far the greatest number of cases of violation of our game laws," the Pennsylvania Game Commission declared in 1908, "killing game out of season, hunting on Sunday, killing song and insectivorous birds, [are] wrongs done by the unnaturalized foreign born resident of this State, mostly Italians."[20]

In countless other state documents, sportsmen's journals, news stories, and conservation-minded books, southern and eastern Europeans were typically characterized as indiscriminate "pot hunters," as opposed to gentlemen sportsmen. "They will shoot for their larders any living wild thing that crosses their path," *Forest and Stream* declared, "from a deer to a chipmunk—from a wild goose to a sparrow. No living creature can escape them, as they are patient, persistent and persevering in their efforts at extermination."[21] Part of the problem was culture, the values and attitudes immigrants (supposedly) brought with them. "They come from lands," the journal explained in another article, "where the destruction of all bird life is regarded as legitimate, and where such life is regarded only as so much food moving about, to be captured by any means whatever."[22]

The "gentlemen" part of "gentlemen sportsmen," however, was really about class. "Pot hunting" was a matter of meeting basic needs in a limited amount of free time, which sportsmen's codes and conservation laws hindered. Although critics were not willing to examine the full significance of that fact, they were sometimes careful to narrow their elitist disapproval accordingly. "The American People are now confronted by the Italian and Austrian and Hungarian laborer and saloon-keeper and mechanic," Hornaday declared, "and all Americans should have an exact measure of the sentiments of southern Europe toward our wild life generally, especially the birds that we do not shoot at all, *and therefore they are easy to kill.*" Having received reports about "Italians in the east, Hungarians in Pennsylvania, and Austrians in Minnesota," he wrote "it seems absolutely certain that all members of the lower classes of southern Europe are a dangerous menace to our wild life.[23]

Besides their threat to wildlife, the working-class immigrants apparently posed a threat to game wardens too. Between 1903, when the nonresident license law was passed, and 1909, when unnaturalized immigrants were banned from hunting altogether, suspected poachers killed at least six Pennsylvania wardens or deputy game protectors, and a number of others were shot but survived.[24] One deputy, Seely Houk, went missing in late March 1906, and his body was found more than a month later near a small limestone quarry in Hillsville. An alderman from a nearby township, O.L. Miller, had complained to the game commission a year before about Houk's vindictiveness toward immigrants and abuse of his authority, and many Italians held a grudge against him, so his bloody end was not entirely surprising to folks in the area. Ultimately, the Pinkerton agents sent to investigate put the blame on members of what they called the Hillsville Black Hand, a secret society of Italian criminals, and a former leader was hanged. But in other cases, attacks on game wardens had nothing to do with criminal elements, and, in fact, none of the other murders were ever solved.[25]

Immediately after the Houk killing, Game Commissioner Kalbfus successfully pushed the state legislature to enact a measure prohibiting unnaturalized residents from possessing a shotgun or rifle and from hunting, ostensibly "to give additional protection to wild birds and animals and game." One immigrant challenged his arrest under the law, and in 1914 the U.S. Supreme Court upheld the legislation, ruling it constitutional.[26] After this, according to Louis Warren, resistance to game laws "became less violent and more covert," and in time, much of the conflict with immigrants over hunting lessened. The American-born, second generation immigrants were citizens and many earned higher wages that made it unnecessary to take to the woods for subsistence. Instead, they joined other local American hunters and turned increasingly to recreational deer hunting, even aiding in the establishment of the Mahoning Sportsmen's Association.[27]

Unbearable Scourge of the South

Among the other groups singled out by William Hornaday for their predilection to violate game laws, particularly their "slaughter of songbirds," were "negroes" and "poor whites" of the South. That observation (and other like-minded attention to certain southerners) belied the notion that such "devilish work" followed from Italian or other European customs rather than from peoples' fundamental need.[28] During the antebellum period, in every state below the Mason-Dixon Line, from the coastal region to the Mississippi Delta, both blacks and whites regarded unimproved land as a commons, open for their subsistence. By custom and law (fence laws required enclosure of crops rather than animals) they used the woods to run cattle and hogs as well as gather nuts, berries, and roots.[29] They also hunted and fished, something that surely provided respite from other labors (especially for black slaves), but employed particular methods to most easily take certain game and fish that were an important food source.

"Mos' ever plantation kep' a man busy huntin an' fishin' all de time," recalled a former Natchez, Mississippi, bondsman named Charlie Davenport, "If dey shot a big buck, us had deer meat roasted on de spit. On Sundays us always had meat pie or fish or fresh game an' roasted taters an' coffee."[30] On these and other estates, however, where masters allowed Saturday afternoons and Sundays to the slaves to use as they chose, almost anyone could venture out, provided he (or she) respect or successfully skirt the few restrictions on where, when, and how game and fish could be caught. James Bolton remembered that slaves were prohibited from hunting at night as well as having guns or dogs of their own. But the night hours were the only time to catch possums and, suggesting frequent rule-breaking, they caught plenty.. His fellow bondsmen borrowed the master's dogs as well, to catch rabbits during the day, and the game that could not be taken this way "we was right smart 'bout ketchin' in traps." To fish in the local creek, they used hook and line as well as basket traps made by the plantation's carpenters.[31]

In the 1850s, historian Steven Hahn points out, there was some support among planters for modifying fence laws and adopting game legislation. This was driven by gentlemen sportsmen's worries over the effects of common rights on game as well as agricultural reformers' concerns with the toll of open-range grazing on livestock quality. To address these interests, counties in Mississippi, Alabama, and Georgia established hunting seasons for deer, turkey, partridge, and quail, and Maryland and Virginia saw passage of local laws as well. Reformers were careful not to overreach with restrictions and enforcement, however, for fear of stirring up the potentially explosive class hatred of whites, who held traditional common rights closely. Additionally, while black slaves' hunting, fishing, gardening, and gathering could interfere with regular staple crop production, it aided the plantation regime too. It allowed bondsmen and bondswomen to produce some of their own food and often helped to prevent or soothe resentment and conflict through extension of various privileges.[32]

With the Civil War and emancipation, long-standing labor and race relations were upended and planters had new reasons to enact laws that limited commons use for independent subsistence. If the white elite were going to see a transition from slavery with their control over land and workers intact, then age-old notions and practices had to be reined in. Even northerners ostensibly sent to reconstruct the South along lines of equality colluded in that effort, blinded by their belief in free labor. Reporting from his subdistrict headquarters in the Gulf coast town of Pascagoula, Mississippi, for example, Freedmen's Bureau officer George Corliss bemoaned local freedpeople's poor work ethic. Many of them "are industrious and frugal," he explained, "while others are inexcusably idle and slothful, [and] some of the latter manage to exist by fishing, hunting, &c."[33] Freedpeople were carving out a space for more genuine autonomy, drawing on customary rights and making use of unenclosed land to thwart labor discipline. They spurned "wage and sharecropping incentives in favor of rude subsistence on game and raised foodstuffs rather than cotton."[34]

In response, there was renewed agitation for game and stock laws, with planters' class interests subsumed under cover of arguments about the "wholesale and ill-seasoned destruction" of fish and wildlife, the diminishing supply of timber, the inefficiencies and costs of fencing practices, and the benefits of improved animal husbandry.[35] In a few states they prevailed, with trespass legislation that fined anyone caught entering enclosed or unenclosed land without the owner's permission, but the elite still had to contend with other small landholding and landless whites. During the brief window of Radical Reconstruction some of those whites joined with blacks in rolling back the restrictions. By the end of the 1870s, though, state governments were once again firmly in the hands of the planters, who resumed efforts to pass conservation measures that served the dual purpose of regulating labor. Before the close of the century, there were game laws in the Black Belt counties of Georgia, Alabama, South Carolina, Tennessee, and Virginia, and they operated on a statewide basis in Mississippi, Louisiana, and Arkansas.[36]

Like legislation in other parts of the United States, game laws in the South prescribed hunting seasons for deer and fowl, prohibited "jack lighting" and various other methods, and curtailed access to private property, while new stock laws required the enclosure of livestock rather than crops and prevented farmers from putting their animals to forage on land they did not own. This requirement made it difficult if not impossible for the landless to keep cows and pigs. At the same time courts eliminated any property claim by sharecroppers in their growing crops, effectively making them rural wage laborers. Similarly, reform legislation lifted protections that certain property once had from debt collection, leaving sharecroppers and small landowners that much more vulnerable to planters and merchants.[37]

These changes did not go uncontested and occasionally newspaper reports mentioned how "outlaws" tore enclosures "to smash" or put out warnings that if anyone meddled with their publicly grazed livestock "they will use their little guns on him."[38] Yet resistance was never as openly violent in the South as it was in New York and Pennsylvania, perhaps testament to opportunities (for whites) and need (for blacks) to quietly evade the law. Certainly, there was much of that happening, as a continued flurry of critical commentary about "the unbearable scourge of the South" suggests. "The pot-hunting negro has all the skill of the Indian, has more industry in his loafing, and kills without pity and without restraint," Charles Askins wrote in a 1909 *Recreation* magazine article. Recently, he claimed, the situation had grown worse, when a higher price for cotton put money in blacks' hands and allowed them to purchase guns, "a gun for every black idler, man and boy, in all the South." With that, "a wail went up from the sportsmen, 'The niggers are killing our quail.'"[39]

The subdued resistance also likely has something to do with the greater power and more vital class interests of conservation proponents. Though some among the ruling white elite did actually want to play out the script of good sportsmen, distinguishing themselves from the lower classes by following particular rules in the field, they were more closely wedded to conservation law and other regulation of access to the land as fundamental to their economic interests. "The great distinction to be ever borne in mind between the game laws of Europe and those of America," President Theodore Roosevelt claimed, "is that that former were passed for the protection of game for a class, while the laws of the republic are passed for the preservation of game for use of all the people."[40] Yet however much the president wanted to think otherwise, fish and game conservation in the South was intimately tied to (black and white) labor discipline and an unchallenged monopoly over natural resources. This is ironic, of course, because within just a few decades after the Civil War, northern investors (of the moneyed kind represented by the Roosevelts and other families like them) managed to turn the region into a colony, extracting its wealth (timber, coal, cotton, etc.) for profit elsewhere.

Raiding Indians and Lawless Whites

Like his friend and fellow outdoor enthusiast Theodore Roosevelt, naturalist John Muir also recognized the importance of state intervention to manage the wildlife and wild places that remained in the United States at the end of the nineteenth century. He was especially enamored of mountain landscapes out West, notable for their power to inspire awe and tend to souls ground down by modern life. "The wildest health and pleasure grounds accessible and available to tourists seeking escape from care and dust and early death" he waxed, "are the parks and reservations of the West."[41] The problem, as Muir well knew, was that these parks and reservations did not actually fit the strict definition of "wild" or "wilderness," since many people continued to occupy them or at least frequently use the natural resources there. "Ax and plow, hogs and horses, have long been and are still busy in Yosemite's gardens and groves," he observed about his most beloved haunt. "All that is accessible and destructible is being rapidly destroyed."[42]

The specific concept of wilderness embraced by Muir and his contemporaries (there were others strikingly different in centuries preceding) was born of a romantic desire to experience both religious redemption and national renewal. Standing in the midst of sublime scenery revealed the handiwork of God, and glimpsing remnants of the unvanquished frontier spoke to the American values and identity fashioned by settlers.[43] What made these sentiments so appealing at the time was the corresponding ambivalence increasing numbers of people felt toward cities and factories, including the wealthy and powerful who gained so immensely from their growth and spread. "The very men who most benefited from urban-industrial capitalism," William Cronon points out, "were among those who believed they must escape its debilitating effects."[44]

The trouble with wilderness, however, is that it was (and is) a profoundly, overly simple notion, setting human against nonhuman, defining people as interloping disturbers rather than integral parts of nature. George Perkins Marsh had said as much in his book, *Man and Nature*, which so significantly influenced the creation of an Adirondack reserve. Likewise, the national parks established according to this idea were not meant to be sites for labor or making a home but rather for escapist, morally freighted recreation.[45] "The first point to be kept in mind … is the preservation and maintenance as exactly as is possible of the natural scenery," Frederick Law Olmsted wrote about Yosemite, "the restriction, that is to say, within the narrowest limits consistent with the necessary accommodation of visitors, of all artificial constructions and the prevention of all constructions markedly inharmonious with the scenery of which would unnecessarily obscure, distort or detract from the dignity of the scenery."[46] Consequently, something had to be done about the folks who ceaselessly desecrated "the gardens," grazing "hoofed locusts" (sheep), gathering stove wood and building timber, and hunting game animals. Because they often refused to desist willingly, coercion and force had to be employed to realize the ideal.

The first of many national parks was Yellowstone, established in 1872, in what was then still Wyoming Territory, and it was there that the federal government set numerous precedents for policing and overseeing protected areas. Among the main attractions of the place were the geysers and hot springs, geothermal wonders expected to attract wealthy tourists venturing forth on newly extended railroad lines. Yet bands of Native Americans (Blackfeet, Crow, Shoshone, and Bannock) roamed the mountains and valleys too, following a well-worn network of paths according to a regular annual cycle. The paths led to obsidian outcroppings that shed workable pieces for arrowheads, knives, and other tools, hunting grounds that promised sheep, bear, elk, and deer, streams swimming with trout and other fish, and sites for gathering wild edibles such as roots, nuts, berries, and greens.[47]

Initially, many whites simply pretended the Indians weren't even there, penning accounts that described the region as untrodden by human footsteps, existing in "primeval solitude," more exactly fitting with their definition of wilderness. Or, when they did admit the presence of people on the land, they characterized them as transitory nomads (leaving no evidence of settled farming, a key measure in their minds), with most of the native people too superstitious to venture near various features. "Owing to the isolation of the park deep amid snowy mountains, and the superstitious awe of roaring cataracts, sulfur pools, and spouting geysers," one of the early superintendents wrote, the pagan Indians "seldom visit it, and only a few harmless Sheepeater [Shoshone] hermits, armed with bow and arrows, ever resided there, and even they are now vanished.[48]

Yet the Nez Perce War in 1877 and the Sheepeater War in 1879, coupled with increased visitation to Yellowstone, forced supporters and administrators to be more clear-eyed about the matter. During the early 1880s, Superintendent Colonel P.W. Norris successfully lobbied Congress for a treaty banning all native people from the park, and he continued making appeals to the secretary of the interior for assistance from the U.S. Army.[49] Toward that end, prominent, eastern conservationists came to his aid. George Bird Grinnell used the pages of *Forest and Stream* to warn about the threat "bands of roaming savages" posed to Yellowstone. He also joined with Theodore Roosevelt to encourage the Boone and Crockett Club to pass a resolution protesting the "destruction of forests and game caused by these Indian hunting parties" and calling for quick government action.[50] Others, including New York congressman Samuel Cox, spelling out what that might mean specifically, suggested that the park be put "under the exclusive care, control and government of the War Department." Subsequently, in 1886 Captain Moses Harris and 50 cavalrymen from Fort Custer, Montana, began patrolling the park from Fort Yellowstone (near Mammoth Hot Springs) and, later, from scattered outposts and "snowshoe cabins."[51]

While the military began to gain the upper hand in dealing with raiding Indians, however, soldiers had to contend with the much more difficult problem of lawless whites (or, "white Indians," as administrators occasionally and tellingly described them). Some of these folks were squatters within the boundaries of Yellowstone, but many more lived right on the edge of the park, in Gardiner, Montana, and in other nearby settlements. "In certain respects," Karl Jacoby explains, "park authorities considered 'white Indians' to constitute even more of a threat to Yellowstone than Indians did." White settlers could not be subdued with all-out war or controlled by banishment to reservations, their actions could not be dismissed as the simple ignorance of savages, and they felt emboldened to defend their behavior as justified by the inalienable-rights tradition and self-sufficiency expectations so thoroughly embedded in American culture.[52]

To enhance the army's legal authority in the park and address locals' persistent hunting, trapping, and fishing there, George Bird Grinnell and the Boone and Crockett Club pushed Congress to pass the Lacey Act. This law, passed in

1894, put Yellowstone under exclusive jurisdiction of the United States (at one time it had been under the jurisdiction of the Wyoming Territory), prohibited killing, wounding, or capturing any bird or wild animal there (according to Department of Interior regulations), and established certain limits on fishing throughout the area. Violators could be punished with a $1,000 fine, 2 years imprisonment, and confiscation or forfeiture of guns and other equipment, to be decided by a magistrate assigned specifically to the park.[53]

Although there had been a prior arrangement with residents of Gardiner that allowed them to take down timber for household use, the army eventually instituted a permit system (requiring written approval for each foray) and then, in 1898, declared a complete ban on gathering any wood. That policy, for various reasons, was fairly successfully enforced. Grazing livestock, though, was another matter. Early on, as with timber gathering, there had been some allowance for running animal herds in the park. But with the new restrictions on hunting, wildlife populations rebounded and the elk, deer, and antelope put more stress on grazing lands, a situation that necessitated the exclusion of livestock. Violators risked fines and having their animals impounded, yet people continued to put their herds there. The army responded by erecting a 4-mile wire fence along Yellowstone's northern boundary, later replaced with a set of 5-foot high steel spikes. They also began using what were only semi-legal methods to make law-breaking less worthwhile. A few offenders were held in Fort Yellowstone's guardhouse for as long as a month, on a diet of bread and water, confined to a large cage. Others caught with their animals in the park were separated from the livestock and marched to the boundary farthest from the herd, which were scattered in the other direction and left vulnerable to predators until the owner could round them up.[54]

Additionally, to better control access to Yellowstone, the army simplified the park's trail system and limited entry to four places so that soldiers could more easily monitor visitors' arrival and departure. The army recorded everyone's name, address, and length of stay, put trigger seals on any firearms, and required off-season visitors (the most suspicious) to obtain a permit. Locals responded by extending unsanctioned trails, erecting footbridges, and building cabins or dugouts, where they could hide for the night before smuggling their contraband. The army then erected its own cabins and guard posts in remote parts of the park, especially useful for patrolling during the winter time, when tourist visitation was negligible and poachers were more active. Still, white settlers knew that not all of the soldiers cared much for their duties, and they played on that awareness and led some into petty corruption.

Or, they waited when veteran troops rotated out and fresh replacements moved in, creating an opportunity for an upsurge in illicit activities.[55]

When efforts to impose the rule of conservation were successful, the ecological consequences were not always good ones, or at least not entirely "natural" by contemporary standards. Suppressing Indian use of fire and stopping conflagrations ignited in other ways meant that when fires did happen and couldn't be put out immediately they often became infernos and scorched everything in their path, including jack pines, which are dependent on smaller fires to heat their cones open and release their seeds. Similarly, campaigns to eliminate lions, coyotes, wolves, and other predators and to more strictly control Indian and settler poaching reduced checks on the elk population. Increased elk caused soil erosion when they grazed in mountain and valley meadows and, since they liked to browse on aspen and willows, beavers had fewer materials to make dams that created lush wetlands, in turn significantly affecting a multitude of other plant and animal species.[56]

Yet despite the limitations of conservation and despite the various ways locals relied on access to protected timber, game, and fish, residents living near Yellowstone did sometimes cooperate with rangers and wardens, and their cooperation increased over time. Much like folks in or around the Adirondacks, western mountaineers made a distinction between subsistence and commercial use of natural resources and ascribed much greater legitimacy to the former than the latter. Profit-hungry hunters and trappers who crossed a particular line by taking too much game or poaching for some marketable part of an animal, such as elk teeth, faced community censure and risked having even neighbors turn them in for their deeds. It was not uncommon for locals to send secret notes to officials, providing the necessary information to catch poachers while keeping the informant safe from retaliation.[57] Eventually, however, that secrecy became less necessary, as common rural people and their urban working-class counterparts moved into a new era marked by widespread support for legislation and regulations meant to conserve and preserve nature.

In Peace and Reverence

"To fully understand the changes in thinking that Oregonians expressed with regard to nature in this period," Lawrence Lipin writes about the late nineteenth and early twentieth centuries, "we must recognize that environmental politics have often been class politics."[58] As was the case in many parts of the United States, prior to the 1920s Oregon conservation laws enjoyed strong support among middle-class businessmen and wealthy elites with newfound interests in sport hunting and angling. Yet they generated widespread opposition among small farmers, market hunters, and commercial fishermen, as well as urban factory workers. This opposition took several forms, including intentional law breaking, threats and violence against game wardens, and organizational resistance.

When longtime game warden Irving Hazeltine confronted a small group of poachers led by Sam Johnson in Wheeler County, they boasted about their catch and ran away. The warden confiscated their boat, but the men were allowed to take it back because Hazeltine failed to go through the courts to make the seizure legal. "I could pepper this man Johnson with shot with no more feeling that [sic] I would have toward a breach cow," he wrote to the central office. The next time he found poachers at Spray Dam, in fact, the warden did shoot, but he knew making an arrest was futile, considering pervasive local hostility. "There was not a jury in Wheeler Co. that would convict any one for taking salmon out of the [fish] ladders at Spray," Johnson told him, and Hazeltine knew he was right.[59] Similarly, in Tillamook County, deputy game warden E.H. Clark arrested two Italians for possessing a shotgun without a license, in violation of the state's own Alien Gun Law, but the elected county attorney refused to prosecute. He claimed the law was unconstitutional, despite the recent U.S. Supreme Court ruling on Pennsylvania's more restrictive legislation.[60]

If officials pushed too hard or too far, the result could be bloodshed, although that was not necessarily punished either. In one case, deputy game warden Arthur Hubbard was murdered in 1914, Lipin recounts, while attempting to arrest Loris Martin. Hubbard had arrested the man before, in 1911, for fishing without a license. Martin had vowed to kill the warden if he came around again, and that's apparently what he did, as Hubbard and Constable A.L. Irwin served a search warrant for illegally hunted venison. During the subsequent trial, the defense attorney successfully painted a negative image of the warden, citing his frequent threats against poachers as well as his habit of entrapping violators. In addition, the county sheriff and his deputy served as witnesses for Martin, who was acquitted.[61]

At the same time, the Oregon Grange and the Oregon State Federation of Labor (OSFL) combined in a battle to stop the "leisure class" from passing legislation that conflicted with "productive use" of nature. "For farmers and workers in extractive industries such as fishing and logging," Lipin explains, "opposition to the efforts to construct a tourist economy was deeply ingrained in a rural value system that presumed fish and animals to belong to those who invested the labor in catching them." With that in mind, in 1914, the legislative committee of the Grange called for abolition of all fish and game laws and passage of new, strictly enforced trespass legislation. Although not as intimately tied to the rural countryside, trade unionists also worked to make the government serve the interests of common people. They mobilized through the OSF "to wrest control of both land and the state from the hands of leading capitalists and corporations" and thereby "provide the basis for a republic of small, independent producers."[62]

During the 1920s, however, urban workers in Oregon (and elsewhere) discarded their emphasis on productive use of nature and embraced the wealthy sportsmen's idea that its recreational use was of greater importance. Beset by the deeply alienating experience of assembly line manufacturing as well as the bustle and dirt of city neighborhoods, factory hands and their families began to venture to forests, streams, and lakes, trips that established and reinforced the new way of thinking about the countryside's flora, fauna, and other features. Articles in the Oregon *Labor Press* responded to this increased interest of the masses to "get away from the complexities of modern life" by printing things like the "ten commandments of the forest," which advised campers to obey wardens and park rangers, to pitch their tents only in designated areas, and to obtain proper permits. If a person followed these rules and approached the forests "in peace and reverence," the *Press* promised, "he shall again find his soul which he loseth in the city."[63]

One particular reason workers were better able to act on evolving desires to experience nature as an escape was an increase in automobile ownership. The assembly line production methods that made escape attractive and necessary also reduced the cost of cars, transforming what had been playthings of the rich into ordinary possessions that even working people could afford. The price of Ford's Model T dropped from $1200 in 1909 to $300 in 1928, and auto registration nationally jumped from a little over a million in 1913 to more than 20 million by the end of the 1920s. This increase was matched by a significant rise in funding by federal and state governments for road building, which extended the reach of cars well into the hinterlands and gave people somewhere to go. "With the improvement of means of travel," Jesse Steiner wrote in 1933, "people are finding it possible to go even further afield in their search for recreation and readily travel long distances during week-ends and vacations to places of scenic interest where their favorite forms of outdoor life may be enjoyed."[64]

The other factor enabling hordes of urban wage laborers and their families to take leisure trips outside the city was the success workers had in winning work-free weekends and extended vacation time. The average workweek of a factory laborer fell from about 60 hours at the turn of the century to 55 hours on the eve of World War I, then again to less than 50 hours by 1920, and still more during that decade and the next.[65] This was something the American labor movement struggled mightily to achieve, partly as a means to reduce unemployment but also, increasingly, with the explicit intention of meeting the growing interest in recreational hunting and fishing, auto camping, and the like. OSFL executive secretary Ben Osborne associated shorter hours with both a "remedy for over-production and under-consumption" as well as "an urge on the part of the people for more leisure and recreation." A two-day week-end, the Oregon *Labor Press* noted in 1925, would give employees "two days to go to the seashore, mountains or rest at home."[66] Similarly, United Auto Workers' Recreation Department director Olga Madar pointed out the way modern work required a new emphasis on the quantity and quality of outdoor leisure. "We need to 'get away from it all,'" she wrote, but "there's more to it than that." Everyone has mental and spiritual "hungers," and those "mental and spiritual cravings which must be satisfied if we are to become complete and happy individuals."[67]

As the twentieth century progressed, in fact, more and more industrial workers developed interests in recreational hunting, fishing, and camping, and that led to widespread acceptance of conservation laws and regulations. Environmental politics continued to be class politics, but there was a grow-ing consensus in the United States, cutting across class lines, about the need for state and federal governments to manage wildlife and preserve scenery. At the center of this new sentiment was the experience workers and their families had with urban living and industrial labor, something Chapter 3 will describe and explain in some detail. The shift in attitudes was also aided by various New Deal programs, which attempted to rescue the economy by putting the unemployed to work expanding and improving state and national parks, mak-ing them more accessible and appealing to the general public, all of which is discussed in Chapter 4. Additionally, in the 1940s and 1950s, support for con-servation became part of the basis for workers and their families to pioneer modern environmentalism, as Chapter 5 will show, providing them with an ecological awareness that sustained a new concern for controlling and prevent-ing industrial pollution.

3

Missionaries Find the Urban Jungle: Sanitation and Worker Health and Safety

Having made the long journey from their homes in Lithuania to the United States, Upton Sinclair's central characters in his 1906 novel, *The Jungle*, were especially startled as a train carried them the last stretch of their journey, from the lush prairie to the hellish bowels of industrial Chicago. On the outskirts of the city there were still fields, but they were "parched and yellow," and eventually the landscape became "hideous and bare," with the exception of ramshackle sheds and houses. "Down every side street they could see, it was the same," Sinclair wrote, "always the same endless vista of ugly dirty little wooden buildings." Passing the first line of factories, with "immense volumes of smoke pouring from the chimneys," the air grew darker and sooty filth covered the ground. The traveling party also began to notice a "pungent odor," which seemed to be getting stronger, soon heavy enough to taste as well as smell. Then they were at its source, standing on a street corner in Back of the Yards, the South Side stockyards district. There were half a dozen chimneys now, "tall as the tallest buildings, touching the very sky—and leaping from them half a dozen columns of smoke, thick, oily, and black as night."[1]

Of course, *The Jungle* is a work of fiction and Upton Sinclair first began writing about the plight of immigrant workers in Chicago meatpacking houses on commission for a socialist magazine, *Appeal to Reason*, which explains why most of the last third is an unabashed ideological diatribe. Yet most of the novel is social realism, descriptive literary journalism that meticulously but poignantly characterizes a people and place in time. Sinclair did months of research for the book, walking the stockyards streets while a bitter meat packing strike played out, interviewing residents about living and working conditions there, and talking with residents of the South Side's University of Chicago settlement house (middle- and upper-class reformers who had moved into the area to help address its many problems). After the research, he went back to New York City and traced out the story of a hard-pressed family that was a composite of what he learned about numerous, actual experiences.

Sinclair's exposé also prompted observers with different political views to make their own assessment, and their reports confirmed what he had to say. By those accounts, the Chicago stockyards and surroundings neighborhoods truly were a living hell. "This world," one Lithuanian American later claimed, "would not have been unusual to Dante."[2] Residents lived densely packed in the midst of foul air, scum-covered waterways, and scattered piles of rotting garbage, compounded by extremely dangerous and unhealthy working conditions in the slaughterhouses and other nearby factories. Not surprisingly, the situation proved deadly from year to year, and disproportionately so, with working-class immigrants and migrants dying at a much higher rate than the city's more affluent, privileged residents. According to a study by Charles Bushnell, one of a number of reform-minded faculty at the University of Chicago at the time, the death rate among children in the Stock Yard District in 1900 was 38.7 per 1,000, while the death rate among children in the wealthier (and politically connected) Hyde Park was 25.7 per 1,000.[3]

Fortunately, by the end of the nineteenth century the unpleasant and deadly situation in Chicago and other American cities had generated growing support for a sanitation (or public health) movement and, by the first decade of the twentieth century, considerable interest in a nascent industrial hygiene (or worker health and safety) campaign. Working-class urban residents and organized labor often played a key part in these efforts, and that experience had a measurable impact on their environmental consciousness, which in turn sustained the role they took in pioneering modern environmentalism in the decades to follow. Yet similar to the tension that plagued the conservation movement, common people did not always see eye-to-eye with the elites leading the urban clean-up and workplace reform crusades.

Part of the reason for disconnect between the groups was that elites tended to cast themselves as missionaries, raising backward people living in impoverished urban wards to a new level of civilization. "Curiously enough," Jane Addams wrote, "the actual activities of a missionary school are not unlike many that are carried on in a Settlement situated in a foreign quarter." This sentiment was particularly evident when native-born reformers were dealing with second-wave European immigrants (from southern and eastern Europe), who they saw as apathetic, ignorant, and lacking moral character. According to Addams, who established the Hull House settlement on Chicago's crowded near west side, the Italians, Greeks, and others living in the district had "little initiative," and the "newly arrived immigrants" were "densely ignorant of civic duties."[4] Ellen Swallow Richards, at one time a resident at the settlement house and now recognized as the "mother of ecology" for her pioneering work on water quality, described these same working-class immigrants as "ignorant, bewildered, and incompetent," needing the attention of a corps of trained men and women if progressive municipal legislation was to be enforced and have any effect once its passage was secured.[5]

To be sure, one of the things that distinguished such Progressive Era reformers as Addams and Richards from others concerned about immigrants was their belief in the possibility for change. Nativists pointed to what they considered essential racial characteristics and threw up their hands, advocating immigration restriction to deal with the myriad problems foreigners supposedly caused. But a growing number of people at the turn of the century pointed to environmental conditions, leavened by remnants of Old World ways, both of which could be transformed. The debate, put more bluntly, was whether "the pig made the sty or the sty made the pig," and settlement house workers tended to agree with the latter formulation.[6] Black "club women" regarded poor, rural black migrants and their neighborhoods in much the same way, and they campaigned for similar improvements.[7] The issue, then, was once again as much about class as ethnicity or race, and the adoption of certain middle-class values was essential for individual social mobility as well as for the health of American democracy. "A tenement dweller exposed to clean streets," as Daniel Eli Burnstein puts it, "would be more likely to acquire habits of personal cleanliness, a livelier personal outlook, and greater civic spirit. The end result would not only be less littering on the streets but also the cultivation of more concern among the poor for complex civic issues that affect the broader community."[8]

Yet even in instances when immigrants did take the initiative to protect their own interests, with what would seem to be the civic consciousness they were said to lack, settlement workers saw the need for guidance from "the better element." In one case, residents of Hull House held a mass meeting to educate their Italian neighbors on the evils of rag picking, the practice of scouring garbage dumps for old rags to sell to a merchant. The reformers sent a delegation to Mayor Creiger and the city council requesting the interference of police and an ordinance was passed and enforced to that effect. But the immigrants "formed a political association, and let the party in power understand that they were voters who would vote against that party at the next election if the interference of the police in their occupation was not stopped." The police, by secret orders, let the rag pickers alone.[9] As the story suggests, the resistance of workers and their families to sanitation measures was frequently driven less by ignorance or some primitive disregard for filthy circumstances than by a need to defend the limited options available for making a living.

On the other hand, there were occasions when ordinary urban dwellers mobilized with reformers to accomplish improved sanitation. Polish women living in Packingtown, for example, repeatedly complained to city officials about the need for water and sewer connections to homes there so that they wouldn't have to carry water from distant hydrants or worry about their children playing in sewage-laden ditches. These were the same ditches that meatpacking companies used to dump the hair, offal, blood, and other waste of slaughtered animals as well. Officials dismissed the women, however, claiming that there weren't enough buildings on the streets to justify an extension. Finally, settlement house workers investigated. They discovered that the area actually had a higher population density than many other parts of Chicago (there were fewer buildings on the block than elsewhere but more people living in them). Subsequently, they joined the Polish women's efforts and by 1910 most Back of the Yards homes had city water as well as city sewer services.[10]

Foreign- and native-born working-class city dwellers also addressed sanitation problems through "sewer socialism," forming alliances with middle-class voters to elect reform candidates who extended municipal control over basic services. This bound solutions to widespread urban environmental problems with efforts to limit the often corrupting influence of private enterprise, setting an important precedent. "The only danger that I can see in the growth of sentiment in favor of collective ownership," Mayor Milton Jones of Toledo, Ohio, explained at a League of American Municipalities meeting, "is the threatened doom of those who seek individual gain at the expense of the people."[11] While in office, Jones was responsible for initiating Toledo's shift to universal garbage collection with a city force, to replace a contract system plagued by deficiency and political patronage and to ensure that garbage collectors earned a decent wage. After his unexpected death in 1904, that agenda was carried on by Mayor Brand Whitlock and other members of a full-fledged Independent Party. It was during Whitlock's second term that the Board of Public Service assumed control of collection.[12]

A similar mix of help from "the better element" and working-class initiative shaped efforts to deal with dangers in the industrial workplace. Power equipment and other technological innovations, assembly line production methods, as well as scientific management efficiency standards might have increased productivity and lowered labor costs, but they worsened familiar occupational health and safety hazards and introduced new ones. Initially, these conditions were addressed by a combination of crusading social scientists like John Andrews and Irene Osgood, settlement house consumer advocates like Florence Kelley and Alice Hamilton, and rank-and-file workers along with various labor leaders. Their advocacy gained traction particularly after the Triangle Shirtwaist fire, March 25, 1911, in which 146 workers died, most of them women. Following the tragedy, the New York Factory Commission conducted an investigation of industrial working conditions, and the state legislature followed up by conducting hearings and enacting 56 laws, many of which other states adopted in some manner or form.[13]

By the 1920s, however, organized labor was in retreat, stumbling in the face of a wholesale assault by employers against workers' collective action, and this changed the role workers and unions played in the emerging field of "industrial hygiene." States were also moving away from resolving employee injury and death claims in the courts to no-fault workers' compensation systems, which established a new incentive for employers to take charge of addressing workplace hazards. Occupational safety and disease studies and the mitigation of recognized problems soon became a nonconfrontational matter of clinical science and industrial engineering.[14] Still, subsequent studies did measurably improve working conditions, and when organized labor revived in the 1930s, unions resumed playing a central part in efforts to make change on the shop floor. Additionally, industrial hygiene became a path for various scientists to begin studying the effects of pollution on communities in general, often with labor's support, laying the groundwork for passing regulatory legislation.

Not a Lady's Job

Like other American cities, Chicago saw dramatic growth between the end of the Civil War and 1920 (the year the U.S. Census Bureau first declared that more than half of all the nation's residents lived in an urban area). By 1880, what was recently a swampy village of 30,000 had more than half a million people living within its limits, and that number doubled to one million within a decade. Every one of these residents generated sewage, garbage, and refuse daily, and the industries that provided employment made even more massive quantities of their own fluid, semi-fluid, and solid waste. To deal with increasing amounts of filth, Chicago had inaugurated a day scavenger service for household waste in 1865. When that proved unsatisfactory, it adopted a contract system 20 years later, although that failed to meet basic sanitation standards as well.[15]

The early ineffectual attempts to collect garbage and refuse were the back-drop for the establishment of Hull House and the residents' campaign to clean up the streets and alleys of the near west side. The settlement house had opened in 1889, when Jane Addams and Ellen Gates Starr renovated a mansion on Polk and Halsted streets, and Addams later claimed she was compelled to establish the settlement by a sense of social futility. She and other young women like her were privileged enough to receive a good formal education, but they found the use of that education restricted by gender conventions. Many of her peers at Rockford Seminary had chosen missionary work over the other limited options (essentially, either teaching or marriage), and Addams compared her work to their approved career choice. "I gradually became convinced," she wrote, "that it would be a good thing to rent a house in a part of the city where many primi-tive and actual needs are found, in which young women who had been given over too exclusively to study might restore a balance of activity along tradi-tional lines and learn of life from life itself."[16]

The near west side was, in fact, one of the most densely populated areas of Chicago, at one time mostly working-class Irish but increasingly crowded by working-class southern Italians, Greeks, and Bulgarians. Early on, settlement residents arranged numerous talks for these neighbors to educate them on the sanitation problems that arose from continuing "peasant" habits in the city. Refuse would not innocently decay in the open air and sunshine in a crowded quarter, they lectured, but would instead cause children to sicken and die. Fearing a cholera epidemic in 1892, the settlement workers also forwarded more than a thousand complaints of sanitary law violations to the health depart-ment. As a result, four local sanitary inspectors were appointed and removed in quick succession, having failed to make any improvements to conditions, but the contractor engaged to collect garbage and refuse continued to neglect his work with impunity. Johnny Powers, the Irish political boss of the nineteenth ward, where Hull House was located, used the contract as a political plum, with little or no expectation that it would be fulfilled.[17]

Frustrated to find an effective means for improving sanitation, in 1895 Jane Addams put in a bid to remove the ward's garbage and refuse herself. Not surprisingly, the bid was thrown out, but Mayor Swift appointed Addams as garbage inspector, causing a great stir among certain local politicians. In the task, Addams took on Amanda Johnson as deputy, and the two made their rounds every day in a covered buggy. Their diligence prompted some com-mentary in newspapers throughout the Midwest, much of it favorable, explain-ing that women were inherently superior to men in such work.[18] Yet not all women were necessarily considered to have the same capacity or desire for what was then called municipal housekeeping. In a speech later that winter, Addams bemoaned the tendency of immigrants on the near west side, particularly the women, to "cling to their old habits and live narrow lives, with scarcely any social intercourse or reception of new ideas." Some residents did eventually become convinced that cleaning up the streets and alleys was an appropriate concern for women, but others, Addams claimed, "remained quite certain that the task of garbage inspection was not a lady's job."[19]

In fact, Hull House residents did not stop at investigations, petitioning, and filling city oversight positions to get the streets and alleys cleaned up. They also became participants in ward elections, trespassing further into the realm of men and altering what it meant to be a municipal housekeeper. Their candidate for one of the two alderman seats in the nineteenth ward won in 1895, although he soon became a loyal supporter of Powers. In the next election, a Hull House put up William Gleeson, an Irish immigrant, to challenge the ward boss himself, but Gleeson lost.[20] In the wake of this defeat, Addams became ill and left for a stint in Europe, so Amanda Johnson took on all the tasks of garbage inspector, performing her duties with evident thoroughness and some success. Powers responded by getting the city council to pass an ordinance eliminating the position across the city, ostensibly to cut expenses. The inspectors were then replaced with temporary appointments, filled at the request of ward leaders, and Powers picked a trusted friend to fill the post in his district.[21]

Hull House residents responded to these sabotage efforts with another city council campaign, but they faced heavy opposition, much of it centered in the nineteenth ward's saloons, where the district's Irish immigrants traditionally gathered for both leisure and politics. Even the wives of saloon patrons and owners, who still could not vote, publicly expressed their support for Powers over the settlement candidate. At one point, a few of these women organized the Ladies Auxiliary of the Nineteenth Ward Democratic Club, and its members elected a Mrs. James McGuirk, wife of a near west side saloon keeper, as president. A Mrs. Frank G. Alberg, the sergeant-at-arms of the club and the wife of another saloon keeper, explained why the members were willing to work for the ward boss, ironically in a way that put their supposed opposition to the expansion of women's roles in question. "He'll keep the streets clean all right," she said, "after the women elect him."[22]

The reform candidate lost the election by a wide margin, but a month after the defeat, Addams met with the mayor and commissioner of public works about the removal of Johnson as garbage inspector. The old inspection system had been restored and new appointments were needed. Officials at city hall would "use every effort to get a satisfactory place for" Johnson, but, the commissioner explained, "he had not yet got the street department organized and until this was done would have to delay the appointment." Only days later, revealing the power Hull House had gained through moral righteousness and good example, he made Johnson chief garbage inspector of the entire city.[23]

Resistance to Hull House–led sanitation was primarily a matter of political calculation, the response by one group (or set of individuals) to defend their monopoly on power. Part of the strategy was to identify reform with women, hoping their steps toward fuller participation in the public sphere would turn misogynist male voters (and complicit female family members) against change. Yet opposition to various reform initiatives, as well as the silence of many who might have supported those initiatives, also stemmed from the sense of superiority and the fear settlement workers exhibited toward neighborhood residents, including the women. Florence Kelley, often held up as most sensitive to working-class immigrants' concerns, demonstrated neither understanding nor sympathy in her description of near west side mothers. "Of the baby's three enemies—milkman, landlord, and unskilled mother," she wrote, "the unskilled mother is the deadliest because her opportunities for doing him harm are continuous and her means of attack so varied." Supposedly, many mothers routinely gave their children spoiled milk, beer, and (when they wouldn't quiet down after being bitten by rats) sleeping draughts. They also fed them bananas, which Kelley and others claimed were dangerous and unhealthy.[24]

Much of elite-led urban environmentalism, including the campaign that played out in Chicago, was part of larger efforts to uplift supposedly deficient ordinary people, to strip them of what was noticeably foreign, and to protect the social order from a radical challenge by diffusing conflict through limited, moderate change. The women taking leading roles in cleaning the city, as they (or their immigrant and African American domestic servants) did their homes, were native-born, middle- and upper-class white women. They initiated and participated in reform campaigns because they considered themselves duty-bound to impart proper urban lifestyles and nurture civic virtue among less fortunate, working-class immigrant urban dwellers. In turn, the immigrants did not always rally to the cause, seeing in it more than just a sincere attempt to improve sanitation and save peoples' lives.

One Chicago settlement house worker who was regarded somewhat differently by neighborhood residents, however, was Mary McDowell. The respect and trust she earned were largely due to the fact that McDowell tended to associate the myriad problems working-class immigrants faced with concentrated corporate power and corrupt city politics rather than individual deficiencies or cultural shortcomings. This social consciousness was gathered from decades of personal experience in a number of movements. She had first come to Chicago with her abolitionist father after the Civil War, and by the 1880s she was immersed in the temperance movement and the campaign for women's suffrage as well as local workers' struggles. While living at Hull House in the 1890s, McDowell took a strong stand in support of striking railroad workers, and in the years to follow she helped organize the Amalgamated Meat Cutters and Butcher Workmen, a local of that same union for female employees, and the Women's Trade Union League. When packinghouse workers went on strike in 1904, she played a leading, supportive role in that drawn-out battle too.

McDowell was keenly aware of the packinghouse workers' plight because in 1894 she also had founded a new settlement house, the University of Chicago settlement, in Back of the Yards.[25] Almost 10 percent of all wage earners worked in that part of the city, and many of the working-class residents were Lithuanians and other eastern Europeans. Conditions for those folks on meatpacking assembly (or disassembly) lines were less than ideal but, as Upton Sinclair's novel suggested, things were little better in the surrounding streets and alleys. The area was plagued by some of the worst air and water pollution in the entire city and whole sections were given over to mounds of garbage carted in from distant (often the most affluent) parts of Chicago.

More than nineteen different companies used a small branch of the Chicago River on the South Side to dump millions of gallons of waste materials daily, and when the larger river's direction was engineered to reverse its flow toward Lake Michigan, the fork ceased to move anywhere. The stagnant section became known as Bubbly Creek, for the gas bubbles that revealed decomposing matter below the surface. "This creek," Mary McDowell wrote, "once an innocent little stream with willows and wild flowers along its bank, had been turned into a cesspool."[26] In addition, what didn't get dumped in the waterway ended up in one of four large clay pits, which had originally served Alderman Thomas Carey's brickyards. The other three holes received garbage and refuse from the rest of Chicago. Not surprisingly, the filth in Bubbly Creek, the rising piles of garbage in the pits, a noxious poorly run garbage reduction plant, the endless animal pens at the stockyards, and the belching smokestacks at the slaughterhouses all made Packingtown a smelly place. Visitors coming down from streetcars immediately put a handkerchief up to their face, and one resident joked that when she first came to the area she thought one of the children she was caring for had dirtied his pants.[27]

Clearly there was need for improvement and the University of Chicago's settlement staff helped encourage greater environmental awareness and channel efforts at remediation by hosting several clubs. The Cleaner Clubs, started in 1896, were made up of immigrant children who went through the neighborhood, recording sanitation problems, taking complaints, and then logging them at City Hall. The Women's Club, composed of first-generation immigrant women, focused on street, alley, and vacant-lot cleanup, including a lot on Ashland Avenue that was used by a packing firm to dump animal hair. And perhaps the most effective club, according to historian Sylvia Hood Washington, was the Neighborhood Guild, a clearinghouse for environmental complaints. The male and female members of this group were particularly concerned about a local glue factory, which produced horrible fumes and maintained pools of filthy standing water, used over and over again. After a great deal of criticism, the company modified its production process to address the bad odor and began to store its water in a rooftop tank.[28]

Following the glue factory victory, McDowell went to city hall in the company of numerous angry immigrant women to complain to the commissioner of health about the clay pit dumps, but he claimed his hands were tied by lack of funds to seek an alternative. The lesson one woman took showed an environmental class consciousness. "Why don't they dump the garbage on the bully-vards?" she asked rhetorically. "Why do they bring it near our homes?"[29] The residents managed to get a temporary injunction against more dumping, and a compromise worked out with a health inspector allowed only dry garbage and required a cover layer of lime. After a few months, however, the compromise was obviously not being followed at the pits and the community campaign soon resumed. In response, McDowell immersed herself in the technical literature about garbage disposal and she made a trip to Europe to study alternative methods, including incineration and recycling. When she returned, the "garbage lady," as some called her, spoke to various groups throughout the city, using stereopticon slides and statistical reports to make her case.[30]

On a sweltering July evening in 1913, just after Chicago women won the right to municipal suffrage, a victory that emboldened some for greater civic engagement, McDowell led an all-female group in a protest at city hall, questioning a proposed incinerator for Back of the Yards. The next day, the *Chicago Tribune* banner headline read "Women Voters Storm Council to Tab Aldermen: More Than 150, Unable to Gain Entrance, Are Forced to Retire." In the end, it was another ingredient in a recipe for success. Eventually, the council approved a small reduction plant and shut down the Packingtown dumps. Mobilizing immigrants, lobbying Chicago residents citywide, confronting the recalcitrant city council, and facing down police had become part of a lady's job.[31]

Graft-Free

Although considerably smaller than Chicago, the city of Milwaukee, Wisconsin, also on the Lake Michigan shore, had its own intractable sanitation problems, including how to collect and dispose of garbage. "Take a stroll of a few blocks in almost any part of Milwaukee," urged one resident, and you will find "heaps of dirt, broken pavements, breakneck crossings, and uninviting pools of filth."[32] Every day the city's "perfect avenues of swill" received all manner of solid waste from householders, overflow from peoples' privy vaults, as well as manure and urine from thousands of horses that pulled carts and carriages. Conditions were as bad as anywhere, but the city government was mired in corruption, and both the Democrat and Republican parties were typically unresponsive to demands for improved basic services, at least those that did not provide a lucrative contract to some favored private investors.

Eventually, following much discussion, years of failed experiments with privately owned crematories and rendering plants, countless accusations and revelations of graft, and several changes in administration, a combination of middle-class business reformers and socialist trade unionists forced the city to take full charge of garbage collection and disposal. Having established the advantages of municipal control in that respect, they continued the struggle and put increasing numbers of socialists in office, reaching the high mark of their influence between 1910 and 1912. Those aldermen, mayors, and others then used their positions to further advance the notion that protecting the interests of all Milwaukee residents was a communal responsibility requiring the expansion of public services.

The coalition of middle-class reformers and working-class radicals was long in coming, however, and the changes they pushed were debated for years before they were implemented. Until 1875, the only garbage removal that happened in Milwaukee was done by roaming hogs or "swill children," immigrant kids sent out to collect usable kitchen scraps to supplement their families' meager earnings. Yet much was left behind, leaving streets, alleys, and backyards "reeking with filth, smelling to heaven." When the city's first health officer recommended replacing the children with a contractor, the aldermen came up with a compromise, allowing each ward to decide on that issue separately, which a few elected to do. By 1878, however, after residents witnessed countless deficiencies by contractors and after some protest by immigrants angered about losing a source of income, none of the wards collected their garbage this way.[33]

At this point, the aldermen finally bowed to the need for a citywide garbage collection contract, though that too generated complaints, between 25 and 30 a day during the hot summer months. Apparently, collectors were less than thorough, irregular in their pick-up schedule, and selective in what they took because they mainly wanted to sell refuse to farmers for pig food or fertilizer. They also dumped waste on vacant lots when it was something they could not entice the farmers to buy. In response, the city briefly took over responsibility for collection. But when people in outlying areas began to refuse city dump carts on their property, worried about the health dangers of that waste, health department officials had to find another means of disposal as well.

For a year Milwaukee simply dumped its garbage in Lake Michigan. This generated plenty of complaints too, and the city council decided to give a contract to the Phoenix Garbage Cremator Company for collection and disposal. Their cremator turned out to be too small, and a new contract was let to the Forrestal Company to build and operate a "Merz" rendering plant, which produced grease and dry fertilizer from garbage. During the summer, however, when affluent residents living near the plant began to complain about the odor and threatened to sue, the health department shut the plant down and forced the city to resume dumping garbage in the lake. Officials reopened the plant in the fall, when the smell would be less noticeable, but they knew they had to come up with a workable alternative.[34]

Seeing their chance, a group of local businessmen organized the Wisconsin Rendering Company and proceeded to lay plans for securing the disposal contract. In the early months of 1892, with elections looming, the mayor and health commissioner arranged a reconciliation between Wisconsin Rendering and Forrestal investors. The two waste disposal companies were consolidated into one, which then submitted a high bid to erect a new Merz plant on the Wisconsin Rendering Company's land, then beyond city limits. Democratic aldermen quickly lined up behind the deal and accusations of graft began to fly. Republican F.C. Lorenz exposed two groups of Democrats who would allegedly receive $45,000 a year because of the company merger. Voters returned most of the incumbents and the bid was accepted, but new rumors of corruption began to circulate, and within two years Republicans routed the Democrats while the rendering company established a record of glaring failure.[35]

Following investigation of the Merz plant, Commissioner Kempster testified that the company still routinely emptied garbage, dead animals, and offal into Lake Michigan. City engineer G.H. Benzenberg confirmed that claim, noting that the shoreline was "liberally supplied with garbage" and explaining that Milwaukee daily produced many tons of garbage beyond the plant's capacity. To remedy the situation, Kempster increased health department monitoring of the company's collection and installed a lockbar on the plant tramway to stop the illegal dumping. In addition to these short-term solutions, he began lobbying the city council for municipal collection and disposal. Then, with the garbage contract set to expire, there was one more controversy, in which the Wisconsin Rendering Company paid off rivals to keep them from making a competing bid and paid assemblymen (some of them stockholders) to grant the company a renewal. This generated even more support for a city takeover. Subsequently, during the 1898 election all of the political parties, Democrats and Republicans as well as the new Social Democrats were each formally pledged to a municipal plant.[36]

Now facing a challenge from the left, aldermen acted quickly to issue municipal bonds for a city disposal plant, which began operating in 1902 and which was replaced by an incinerator with greater capacity just a few years later. During that time complaints about collection dropped sharply and accusations of corruption over disposal were nonexistent. Democrats and Republicans seemed unable to give up on graft, though, and a flurry of indictments against officials from both parties in 1904 and 1906 gave the graft-free Social Democrats a real boost in subsequent elections. The persistent corruption ultimately drove middle-class reformers to join with tradesmen and others to put city government in the hands of the socialists. In 1910, they not only won a strong majority on the council but also won the mayor's office, the city attorney and city treasurer posts, one-fourth of the school board, and two-thirds of the county's delegation to the state legislature, besides sending Victor Berger to Congress.[37]

Once in office, the socialists had a newly established Bureau of Economy and Efficiency study the city incinerator, a task led by John R. Commons, a University of Wisconsin economics professor. Following his recommendations, Milwaukee consolidated garbage collection and disposal under a single authority within the public works department.[38] This was in addition to many more additional changes, large and small, most of which assumed that city government was supposed to protect the health and welfare of all citizens rather than favor the wealthy elite with special privileges. Even when the socialists lost their hold on the city council in 1912 (still retaining the mayor's office for three more decades) the principle remained a key part of the city's governance. This provided legitimacy for a whole host of other health-related measures, including distribution of diphtheria antitoxin to poor families, more effective food inspection, school nurses and regular medical examinations for children, and milk vendor licensing. In the long-term, it also set yet more precedents for state and federal involvement in guarding environmental quality.

Desperate Work

During the seeding and ripening of an urban sanitation movement in the United States—something that happened in varying degrees from east to west and north to south—a related industrial hygiene campaign emerged to address workplace injury and disease, often involving many of the same people. This campaign included Commons, who was not only a university professor but also a politically engaged social activist. In 1911, shortly after the Triangle Shirtwaist Fire in New York raised public awareness about occupational dangers, he and other university faculty assisted Wisconsin state legislator Robert LaFollette in passing one of the country's first workers' compensation laws. The legislation obliged employers to follow various standards meant to protect the safety, health, and welfare of employees, penalized employers if workplace injuries resulted from failure to follow the standards, and provided for no-fault claims by workers to compensation in the case of injury, illness, or death.[39]

Commons was involved at the national level as well, as secretary of the American Association for Labor Legislation (AALL), founded in 1906. Although its objectives were wide-ranging, the organization probably did more than any other to stoke general interest in industrial hygiene, facilitate formation of collaborative networks, and press the federal Bureau of Labor and U.S. Public Health Service to act. "Between 1908 and 1912," Barbara Sicherman explains, the AALL "established a national commission on industrial hygiene, sponsored two conferences on industrial diseases (the second included a joint meeting with the American Medical Association, marking the first session devoted by that body to the subject), and mounted an exhibit, a favorite device of the era for conveying information to the public."[40]

Perhaps the organization's most important contribution in this period, however, was a study of phosphorous poisoning in the match industry. It was conducted by executive secretary John B. Andrews and assistant secretary Irene Osgood, both crusading social scientists, rather than medical doctors, and inclined to make their case by collecting information from a variety of sources. Their report was published by the Bureau of Labor in 1910, and Congress followed up in 1912, passing a law that established a prohibitive tax on matches of white phosphorous and banned import and export of the compound, effectively eliminating it from the industry. This made novel use of the federal government's police powers to address a specific problem in the workplace as well as to bring some balance to the relationship between employers and employees. Likewise, it pioneered a field-based model for occupational disease research that enjoyed considerable favor until the 1920s, when industrial hygiene shifted to the laboratory.[41]

One famous practitioner of "shoe-leather" epidemiology was Alice Hamilton, a native of Fort Wayne, Indiana, professor of pathology at the Woman's Medical School of Northwestern University, and longtime resident of Hull House, Jane Addams's settlement on Chicago's near west side. In 1908, both John Commons and Irene Osgood had consulted her at the beginning of the white phosphorous study since Hamilton had already begun to launch a career investigating workplace dangers and disease and quickly established herself as a leader in the field. Recognizing her growing professional reputation, that same year the Illinois governor appointed Hamilton to the state's Commission on Occupational Diseases, but after a preliminary investigation demonstrated need for a wide-ranging state study Hamilton resigned to direct the survey.[42]

Like the other settlement house workers in Chicago, Hamilton both challenged and accepted certain traditional gender conventions in the way she went about her work. "Although she chose to work for the most part in a world of men," Sicherman explains, "by emphasizing the human side of science and by relying on personal persuasion as an instrument of change she was adopting a classically 'feminine' strategy." In fact, she often found that her gender sometimes aided interactions with factory owners, men who saw women as "the guardians of the nation's morals." Like Addams and other well-meaning, native-born, middle- and upper-class reformers of the day, Hamilton also ventured onto the shop floor with the notion that she was helping the most vulnerable in the most "dangerous trades," typically foreign-born "wops" and "hunkies," as one employer described his workers to her. Without her involvement, she believed, the immigrant workers didn't have a voice or a chance.[43]

Hamilton "was a true progressive in her conviction that the system could be improved by the exposure of evils and the efforts of forward-looking men and women to correct if not eliminate them." Yet, her work was not always so easy, and she had to use all her wits to get access to factories run by wary owners, to convince workers fearful of losing their jobs to talk to her, and to find basic injury, morbidity, and mortality information. Soon after launching the Illinois survey, in April 1910, she was feeling overwhelmed and pessimistic. "This industrial disease work is like trying to make one's way through a jungle and not even being able to find an opening," she wrote. "I go to the factories, white lead and lead pipe and paint so far—and I see conditions which make for lead poisoning and then it is the most desperate work finding any. Of course the foremen deny everything and the men will not talk and they live in all parts of the city and employ any number of physicians ... I shall never be able to get more than an approximate statement about any place."[44]

The Illinois study, in which Hamilton led 23 physicians, medical students, and social workers, focused on determining the manufacturing methods that used lead and the resulting symptoms of lead poisoning among laborers. The various participants also investigated the dangers of arsenic, carbon monoxide, cyanide, and turpentine as well as health hazards in brass manufacturing and zinc smelting. In their final report, presented to the governor during the first part of 1911, they called for workplace health and safety legislation that included special protections for employees of the most hazardous industries. Subsequently, before the year was out, Illinois had a law that required employers to provide safety measures and monthly medical examinations to employees who worked with lead and arsenic, in the manufacturing of brass, or in the smelting of lead and zinc. And it required them to report all cases of illness to the Department of Factory Inspection, which was empowered to follow-up with prosecutions for standards violations although there was no provision of compensation to the sick or injured.[45]

Following her work in Illinois, Hamilton was made a special investigator in what was then the federal Bureau of Labor. In that post, over the course of the next three years, she did studies on lead poisoning in the pottery, tile, and porcelain-enameled sanitary ware industries, investigated the manufacture of storage batteries, and began probing into workplace dangers of the rubber industry.[46] In every case, she applied a well-tested formula, which included making a visual inspection of the shop floor and sifting through clinical information from hospitals and dispensaries, and conducting personal interviews. Yet by building a solid record of thoughtful and honest accounting, she helped transform industrial hygiene "into a more specialized technical field, uncoupled from discussion or understanding of its broader legislative or social dimensions." When Hamilton was appointed assistant professor of industrial medicine at Harvard in 1919, Christopher Sellers notes, the science of occupational disease was increasingly based on "premises, style, and methods quite alien to her own."[47]

Two other factors forced industrial hygiene's shift from field to laboratory, one of which was a dramatically changed social context during and after World War I. That event absorbed much of the attention Progressive reformers had been giving to assimilating immigrants, cleaning up streets, and making city government more efficient. Even opponents like Jane Addams were overly busy traveling on peace missions and lecturing about the war's folly. Meanwhile, American employers initiated an all-out attack on radicals, particularly the Socialist Party and Industrial Workers of the World (IWW), using their war opposition (which was winning them favor among a skeptical public) to more effectively question their purpose and legitimacy. Pressed by capital, Congress passed the Espionage and Sedition Acts, which criminalized the radicals' views, and subsequent raids, arrests, and imprisonment made it virtually impossible for the Socialist Party and IWW to continue functioning (though Eugene Debs managed to run for president from jail in 1920). Finally, in the wake of the war, with radicals mostly out of the way, employers took aim at organized labor in general, stepping up attacks on trade unions affiliated with the conservative American Federation of Labor and successfully reducing if not eliminating workers' role in deciding wages, hours, and conditions for most of the next decade.

The second, additional factor that changed the orientation and approach of occupational medicine was the spread of workers' compensation legislation. By 1915, 23 states had some form of a law replacing the process of establishing responsibility and making reparation for injury or death through civil court proceedings with a no-fault workers' compensation system in which employers carried insurance to cover their liability. This legislation gave employers (and insurance companies) a new incentive to care about workplace hazards. Now physicians, safety engineers, and others were hired to prevent accidents that might lead to compensation claims and to maintain affordable premiums for manufacturers and protect the earnings of insurers. As states began to extend their laws to cover some or all occupational diseases, even more medical and engineering experts were needed to solve problems before they led to illness and generated claims for compensation.[48]

With increased emphasis on prevention, academic institutions began to receive corporate support to establish and operate complementary research programs. The most important and influential was the Harvard Division of Industrial Hygiene, under the watch of David Edsall, with a group of key faculty that included clinical scientist Joseph Aub, physiologist Cecil Drinker, and Alice Hamilton. Drawing on their own particular disciplines, they adopted "a cognitive and practical framework for dealing with industrial causes of disease that both corporate officials and their fellow professionals could embrace." This new (or transformed) generation of industrial hygienists delocalized the study of the workplace, transferring concern from workers on the shop floor to experimental animals in the laboratory, lending it the stamp of objective rigor as well as prestige.[49]

Whether due to the divorce of occupational medicine from its important social dimensions, or in spite of it, members of the Harvard cohort quickly made important contributions to their field. In the most celebrated case, Alice Hamilton drew on her many contacts in industry and convinced the presidents of several lead companies to fund a three-year study on lead poisoning. Demonstrating the advantages of working under controlled conditions, Joseph Aub and his associates "discovered how lead was absorbed, stored, and eliminated from the body and also developed an effective treatment for lead colic." Additionally, they conclusively determined that lead was more toxic when inhaled than when swallowed, a discovery that overturned a common misconception and pointed the way to better protection for workers.[50] How that information was put to use, however, was a different question.

The laboratory-centered industrial hygiene did seem to pose somewhat less of a threat to industrial manufacturers, their control over production, and the bottom line. Yet over the course of two decades occupational medicine spawned another field, environmental health, which was not so benign to corporate interests. In fact, many of the scientists who went on to play a leading role determining the effects of industrial air and water pollution on whole communities got their start investigating occupational diseases. "In their confrontation with the microenvironment of the factory," Christopher Sellers argues, "they concocted what are arguably our most important means for regulating the environment as a whole." Early in his career, for example, Wilhelm Hueper determined the chemical responsible for workers' bladder cancers in Du Pont's dye works. Later, as head of the Environmental Cancer Section of the National Cancer Institute, he went on to study the carcinogenic role of other industrial chemicals, gradually widening his perspective to encompass the health and well-being of people beyond the workplace.[51]

The practical implications of this shift in concern were dramatically demonstrated in 1948, a few days before Halloween, when air pollution from a zinc works in Donora, Pennsylvania, was trapped by a thermal inversion. The poisonous cloud killed 17 people and left thousands more struggling to breathe, gasping through the day and into the night, until finally the weather conditions changed. But this was not the first time local residents had been aversely impacted by pollution from nearby manufacturing plants. Starting in the 1920s, landowners, tenants, and farmers periodically sued for damages they attributed to smelter pollution, including crop loss and sick livestock, and more than once courts made legal judgments in their favor.[52]

During the 1930s, workers in the area were swept up in a nationwide labor movement revival, and they organized locals affiliated with various industrial unions. By mid-century six of the seven city councilmen in Donora were United Steelworkers (USW) members, and when the zinc works disaster struck, they used their combined political power and economic muscle to determine culpability. They feared that any government action would put people out of work, but they also understood the need to protect the health of the community (many smelter employees and their families). Along with the USW they called for an independent investigation by the U.S. Public Health Service. After the first report proved inconclusive, the councilmen and union initiated their own environmental health study, with $10,000 pledged by USW founder Phil Murray. A Short timelate, with urging from Public Health Service officials, Congress passed the first federal clean air legislation in 1955.[53]

4

Green Relief and Recovery: By Which Working People and Nature Get a New Deal

Looking back on the first year's work by the 110th Company of the Civilian Conservation Corps (CCC) at Harold Parker State Forest, near Andover, Massachusetts, editors of a local newspaper believed there was reason for acclamation. The company had been established as part of a federal relief program in the summer of 1933, bringing 212 unemployed young men from across the state to repair the worn-out land. Many of the boys were undernourished and sickly when they arrived and the woods were originally "waste land," farmed to exhaustion, heavily logged as well as ravaged by fire, purchased by the Forest Commission in 1919 for only $5 an acre. By June of 1934, however, the boys looked "just like boys who have lived a year in a forest should look, bronzed, rugged, clean cut—fine specimens of American manhood." Their initially untidy camp was now a set of neatly arranged wooden barracks. "And the forest has changed too," the *Andover Townsmen* reported, "which is a story in itself."[1]

Much of the 110th Company's efforts were aimed at turning Harold Parker into a leisurely escape, complete with several fishing ponds, bathing beaches, hiking trails, access roads, and new groves of white and red pines. The boys handily accomplished the task and left a lasting legacy in the form of an accommodating infrastructure that enticed residents from Boston, Lawrence, Lowell, and other neighboring industrial cities to find escape in nature there. "Every week-end," the *Lawrence Eagle Tribune* explained in 1937, "hundreds of cars from the Hub [in Boston] carry merry families to the woodland playground carved out of the rough by CCC boys."[2] The young men's labors not only transformed their bodies and the natural landscape but also qualitatively improved the lives of eager, frequent visitors for decades to come.

At the time, the beginning of what became known as the Great Depression, the immediate need for the Civilian Conservation Corps and other relief programs was glaringly clear. By 1933, nearly 40 percent of the nonagricultural labor force in the United States was out of work, with much higher percentages in places where the local or regional economy was tied to the waxing and waning strength of one particular industry. High unemployment and "short time" (or reduced hours) for the few employees who managed to keep their jobs meant widespread poverty, overwhelming private welfare organizations such as Catholic Charities and the Salvation Army. Some of the people who defaulted on mortgages and lost their homes or failed to pay their rent and found themselves evicted even began to establish so-called Hoovervilles on the outskirts of cities. These were ramshackle communities made from cast-off tin, wood scraps, and cardboard on vacant lots, named in blame-tainted honor of the sitting president.

Yet while his understanding of the reasons behind the economic collapse and how best to respond were lacking, Herbert Hoover bore only a minor personal responsibility for the Depression's onset and the severe worsening of conditions. The main causes were underconsumption and overproduction, perennial problems inherent to industrial capitalism, a system of profit-oriented production in which private corporations are constantly seeking to outdo their competitors by lowering labor costs, increasing efficiency, and capturing markets. The American economy had repeatedly seen similar periods of collapse for the same reasons, although there were specific factors that made the situation in the 1930s notably bad and worrisome. European countries were defaulting on loans from World War I as the reparations plan in the Treaty of Versailles fell apart. A recession in agriculture that started just after the war was complemented by the poor performance of "sick" industries such as coal and textiles as early as the 1920s. And lastly, capital's war on radicals and organized labor during the same period undermined the ability of workers to demand a more equitable share of the wealth, while unregulated banking and stock trading practices enabled the rich to lose billions of dollars of other people's real life savings as well as their own paper stock profits.

Hoover's victorious opponent in the 1932 presidential election, Franklin Delano Roosevelt (FDR), came into office with the understanding that he would have to save American capitalism, but he was without a coherent plan to do it. On the campaign trail, the news media had branded his vague positions as a New Deal, distinguishing him from the incumbent, though he was on record clearly favoring the old notion of balanced budgets. Actually, once he sat in the Whitehouse, FDR temporarily put that idea aside and pursued innovative policies that established a new role for the federal government in priming, sustaining, and regulating the national economy. Many of those initiatives channeled public spending to put the unemployed to work and to repair a ravaged rural landscape, simultaneously addressing economic and environmental problems.

The Tennessee Valley Authority (TVA), for example, a public corporation established by an act of the Democratic-controlled Congress in 1933, was charged with building dams and hydroelectric power plants in the Tennessee River Valley as part of a larger effort at regional planning. Construction provided immediate employment in the impoverished area, dams controlled flooding and improved navigability of waterways, and power plants generated cheap power. The power plants put the TVA in competition with private utilities, provoking conservatives to warn against "creeping socialism," but commercial users benefited along with valley residents, insulating the agency somewhat from reactionary criticism. The TVA also gained support by lending expertise and resources to repairing the region's eroding soils and cutover forests. Locally hired field agents supplied farmers with subsidized fertilizer and taught them about crop rotation and various methods to improve yields, while others were put to work replanting forests and controlling forest fires.

Still, perhaps no other element of the New Deal was more important in transforming the American landscape and affecting working people's environmental consciousness than the Civilian Conservation Corps. The quick and extraordinary changes witnessed at Harold Parker State Forest in Massachusetts happened in hundreds of more state and national forests and parks and eventually on private farmland and along coastal shorelines the length and breadth of the country. "They are making a new kind of American man out of the city boy in the woods," the novelist Sherwood Anderson remarked after visiting a camp in Pennsylvania, "and they are planning at least to begin to make a new land with the help of such boys."[3]

The 3 million young men who participated in the CCC between 1933 and 1943 planted 2 billion trees, effectively reforesting whole parts of the United States, and they slowed erosion on 40 million acres of farmland with equally impressive results. By helping farmers combine both terracing and contour furrowing, Neil Maher notes, they increased "wheat yields on the southern Great Plains by 3.5 bushels per acre, bean production in New Mexico by 78 pounds per acre, and grain sorghum growth in Texas by an astounding 262 pounds per acre."[4] Likewise, the many CCC companies scattered about the country greatly enhanced the nation's resources for outdoor recreation. By 1935, the corps was working in state and national parks, giving increased attention to constructing picnic shelters and sanitary facilities, adding roads and bridges, building administrative buildings and equipment houses, blazing hiking trails, digging reservoirs, and installing swimming pools. Subsequently, visitation to national parks alone increased from less than 3.5 million in 1933 to 16 million in 1938 and to 21 million in 1941.[5]

As Sherwood Anderson suggested, participation in all of the different conservation work also proved to be formative experiences for enrollees, restoring their health and fitness, advancing their "Americanization," and nudging along their environmental consciousness. Similarly, improvements in reforestation and soil fertility, favorable coverage by local and national media, government propaganda literature and films, and especially rising levels of park and forest visitation all contributed to making the CCC part of ordinary Americans' changing relationship with nature. "For most of the nation's history, from Thomas Jefferson to Frederick Jackson Turner, work in nature had been celebrated as virtuous," argues Paul Sutter, "but as industrialization degraded work, as urbanization moved more Americans away from a direct working relationship with nature, and as the frontier waned, Americans increasingly invested leisure in nature with the sorts of virtues that work in nature had once embodied." The New Deal, especially the Civilian Conservation Corps, successfully incorporated this new cultural meaning of outdoor recreational leisure into the politics of national recovery.[6]

A New Day

Undoubtedly, one of the main influences that led Franklin Roosevelt to establish the Civilian Conservation Corps was an early dedication to forestry, a personal passion he inherited in part from his role model and older cousin, Theodore Roosevelt. At his Hyde Park estate, in New York, FDR was very much engaged in carefully managing its wooded sections, going well beyond the amateur dabbling of a "gentlemen" farmer, despite a disability that prevented him from walking the grounds (instead he drove a car on narrow access roads). He worked closely with hired hands to select, plant, and care for trees best-suited to the soil and climate, repairing areas that had not always been so gently used, learning and adapting as experiments and trials played out.

The other major shaping force, not unrelated to FDR's interest in forest conservation, was Roosevelt's long involvement with the Boy Scouts. Founded just after the turn of the century, the Scouts were meant to address the needs of boys growing up in cities, with all of their supposed enticements to delinquency, by providing the youth with opportunities for exposure to nature. This reflected the environmentalist thinking of Progressive reformers who believed that surroundings shaped social behavior. According to this philosophy, sending young men from filthy, crowded neighborhoods to rural camps, however temporarily, provided a much-needed curative to the unhealthy and corrupting facets of modern urban life.[7]

As the first indications of serious economic hardship became apparent in New York at the end of the 1920s and beginning of the 1930s, then Governor Franklin Roosevelt saw a chance to promote both forest conservation and the Boy Scouts' concern with restoring youth through government intervention. In September 1931, he established the Temporary Emergency Relief Administration, which not only provided food, clothing, and shelter to those in need but also created a work program, including 10,000 jobs converting abandoned farmland into public forests. Shortly after this, Michigan, Indiana, Mississippi, Virginia, Oregon, Washington, and other states began similar forestry work-relief initiatives of their own, opening the way for establishing a national program.[8]

Within the first 100 days of Roosevelt's first term in the White House, the Democratic-controlled Congress passed a bill creating the Civilian Conservation Corps. Organized labor objected, fearing the program would displace workers and depress wages, but the president brought unions around by appointing Robert Fechner as director. Fechner had been a leader of the International Association of Machinists and a vice president of the American Federation of Labor, and he in turn appointed a fellow machinist, James McEntee, as assistant director. Together, they oversaw creation of the first camps and initial recruitment. They set quotas for each state by population and limited enrollment to unemployed, single men, between the ages of 18 and 25, whose families were already receiving public assistance. In an effort to aid family income and stabilize the economy, the CCC boys had to send almost all of their $30 monthly paycheck back home, but they really needed only a few dollars for personal expenses anyway, since they ate in common mess halls, slept in tents or barracks, and often organized their own evening and weekend entertainment.[9]

The first CCC camp in the nation was in Virginia, but the next three to follow were in Pennsylvania, and no other eastern state had more camps by the end of the decade. This success was due in part to Gifford Pinchot, who had established himself as the first professionally trained forester in the United States, headed the U.S. Forest Service under President Theodore Roosevelt, and sympathized with Progressive reform ideals, which he carried to the governor's office in the early 1920s. Early on, Pinchot created the state's Department of

Forest and Waters, overseen by one of his forestry protégés, Lewis Stanley, and a decade later, in 1933, he set up the State Emergency Relief Board. Both of these agencies helped facilitate quick establishment of CCC camps and efficient coordination of initial recruitment. One other important factor was that the state had extensive public land, two million acres total, including half a million acres in the Allegheny National Forest, with many potential sites to initiate projects. Much of the public land was newly acquired and in great need of repair, abandoned to tax delinquency, clear cut and unsightly, with raw stumps, eroding soil, and volatile brush.[10]

In terms of economic need, Pennsylvania also stood out for being among the most hard-hit by manufacturing's collapse. Between 1929 and 1933, more than 12,000 of the 17,000 factories and mills in the state closed, a drop in industrial capacity second only to New York, and those plants that remained operated on a curtailed basis. The effect this had on employment was devastating, leaving 1.5 million residents without work and putting many more on half-time or less. Among those unemployed was Joseph Speakman, one of the first enrollees placed in a camp in the Moshannon State Forest. In 1933, he was in his mid-twenties, living at home with his parents, with only an elementary school education and no special skills to give him an advantage over other job seekers. On June 20, he signed up at an army recruiting station in Philadelphia, traveled out to Fort George Meade, in Maryland, for conditioning, then went to the CCC camp, where he stayed for a full 6-month stint, helping his family with the pay he sent home and remaking himself through outdoor labor and plentiful food. "My older cousins have told me that when my father returned home, he had been physically transformed into some kind of bodybuilder," Speakman's son recalled. "He later boasted to me that he had put on twenty pounds of muscle, engaging in competitive bouts of wood chopping after work hours."[11]

Beyond Pennsylvania, there were millions of others in dire need and yet, for the fortunate young men who managed to get into the Corps, there was now some reason to hope. "Before joining the C.C.C.," one recruit wrote in 1934, many were "in the blackest depths of despondency." But having found a lifeline, the sky was brighter, the dawn was apparent, and there were real prospects for "a new day and new era filled with many wonderful and untold opportunities for us all."[12] R.D. Morehead's father, a Texas cotton farmer, basically told him he had to leave home and join the CCC for the sake of the rest of the destitute family. "We had six boys," Morehead said, and "to this day I don't know how my dad fed us. We ate like a bunch of thresher hens." Having demonstrated need, within a week's time he was working alongside other recruits in the Grand Canyon.[13] Likewise, Howard Holt remembered that "times were awful bad in Berlin [New Hampshire]," not just for a few but for many. "A good portion of the students in the high school ... wore welfare pants and a big heavy sweater," he noted, and there were no jobs other than work projects through the Works Progress Administration, the National Youth Administration, and the CCC. "It was almost a matter of if you wanted to eat you better go to the Civilian Conservation Corps."[14]

In fact, a good deal of emphasis was put on restoring the health of enrollees, who often came to a camp undernourished and scrawny even if they weren't from the city, the environment viewed as the ruin of manhood in the modern age. When recruits were first inducted, they underwent physical exams and received smallpox, typhoid, and para-typhoid inoculations as well as a pneumonia antigen. During the length of their stint, the enrollees also received regular hearty meals, although the field lunches prepared for traveling work crews were apparently sometimes wanting. At Camp S-51, located in the Cloquet Valley State Forest, near Brimson, Minnesota, the boys had a running joke about the "horse cock" or "pony pecker" sandwiches, made with cold meats, when they would have preferred peanut butter sandwiches instead.[15] In any case, there was a doctor at every camp, to oversee general health conditions and to deal with injuries and sickness, including venereal disease. At first, recruits who contracted syphilis (presumably from visits to a local town) were summarily discharged. Within a couple of years, however, a new policy allowed afflicted boys to stay to receive extended treatment and established a procedure for supplying prophylactics.[16]

The corps also worked a cultural transformation on recruits by creating the circumstance for interactions between young men from different racial and ethnic groups. The letter of the law creating the CCC required racial integration, but Director Robert Fechner (who described himself as "a southerner by birth and raising" who "clearly understood the Negro problem") allowed southern states to segregate African American enrollees in separate camps and to put whites in all positions of authority in the black camps.[17] Other, ostensibly "integrated" camps lodged whites and blacks in separate barracks and put them to work on different projects. Still, a stint in the corps did sometimes include an experience with race mixing and racial equality. One black enrollee assigned to a camp near Sacramento, California, recalled that work assignments in the kitchen, driving trucks, and in the field were divided equally by race. "My commander had been in the Navy and treated all enrollees the same," he said.[18]

Perhaps more profound was the Americanization that happened when different groups of mostly second-generation immigrants interacted with one another as well as with more long-established native born. The United States had enacted immigration laws establishing restrictive quotas in the early 1920s, effectively shutting down the flood of newcomers prior to that point in time, and this meant the younger generation was less firmly rooted in the languages and traditions of another homeland and ready to be assimilated in the right context. Sharing sleeping areas, work routines, meals, weekend excursions to town, and other aspects of camp life dissolved many social barriers and contributed to creation of a common American culture. Or, at the very least, it helped boys learn how to get along with one another on terms of mutual respect. Vernard Wilbur, for example, later described his CCC company out of New York City as "Jewish kids, Italian kids, Irish kids, and probably the best mix of nationalities that you could find."[19]

Firm Believers

Of course, the other major change experienced by enrollees had to do with effects of their exposure to nature, although that typically took weeks or months. Many were not too happy when they first arrived at their assigned camp, especially the boys who went to work on projects out west. Hobart Feltner traveled from the "lush forests and grassy meadows" of Kentucky to the "sparsely vegetated, dusty landscape" of the Colorado Plateau in Utah and initially considered it "the damnedest country" he had ever seen. He felt no fondness for the desert's "briar stuff" and found it all "hard to look at." Ed Braun, from Ohio, had a similar reaction after getting off the train with 150 other enrollees bound for a Division of Grazing camp in Utah. Their barracks leader formed the boys into a line and marched them for an hour to the camp. "It was situated 500 miles from Nowhere surrounded by Nothing," Braun remembered. "There wasn't a tree as far as the eye could see."[20] Yet lush landscapes provoked similar sentiments. Robert Ross was stationed in the forested Ozarks mountains of Arkansas, and still he experienced a sense of repugnance. "Mountains surrounded me and hemmed me in," he recalled, "bushes with thorns on them, and the clinging vines that snarled and twisted around one's feet ... This was all so foreign to me, I hated it at once."[21]

Even absent feelings of aversion and isolation, almost all the young enrollees were unfamiliar with the flora and fauna in the places they were sent, and this was particularly true in terms of the wildlife that inhabited the woods and canyons. In some cases their naïveté had humorous consequences. George Weeks explained that his Glacier Park, Montana, camp was overrun by "BEARS, BEARS, BEARS." One day he and some other recruits put out a bucket of syrup as bait and that did the trick, attracting a bear that seemed to have its head pretty well jammed. It pulled free, however, when the young men gathered close, and all the onlookers scattered in panic.[22] Charlie Pflugh, who was with a Pennsylvania contingent at Chevalon Canyon, in Arizona, had a similar experience with a badger, which only a few of the recruits had ever heard of or seen before. He and others trapped one in a burlap sack, which they wedged between themselves in the back of a truck on the way back to camp. It didn't take long before the badger wanted out, so he ripped a hole in the sack and escaped, looking "mean as the devil." Pflugh and the others yelled for the driver to stop, but everyone decided to jump out with the truck running. Later that evening, they watched a movie about wild animals in the area, one that confirmed what they had already learned about the ferocity of badgers when cornered.[23]

Eventually, as happened with Pflugh, corps enrollees adjusted to their new environment and learned a thing or two (or much more) about nature. The work they did from day to day was especially critical to that change. Most of the camps established in the first two years were administered by the U.S. Forest Service and located in national and state forests. There the CCC worked with a professional staff, including trained foresters, landscape engineers, and what were called "locally experienced men," who arranged and oversaw projects for planting and thinning trees, eradicating tree pests and diseases, preventing and extinguishing forest fires, and other important tasks. In Pennsylvania, Joseph Speakman and fellow recruits devoted a considerable amount of time to fighting pine blister rust, which had come from Europe in 1905 and was devastating the state's valuable white pine trees. To eliminate the disease, crews had to go through the woods pulling gooseberry and currant bushes, the initial host plants for the rust, absorbing a basic lesson about the interrelationships between living things.[24]

In fact, labor in the forests could and did turn enrollees into conservationists. "The work we do in the Great North woods gives us a greater understanding of what the word 'Conservation' really means," wrote Fred Harrison in the mid-1930s. "I am now a firm believer that conservation is necessary for the preservation of our forests."[25] A number of the young men even sought out related careers, sometimes within just months of their stint's end. Robert Woodward wrote New Hampshire state forester Steve Boomer in the summer of 1935 for a summer job, listing off his knowledge about blister rust eradication, and Boomer put him in charge of a crew. Later, when his boss retired in 1956, Woodward took his job. In another case, Howard Holt accepted a clerical job with the Fish and Wildlife Service in the same office where he had worked as a CCC recruit, right after his discharge.[26]

By the middle of the 1930s, CCC recruits were hard at work on farms as well, learning firsthand the great need to save the nation's soil. Under the charge of Soil Conservation Service engineers and other knowledgeable overseers, they demonstrated the merits of both vegetative methods and physical alteration of fields to regulate the movement of water and wind. At the Coon Creek Demonstration Area, in Wisconsin, the largest in the country, enrollees helped farmers cut 1,700 acres of terraces, plant alternating strip crops in more than three-fourths of their fields, lay contour lines to guide crop rows that ran perpendicular to sloping land, and build check-dams and diversion ditches. They also replanted trees on steep slopes and converted 10,000 acres of sloping pasture into woodland. As a consequence, during the next several years upland erosion rates decreased by 75 percent and sedimentation dropped by 98 percent. The resulting improved soil fertility translated into higher yields and increased land values, which encouraged once-reluctant banks to extend credit again.[27]

With involvement in these types of efforts, the CCC boys often gained an intimate knowledge of best farming practices as well as the benefits of applying them. Troy Crosier, enrolled in Camp Dixon Springs (in Illinois) during 1937, had grown up helping his aunt and uncle on their farm every summer and over holidays. He also recalled that farmers in the area were usually hesitant to do anything different or try something innovative, claiming only half-jokingly that they knew all they needed to know since they'd already worn out two or three farms. After a stint in the C's Crosier was ready and willing to take another approach. He bought a farm from a widow, who had overworked it for 30 years, and applied the various "good farming skills" the corps had taught him. He "cleaned it up, fertilized it, fenced it, and made a showplace out of it."[28]

Part of what aided quick and successful absorption of forest and soil conservation techniques were the evening and weekend hours some enrollees spent studying with their peers in organized classes or reading books in a camp library. By 1934, more than 85 percent of the boys attended camp educational activities and, judging by the popularity of specific courses, they were particularly interested in natural resource management. Likewise, after the American Tree Association donated 250,000 copies of its textbook, *The Forestry Primer*, to the CCC, requests for more flooded in from camps throughout the country. "Our Ohio boys are anxious to learn all they can," wrote an educational adviser at a camp in California, "and your publication is a valuable help."[29]

Besides the technical skills needed to use the environment in a sustainable fashion, organized and self-directed study also led a few recruits to test their hand at nature writing, employing a literary romantic style not unlike the working-class romantic writing New England mill girls developed in the nineteenth century. Looking out his window at a Pennsylvania camp in 1935, gazing at the nearby mountains through the falling snow, one unnamed recruit waxed eloquently about "those wooded hills whose beauty has never ceased to impress me with their magnificence." Provoked by the scenery, he thought about the months he and the other boys had been in the C's, a brief interlude yet a "lifetime" if judged by "the wealth of experience, the gain in mental and physical attributes" it had meant. "Little did we realize then," he added, "that there was untold unhappiness awaiting us in this forest refuge, away from the artificial pleasures of the city."[30]

Outlets for the young men inclined to think and write this way included the numerous camp newspapers, often part of journalism courses, and the national weekly CCC publication, *Happy Days*. The weekly had a regular column on wildlife, "Outdoor Neighbors," and it printed features on the national parks, but it made room for more wide-ranging contributions too. In one example, E.D. Rennacker described sitting on a hillside at a camp in Fairfax, California, finding solace in "Nature" for a general feeling of "despair," or perhaps more specifically for the despair brought on by the Depression. "The quiet hills and deep ravines," he wrote, "revive my memory of scenes I had forgotten in the strife of civilization's noisy life." Above him spread the branches of a "huge oak tree, years older by many seasons than me," and as he leaned back against its bark he had "no fear of the gathering dark."[31]

Interestingly, many of the enrollees' poems seemed to be a popular medium for expressing a preservationist (protection) rather than conservationist (management) sentiment, relating awe and wonder before the grandeur and beauty of untouched nature. Anthony Yourch, from Company 130 at Baxter State Park, in Maine, wished for a "power over words great enough to cause another individual the same pleasure which was my good fortune to experience as I marveled at the view from Mount Katahdin." Similarly, Truxton Hosely, of Company 295 at Camp Walker River, in Nevada, praised a stately pine, "unharmed, lonesome, free," and cursed anyone who might cut it down or otherwise harm it. Gerald J. McIntosh, posted to Mt. Nebo, Arkansas, even went so far as to rethink the tradition of cutting trees for Christmas. He contrasted the loud cry of the "huckster," avariciously selling trees for a mere fifty cents, with "the stately trees back in the forest green, that I had left the day before—May God preserve the scene!"[32]

Another indication of how the corps experience was changing enrollees' attitudes and values was the way they spent (and later described) some of their leisure hours. Always, at every camp, nearly every weekend, young men were eager to visit a nearby town, do some drinking, and pass the time with other male and female companions (based on a survey of 419 enrollees, the American Educational Council confirmed local residents' fears that recruits were "not high in moral quality," and on matters of gambling, sexual behavior, and the use of alcohol, they concluded that the "majority of CCC enrollees might almost be described as immoral.").[33] Yet the enrollees did make an effort to explore and enjoy the local landscape, even places around some of the western camps that initially inspired aversion and loathing. Jake Barranca used to hike around the Grand Canyon to look at rocks, flowers, and animals. He had a special fondness for a particular blooming cactus, and one of his most cherished memories was watching eagles in flight and at their nesting sites. Ed Braun, on the Colorado Plateau in Utah, recalled "roaming around the desert chasing little critters."[34] Charlie Pflugh, a displaced easterner from Pennsylvania, remembered that "wildlife was plentiful throughout Chevalon Canyon, in Arizona. "You always had to keep your eyes open," he said. On Sunday afternoons, he usually took a walk in the woods with a buddy to see what we could see, and they were "hardly ever disappointed."[35]

Besides the way it affected enrollees, the Civilian Conservation Corps had a measurable impact on local areas close to the camps and on Americans in general across the country. One of the most direct results was the immediate economic stimulus provided by enrollees' discretionary spending as well as purchases of camp supplies. The C's had to send $25 of their monthly $30 pay back home (which served as an economic stimulus there), but the remaining $5 that they spent for themselves was enough to be felt by town movie theaters, stores, restaurants, and laundries. The camps bought food, gasoline, and hardware from local merchants and contractors as well. In addition to these aids to nearby depressed economies, the corps hired local men, usually older than the recruits, with families of their own, though unemployed like them. The work saved the men from destitution and put an income in their hands that supported their communities.

When floods and fires created demands for assistance, corps enrollees proved their value in that respect too. In 1936, Andover, Massachusetts, saw the worst flooding in its history, as the Merrimack River backed up into the Shawsheen, which spread through several villages and forced the evacuation of more than 100 homes. After the waters receded, recruits from the Harold Park State Forest camps descended on Shawsheen Village with shovels to clean up and a local newspaper printed a picture of their service on the front page. Others helped during the 1937 flood on the Ohio River. One group from Dixon

Springs, Illinois, including Troy Crossier, got stranded while trying to make
their way back and signed on to stick around for the next five weeks to assist
the Red Cross in moving people out.[36] More in line with the work enrollees
were doing in forest camps, companies were also called out to fight forest fires,
which were particularly bad during the 1930s, when summer weather turned
hot and dry in many parts of the country for several years in a row. The peak
fire season in the Cloquet Valley State Forest, in Minnesota, was 1936, and during the first part of August several fires there got out of control, traveling fast
and leaving destruction in their wake. "I called on the CCC men available to
go to the Palo-Markham fire to help the people that lost their homes" forester
J.C. Ryan recalled. They worked all night gathering up belongings, caring for
livestock, and providing whatever aid was needed, all of which garnered "a lot
of praise from the news media."[37]

The Civilian Conservation Corps made another, more important impression
on local communities by showing the merits of various forest- and soil-man-
agement methods and spreading knowledge about basic principles of ecology.
Americans in every region, Neil Maher explains, "saw CCC enrollees working
near their homes, read about Corps camps in local newspapers and national
magazines, and even watched full-length feature films portraying CCC conservation projects."[38] In a survey of 531 farmers who had been involved with soil
conservation efforts in the upper Mississippi Valley, for example, nearly every
single one agreed that vegetative and landscape engineering methods were
solving their erosion problems and, consequently they planned to continue
farming that way in the future. Just as telling, a large majority of those farmers
who had refused to sign cooperative agreements in the region began practicing
soil conservation on their land, and many techniques started to spread to areas
well beyond designated demonstration areas.[39]

With few exceptions, by decade's end federal intervention to repair and
maintain the natural environment was no longer routinely questioned or skew-
ered as wayward socialism (or the germ of fascism), or if it was socialism then it
was a sort that most people could support. It had achieved the same legitimacy
as public libraries, city water, and the postal service. In 1936, 82 percent of
Americans surveyed wanted the corps to continue its work on farms as well as
in forests and parks, and three years later this support was even higher, cutting
across party lines and regional divides. In effect, the corps had overcome the
resistance to conservation that was so prevalent among common people in the
late nineteenth century, and it consolidated reconciliation between them and
"professional conservationists from scientific and government circles." That, in
turn, shored up the base for post–World War II environmentalism.[40]

Nature Democratized

Even when the CCC was shut down in 1941 to free up labor and resources for war production and military service during World War II, the program continued to shape people's thinking and values. The millions of Americans who ventured to state and national forests and parks improved by the CCC relied on the new amenities left by the corps. At Harold Parker State Forest, as noted, the two CCC companies had completely transformed the area in the course of a few years. They planted 50,000 white and red pines, made 10 miles of footpaths, and built nine ponds, five of which they stocked with game fish such as trout, yellow perch, and hornpout. Additionally, they established a dozen campgrounds, each equipped with rubbish barrels, picnic tables, and sanitary facilities, along with a total of 67 stone fireplaces. There were only a couple access roads, however, and parking spaces were located on the outskirts of the forest. "Throughout the entire project, the utmost care has been taken to insure that the woods be kept in a primeval state," one local newspaper reported, "unspoiled by gasoline fumes and hurried drives." The camp supervisors were also "careful to preserve the best features of nature, and eradicate the scars on the land inflicted by the labor required to produce the materials necessary for the job."[41]

To be sure, the CCC did generate a certain amount of persistent and difficult-to-ignore public grumbling by highly regarded conservationists and preservationists. Taking the lead in this was Aldo Leopold, known for his work in game management and later for his posthumously published *A Sand County Almanac*, as well as Robert Marshall, a socialist and founding member of the Wilderness Society. Leopold supported President Roosevelt in much of what he was trying to do with the New Deal, but he developed an ecological critique of work by the corps that sparked a movement within wildlife circles and the park service. This opposition saw CCC forest fire suppression, disease eradication, tree planting, and other projects as reckless, specifically for ignoring facets of balance in nature. Marshall also generally believed in the New Deal yet made his own, slightly different criticism of the corps, one that was a bit ironic considering his socialist political leanings. He saw the democratization of nature aided by the CCC, particularly the road building as well as campground and picnic shelter construction that made it so much easier and enjoyable for millions to visit the outdoors, as an unacceptable threat to wilderness.[42]

Nevertheless, by the end of the 1930s and during the decades following, various trends came together to make for an astounding increase in the number of working-class Americans seeking escape in natural settings, near and far, to picnic, camp, hike, hunt, and fish. Automobile ownership spiraled upward as assembly line production lowered the price of cars and state and federal governments poured money into expanding highways. More people migrated from rural farms to labor in urban factories (some to work on assembly lines) and experienced a sense of alienation from their work as well as the environment. A few enlightened companies (or those wary of independent unions getting organized) provided workers with more leisure time as part of "welfare capitalism" plans, and a revived labor movement (namely unions in the Congress of Industrial Organizations) won contracts that accomplished the same end. Finally, projects by the CCC and other New Deal initiatives and continued improvement efforts by park, fish and game, and other state and federal government agencies enhanced amenities at parks, forests, and wildlife reserves across the country.

As result of all these myriad factors, visitors to national parks increased from 21 million in 1941 to 56 million in 1955, with the exception of a slight decline during World War II. Similarly, visitation at national forests for recreational purposes was 27 million in 1950, a number that continued to climb through the second half of the twentieth century.[43] And the national statistics were mirrored at the state level as well, including increased purchases of hunting and fishing licenses. In Michigan, where the many auto plants and subsidiary industries sustained an ever-expanding community of working-class sportsmen (and sportswomen), deer hunting licenses jumped from 36,000 in 1924 to 170,000 in 1939, small game licenses nearly doubled from 282,000 in 1924 to 538,000 in 1939, while fishing licenses more than doubled from 290,000 in 1933 to 657,000 in 1939, and the 1940s and 1950s showed a persistent steep increase in applications in each category.[44] "Vacations in the woods, amid scenery and nature," Lawrence Lipin explains, "had come to be understood as part of what was being defined as 'freedom and life.'"[45]

Of course, the nature that so many ordinary people found wanting in their lives was not the same one previous generations knew. They ceased to connect the land to work and instead came to regard it as separate and beyond, a place to flee certain objectionable aspects of urban-industrial life.[46] This retreat to the imagination and the actual escape outdoors that it prompted were also part of the summer camp experience, which more and more children from urban, working-class families had the chance to know. For a week or more at a time they went to recreational sites carved out of the woods to play in ways that called up a remote past, particularly the traditions and practices of Native Americans and European pioneers. They did this all the while free from any real threat of wild animals, hunger, sickness, cold, drought, or violent attacks.

In the late nineteenth century, when summer camps first started, they were almost exclusively the domain of well-bred, privileged boys from large cities in the Northeast. Teachers, clergymen, and physicians began testing out the concept as a means to properly socialize youth, particularly to counter the influence of urban, modern life on boys' bodies and minds. Their ideas were based on the assumption that immersion in nature was inherently healthy as well as ideal for character building, an environment where they could become strong and self-reliant. One camp brochure from the 1890s, historian Michael Smith explains, expressed this faith in nature perfectly. "A camp in the woods bordering on a beautiful lake, breathing the healthful, bracing air of the pines, viewing Nature in her ever-changing moods, living a free, outdoor life, and having at all times the sympathetic companionship of young men of refinement, experience, and character," the sales pitch read. Is this not the ideal summer outing for a boy? The outdoors Nature offered the "essential realities" of woods and water, wrote one camp advocate, as opposed to "the artificial realities and conventionalities" of "routine living, especially in our cities." Embedded in this perspective, however, was the notion that even a brief exposure to nature was a critical part of learning to function in the real world back home.[47]

Within a few decades, the number of summer camps grew from a few hundred to more than a thousand, and much of that growth was due to the beginning of scouting in the United States, a development that began to open camps to the working class. Ernest Thompson Seton established the Woodcraft Indians in 1901, part of an attempt to occupy young trespassers on his Connecticut estate with Indian stories and camping, while Daniel Beard created the Sons of Daniel Boone in 1905, an effort to recover and pass on the supposed skills of frontier pioneers. These two organizations were folded into the Boy Scouts of America several years later, and Seton and Beard (like Franklin Delano Roosevelt) were both active in the Boy Scout leadership. By 1920, 45 percent of all Boy Scouts, over 160,000 boys, a good portion of them from working-class families, spent some part of their summers at one of the inexpensive camps scattered throughout the Northeast and Midwest. With the founding of the Camp Fire Girls in 1911 and the Girl Scouts in 1912, camps for girls with a similar socioeconomic background also became more common. In addition, the Scout-run camps were complemented by the increasing number of camps offered through settlement houses (like Jane Addams's Hull House and Mary McDowell's University Settlement) as well as other urban charitable organizations (including the Y.M.C.A. and Y.W.C.A.), which welcomed racial minorities.[48]

It was difficult for laboring families to provide their sons and daughters with any kind of vacation during the 1930s, and the charitable efforts did not adequately fill the gap, but with the return of prosperity during and after World War II, summer camps resumed their popularity as a rite of passage and essential socialization for youth. In a number of cases, new camps were public programs, following precedents set by state and federal governments during the New Deal, providing relief to unemployed youth through conservation work projects. In 1949, for example, the Michigan Department of Conservation established 16 group camps around the state that immersed campers in the study of fish, game, and forest conservation from the beginning of June to early September. "These children are learning that the soil and water and woods and wildlife that God gave so freely to this country are theirs to use, but to use intelligently so that others may also use it," wrote the assistant secretary of the Wayne County Sportsman's Club, an organization of mostly working-class hunters and fishermen based in Detroit. Revealing a persistent concern with socialization for adequately navigating the challenges of modern life, he added that the boys and girls were learning to work and live together, "and it is with them that America's hope for the future rests."[49]

With a similar approach the expansion of summer camp options was aided by organized labor as well. By the late 1940s, one of the camps available to working-class kids was run by the United Auto Workers, the industrial union representing employees at Ford, Chevrolet, General Motors, and their suppliers, largely in the upper Midwest. The UAW leadership took a strong interest in the leisure of the rank-and-file members and, to guide this interest, in 1939 they established the Recreation Department. Then, in 1946, department head Olga Madar worked with President Walter Reuther to start a summer camp at the union's "Franklin Delano Roosevelt—CIO Labor Center," eight miles north of Port Huron, Michigan, on the Lake Huron shore. It was open to boys and girls ages 8 to 14, black as well as white, provided their parents were UAW members.

Promoting the new initiative to UAW Local recording secretaries, in a letter and a brochure, Madar listed a variety of activities that would be led by trained counselors, including swimming, tennis, overnight hikes, campfires, softball, and volleyball. The brochure's cover emphasized the affordability of the camp announcing "Now UAW-CIO Members Can Afford to Send Their Children to Camp Too." In fact, typically at least part of the $10 fee was covered by a respective local union, while the International subsidized general operating expenses. On the inside pages, the brochure described the buildings and grounds, which were ample for play and meeting and included a large dining hall, a working kitchen, an infirmary, and a canteen. There were also 200 hundred acres of woods with plenty of trails, as well as a good beach, a long stretch of sand on the lake. The idea, Madar persuaded, was to give children a space "to learn to live and play together the CIO way."[50]

After filling the Port Huron camp beyond its capacity in the first two years, in 1948 the Recreation Department partnered with Toledo UAW Local 12 to operate a summer camp at their site, on Sand Lake, in Lenawee County, Michigan, 65 miles west of Detroit. By moving to Sand Lake, the union could host 125 children a week from June 19 to August 14, allowing more than 1,000 girls and boys to attend. This camp, like Port Huron, would provide ample opportunity for swimming and boating, hiking and nature study, as well as various recreational sports, in addition to training in handicrafts, folk dancing, drama, and music. These group activities, parents were assured, were meant to give the children "insight into democratic living." Attendance was not what had been expected, however, due to some confusion over registration procedures, and the UAW Recreation Department decided to move the International-sponsored summer camp back to the Labor Center, even while Local 12 continued to operate theirs as well.[51]

Throughout the rest of the 1950s, the Port Huron camp hosted hundreds of boys and girls for four weeks every summer, with a consistent emphasis on social and civic development in the outdoors. It was important for children to leave their cities and towns for life near woods, fields, marshes, and beaches, one report explained, "to develop in the boys and girls a love and appreciation of the natural aspects of the world." At the same time, the more natural landscape was meant to be a site for instruction in effectively navigating modern, urban-industrial life. "The day has passed," the report noted, "when camping should be regarded as primarily a way of release from the harsh realities of city life." Instead, the staff was instructed to observe campers' thought and habit patterns, to encourage those with social value and discourage those that were destructive to the individual and society. "It is possible and highly desirable," the report suggested, "to develop altruism and the best ideals of democratic thinking in camp."[52]

Later, in 1962, the same year the newly formed Students for a Democratic Society used Port Huron to draft their radical statement of principles, the Recreation Department was still running the UAW's summer camp with the goal of promoting social democracy. "It is the 'togetherness' of nature and wholesome group living," the updated brochure read, "that make a camp vacation a never-to-be-forgotten experience." The program provided young people with "the chance to practice some of the beliefs and principles for which our

organization stands." Besides typical outdoor activities, boys and girls prepared their own newspaper and participated in a weekly Camper's Council, "to
give the youngsters a chance to express their needs and interests ... in the total
organization of the program."[53] Not coincidentally, these were skills and attitudes that helped sustain UAW support and mobilization for industrial democracy, racial equality, an end to poverty, and, not coincidentally, environmental
reform.[54]

5

A Popular Crusade: Organized Labor Takes the Lead against Pollution

As the promotional materials for the United Auto Workers' (UAW) summer camp suggests, during the mid-twentieth century at least some segments of the American labor movement were very much concerned with the ways urbanization and industrialization were changing peoples' relationship with nature. For the UAW this awareness had a lot to do with progressive leadership, particularly Walter Reuther, the union's president from 1946 to 1970. Even beyond labor circles he was known for his passionate interest in resource conservation and pollution control, always colored by an equally fervent class consciousness. When Rachel Carson was too ill from breast cancer to address the National Wildlife Federation's annual meeting in Detroit in 1963, the organization invited Reuther in her place. He gave a speech about expanding and enhancing recreational resources for workers, retirees, and the unemployed in a manner that clashed with the restrained tone and apolitical advocacy of *Silent Spring*, published only a year before. "There is a feeling of utmost urgency," Reuther noted, "in the war against selfishness, greed and apathy in meeting the ever-increasing outdoor recreation needs of the people." One way to meet those needs, he continued, was to increase grants to local communities under the open-space provisions of the Housing Act, highlighting a potential role for the federal government.[1]

Reuther always claimed that his interest in environmental issues was both personal and social. On the one hand, he was an avid fisherman and when he moved to a neighborhood along Paint Creek at the end of the 1950s, it was partly for the chance it gave him to angle for trout only 25 feet from his front door. Within a few years, however, the creek's fish disappeared, killed off or run out by filth from an upstream community's antiquated septic tank system. His response, not surprisingly, was to organize the Paint Creek Citizen's Conservation Committee, which filed a lawsuit. "A lot of people have gotten discouraged," the union leader admitted, "because it's a hard fight to go into the courts." Common folks often lacked resources for that kind of battle, Reuther explained, and they had to deal with a whole range of other problems in their lives. Nevertheless, he thought it was worthwhile to persevere in the face of such formidable obstacles, pointing to his own struggle as a lesson.[2]

On the other hand, Reuther also saw his environmentalism as an essential element of both progressive social unionism and broad-minded Cold War liberalism. "What good is getting higher pay, what good is it to get a shorter work week so you have more leisure time, or longer vacation periods," he asked in a rhetorical fashion during one speech, "if the lakes you want to take your family to are polluted and you can't fish in them, or swim in them, or, if the air is poisoned, and if our cities are becoming big asphalt jungles, turning the green parks into parking lots?" Free people shouldn't have to live that way, he went on, yet "that's the kind of world we are going to give them if we continue to neglect these basic problems." As part of the union's effort to follow through on these sentiments, the union had established a Resource and Conservation Department, with staff in all areas of the country, taking over and expanding the work of the older Recreation Department. Likewise, it had convened a series of conferences, including the 1965 United Action for Clean Water Conference, attended by more than 1,000 delegates from the United States as well as Canada, representing a range of unions and organizations.[3]

What's interesting is that the union representing workers who made cars, one of the more noxious threats to the environment in the modern era, was in the environmental movement's vanguard, if not its single-most important organizational pioneer. And (usually) this was not a self-serving or calculated attempt to deflect public criticism or undermine stronger regulatory efforts. The UAW leadership as well as most of the rank-and-file truly believed in making what Reuther called "a decent, wholesome living environment for everyone," whether that meant changing individual behavior or reigning in corporate polluters.[4] Perhaps equally remarkable to those who tend to see labor and environment as mutually exclusive commitments is the fact that the auto workers were not alone. As historian Scott Dewey contends, decades before the first Earth Day confirmed the environmental movement's arrival, a number of unions exhibited "a sophisticated understanding of environmental issues" and adopted "relatively radical positions that were strikingly at odds with the views of the employers with whom they were supposedly allied."[5]

The explanation for many workers' early engagement with environmental issues and some key unions' willingness to back reform lies primarily in the shift common people made from rural farms to urban factories during the nineteenth and twentieth centuries. That experience, one shared by countless native-born Americans and immigrants alike, brought about a new relationship with labor as well as nature. In a word, industrial wage workers experienced a profound alienation from both. They no longer knew soil, water, air, plants, and animals directly, through daily, regular use to meet basic needs, and this lent new meaning and appeal to certain leisure activities such as gardening, hunting, and fishing. At the same time, as workers endured the constant irritations, ugliness, and dangers of city life, they began to recognize the need to establish limits that would check industrial and municipal pollution and give them even more reason to seek escape in the outdoors, to hunt in game refuges, visit parks, camp in forests, fish and boat on lakes, and enjoy other similar recreational activities.

Of course, by the 1940s there was already a long history of worker concern for pollution dating at least to the early nineteenth century, when manufacturers began using rivers to dispose of industrial waste, and extending to the early twentieth century, when Progressive reformers helped mobilize urban communities to improve local sanitation. Likewise, in the interwar years, industrial-hygiene advocates had lent attention to recognizing and eliminating workplace hazards, an effort that pushed some scientists to identify dangers beyond factory gates, a link that many workers were ready and receptive to understand. Americans in general and workers in particular did not suddenly discover bad water and air in the 1960s, and they were not venturing out onto entirely new ground when they organized to do something about environmental problems. It's nearly impossible, actually, to say when exactly an environmental movement truly began, since there were so many numerous, early precedents.

Also, escape to nature was enabled by projects the Civilian Conservation Corps (CCC) and other New Deal programs accomplished in the 1930s, ranging from reforestation to dune construction, something that must be counted among the factors behind the rise and development of a working-class environmental movement as well. Wilderness advocates sounded their objections, but the 125,000 miles of new roads, 40,000 vehicular bridges, and 8 million square yards of parking lot space built by the CCC in the national parks alone certainly facilitated ease of access to woods and water for workers and their families.[6] In the years following the Depression, state and federal agencies continued to expand and enhance parks, forests, game reserves, lakes, beaches, and other sites, often at the urging of organized labor.

"One of our major concerns in Oakland County," declared Ken Morris, a UAW representative speaking at a Michigan department of natural resources hearing in 1970, "is that there are approximately 488 lakes and only approximately 18 public access sites." The problem was the inconvenience this imposed on a particular segment of the population. "What this means to workers and lower-middle class citizens, is that they must go far from their homes, traveling long distances," Morris continued, "to make use of lakes which are not for the exclusive use of those who own property around the lake itself. Each one of these lakes are [sic] a public body of water and reasonable public access ought not to be limited by a few who fear other possible problems." Paul Massaron, another UAW representative, echoed these points later the next year at a Water Management Needs Conference, where he explained why auto workers had joined with others to push the state waterways commission to continue its public-access acquisition efforts. These kinds of remarks, not unusual for the time, were merely one more way in which class struggle was folded into environmental politics.[7]

Something Much More Fundamental

While much of the American economy was organized around textile production at the beginning stages of industrialization, by the post–Civil War period it was railroads that drove expansion and growth. Then, beginning in the years leading up to World War I, auto manufacturing and its subsidiary industries (steel, rubber, glass, etc.) took center stage, primarily in major cities of the upper Midwest. Just as agriculture was becoming increasingly mechanized and farmers were consolidating landholdings, in the face of declining prices and overproduction, industrial capitalism was creating jobs that could absorb at least a portion of the newly redundant rural labor. Like the young women from New England farms a century before, who packed their bags for mill work in Lowell, Chicopee, Manchester, and elsewhere in that region, rural dwellers from scattered farms throughout the eastern part of the United States gathered their families and headed to Pittsburgh, Akron, Detroit, and various cities and towns in the westward-shifting industrial belt. Peasants from southern and eastern Europe as well as Mexico made their way to the new urban factories and mills in great numbers too (at least until quotas established in the 1920s slowed their entry), adding yet another wave of immigrants to the available labor pool.

By the interwar years, wages for auto workers were comparatively high, especially after the five-dollar day became a standard rate throughout the industry,

and hours were not inordinate, with an average 50-hour week. But auto manufacturers had dramatically transformed production since the 1890s, when cars
were custom-built playthings for the wealthy. To increase worker productivity
they introduced the moving assembly line and continuously sought ways to
deskill labor, in accordance with Frederick Winslow Taylor's scientific management principles. Consequently, work became extremely repetitive and
mind-numbingly dull and allowed little if any opportunity for creative self-
expression. Amidst the overpowering noise of constantly moving machines
employees went through the same motions, the same "one best way," over and
over, all day long, filling every hour with tension. There was no outlet for even
slight relief on the line, as foremen enforced draconian rules prohibiting talking, sitting, singing, and smoking.[8]

Conditions in the auto plants, coupled with a longing for the rural countryside only recently left behind, explain why so many working men (and a
few women) were newly drawn to recreational hunting and fishing at the time.
During the nineteenth century, sportsmen's ranks in the region, as elsewhere,
were dominated by "prominent citizens of the professions, of business and of
industry of that day."[9] By the 1920s, however, this situation was beginning to
change, particularly in Michigan, where license records show a substantial,
consistent increase in the years before World War II.[10] After the war, even more
workers took to the fields, forests, streams, and lakes with rifle, bow, rod, or
traps in hand. In 1948, Wayne County residents—including line employees
at River Rouge, Highland Park, Hamtramck, and other Detroit car plants—
purchased 274,800 hunting and fishing licenses, an increase of 22,000 from
the year before. Genesee County residents—many of them workers at General
Motors in Flint—purchased 50,000 deer and small-game licenses, putting
them second to Wayne County in the number of state-sanctioned hunters. And
Oakland County, just north of Detroit and including the city of Pontiac, was
second in fishing licenses, with 59,000 sold.[11]

The greater popularity of hunting and fishing in Michigan, through the
interwar years and after, was enough to sustain a vibrant network of mostly
new or recently founded working-class sportsmen's clubs. Some of them, like
the Genesee Sportsmen's Association, had membership lists in the thousands
and published monthly newsletters with an even larger circulation. Toward
the end of the 1930s, they also banded together to form the Michigan United
Conservation Clubs (MUCC) to guard and advance sportsmen's concerns at
the state level. This organization was headed by Vic Beresford, secretary of the
Wayne County Sportsmen's Club, based in River Rouge. Within ten years, it
had 250 affiliates and easily rivaled the Michigan Izaak Walton League, which

was a decade and a half older and tended to attract members with an elite background.[12]

One indication of newer sportsmen's groups different composition are the advertisements in their monthly newsletters, ranging from bowling alleys and hardware stores to filling stations and grocers, places with particular appeal to a working-class readership. Similarly, various columns included items advising members to support proposed legislation that would end bans on Sunday hunting, a policy that still prevailed in a number of counties across the state. Only a little more than half of the downstate hunting areas were open on that particular day of the week, editors of the *Macomb County Sportsman* complained, even though it was "the only day when many hunters can go afield." Another article considered the threat posed by wealthy individuals and private clubs, who could afford to buy available outdoor lands and bar them from public access and so deny "the common man of moderate means" a place to hunt and fish. The clubs also showed their alignment with workers' interests in other ways, such as by making arrangements to encourage and enable the participation of all members. The Genesee Sportsmen's Association, for example, held mid-morning meetings for Flint auto workers coming off the second and third shifts on the same day as the regularly scheduled evening meeting.[13]

The tens of thousands of ordinary Michigan residents who joined the new sportsmen's clubs were, at least originally, primarily interested in fish and game conservation. They worked hand in hand with the state department of conservation to maintain the deer population in public hunting grounds, collaborated with farmers to control foxes and expand pheasant habitat on their property, and promoted the use of rod and boat license fees to raise revenue for stocking ponds, lakes, and streams with fish. Those efforts enhanced the chances factory hands had to get out of the cities and connect with the nature that seemed otherwise absent in workers' lives, an experience that frequently prompted romantic musings. "A promising opening day turning to rain and sticky snow which clung to alder and willow and hapless fishermen," read one club newsletter article on the start of trout fishing season, "the grace and whiteness of birch against the somber darkness of spruce and hemlock ... a limpid stream with the daring of youth merrily kissing each stone and waltzing away ... violets and marigolds forming patterns on Nature's carpet ... the musical ring of distant bells of ranging cattle ... the tight line and a rainbow of great vigor and determination ... the solace and comfort of intimacy with Nature ... That's trout fishing!"[14]

By the 1940s and 1950s, however, members shared a growing apprehension about pollution, particularly municipal sewage and industrial waste, and they began to mobilize to address the issue through the county clubs and MUCC. Hunting and fishing clubs have outlived their usefulness, the *Kent League Sportsmen* put it, "if they [are] organized merely for the stocking, feeding and protection of a single species, without regard to their obligation to the public, without respect to nature and science, without regard to human rights."[15] As part of the shift in focus, Genesee County sportsmen became increasingly concerned with heavily degraded sections of the Flint River, off-limits to swimmers because of a high bacteria count from untreated sewage waste and likely contaminated with noxious industrial waste as well. In response, the local club president established a Water Pollution Committee. Various groups also started a petition campaign in response to a large fish kill in the Kalamazoo River, caused by Union Steel's repeated release of cyanide into the water. This actually became the first case settled under a new antipollution law, passed in 1949, with the critical support of sportsmen's clubs and the MUCC, despite the efforts of industry lobbyists in opposition.[16]

Yet there was still much to do to clean up Michigan waters, as the water resources commission established by the antipollution law explained in a comprehensive report. Large parts of at least 25 major rivers in the state were so fouled by municipal and industrial waste that they were hazardous for recreational swimming and allied purposes. This included the Detroit River from downtown to Lake Erie, River Rouge from Michigan Avenue to the Detroit River, much of the shore line around Lake St. Clair, the full length of the Saginaw River, and the Kalamazoo River from Albion to Lake Michigan. To clean up these and other waterways and to begin to address the equally pressing problem of air pollution, working-class sportsmen needed the assistance of other organizations, and they got plenty of help from their union, the United Auto Workers (UAW).[17]

Established in 1936, the UAW was born from a larger, national resurgence of organized labor in the 1930s. Throwing off the quiescent trade unionism of the American Federation of Labor, the newly founded Congress of Industrial Organizations (CIO) initiated organizing campaigns in auto, steel, rubber, and various key industries, often led by socialists and communists, and sometimes won with the use of sit-down strikes and other radical tactics. There were hundreds of such strikes at auto plants throughout the upper Midwest, and after an especially hard-fought battle at Ford's River Rouge in 1941, the UAW had contracts with all three major auto manufacturers as well as many suppliers. During the war years, autoworkers squeezed by heavy production demands and high inflation also staged thousands of unsanctioned wildcat strikes. But with the onset of the Cold War and the second Red scare, the UAW and other CIO unions tried to defend themselves against conservative attacks by restraining and even purging their radicals. Consequently, the end of the 1940s saw most shop-floor militancy replaced with a more orderly, centralized bureaucratic unionism.

Walter Reuther, who was elected president of the UAW during the transition period, played an important role in the anticommunist housecleaning and leadership consolidation. Still, Reuther, his brothers, and many others in the UAW were old-style socialists, committed to a brand of unionism that went beyond a narrow concern with wages and hours and embraced a whole host of social issues. Their social democratic vision was, in fact, what led the UAW leadership to lend so much support to worker education and recreation, which helped establish a foundation for developing autoworkers' environmental consciousness, and it was what drove them to position the UAW as a foremost labor advocate for local, state, and national pollution controls.[18]

The UAW executive board had established an Education Department in 1935 and a separate Recreation Department as early as 1939. In 1946, the same year that Reuther became president, Olga Madar was named acting head of the Recreation Department, and she enjoyed considerable support for her work, overseeing a wide range of union-sponsored leisure activities. Her charge was to enable and enhance the way members spent their time off the job, which she saw as much more than time for loafing or playing. It was, in her view, a critical part of feeding mental and spiritual hungers that modern industry failed to account for in its drive to produce goods ever faster and cheaper. "What about the man in the shop who inspects bearings, hour after hour, day after day?," Madar asked at one point. "What about the woman who does nothing throughout her working weeks and months but put fasteners on to automobile doors? There's nothing creative, or combative, competitive, adventurous, or social about this." To fill the gap, she recommended lying on a river bank and looking at the sky, turning the soil to plant beans in a garden, and hunting deer in a forest, all of which drew their value from the activity itself rather than any monetary gain.[19]

Reuther echoed these sentiments in his own way in various public speeches, internal memos, and published articles, and they became a part of the distinctive working-class environmentalism he sought to promote and implement as policy. By the 1960s, his task was made easier by the fact of John F. Kennedy's election to the White House and Stewart Udall's appointment as secretary of interior. The victorious Democrats looked to organized labor for votes, of course, but theirs was a bond of ideas too, molded around a Cold War liberalism. After Kennedy was assassinated in 1963, Reuther found an even more sympathetic ally in Lyndon Johnson. The two men shared a commitment to ending poverty and racial inequality as well as a common interest in natural beautification and environmental quality.

When Johnson gave his Great Society speech at the University of Michigan in 1964, Reuther was sitting on stage, listening intently. The next year, opening the UAW-organized Clean Water Conference, the union president invoked Johnson's own words. "A great society," he quoted, "is a society more concerned with the quality of its goals than the quantity of its goods." Reuther argued for the need to reject the marketplace as the only measure of good and to adopt a new value system. "We look at something much more fundamental," he explained, "the enrichment and the growth and development of the human spirit, and yet, if we go on as we have been going on, we will destroy the kind of living environment in which the free human spirit can flourish." To avert disaster, he said, there needed to be "a popular crusade not only for clean water, but also for cleaning up the atmosphere, the highways, the junkyards and the slums and for creating a total living environment worthy of free men." This "massive mobilization of citizens" had to happen at "the community, state, and national levels and challenge recalcitrant governments as well as irresponsible industry."[20]

As the 1960s progressed and a range of social movements began radicalizing various segments of the American population, the UAW president grew even more zealous. Speaking at the annual conference of the Water Pollution Control Federation in 1968, Reuther offered up an apocalyptic vision to the audience, framing the nation's environmental crisis as "a crisis in our value system," connecting environmental problems to economic and social problems, and warning (again) of the disaster that would come without immediate, radical change. "If we continue to destroy our living environment by polluting our streams and poisoning our air," he said, "we put the survival of the human family in jeopardy.... We may be the first civilization in the history of man that will have suffocated and been strangled in the waste of its material affluence— compounded by social indifference and social neglect."[21]

Meanwhile, in 1966 Olga Madar was made a member of the UAW executive board, and in 1967 she was put in charge of a new Conservation and Resource Development Department, which effectively served as a center for promoting environmental education and activism. The department was established, Madar explained, "because our members and their families are directly affected by the environment around them, both inside and outside of the plants in which they work."[22] In her testimony before a congressional subcommittee considering stricter air pollution legislation, she declared that autoworkers were "first and foremost American citizens and consumers," who had "to breathe the same air and drink and bathe in the same water" as other Americans. That, she continued, was why the UAW supported emission controls on cars, in contrast to the auto industry's obstinate opposition and despite a possible adverse impact on employment.[23]

Realizing that testifying and lobbying were not enough to bring about change, Madar also put the Conservation and Resource Development Department to work facilitating community action. One campaign, the Down River Anti-Pollution League (DAPL), encompassed Wyandotte Lincoln Park (predominantly white) as well as River Rouge and Ecorse (mostly black), where working-class residents had long-complained about local air and water quality. Gases in the air apparently burned eyes and noses, caused serious respiratory problems, and peeled paint from house siding, but industrial and municipal waste in the water had equally if not more unpleasant effects. "Not only has pollution in our streams, lakes and rivers severely cut back our fishing, swimming and boating activities," acknowledged a DAPL flier addressed to members of Local 174, "but the filth is so bad that even extensive chemical purification may be unable to provide us with reasonably clean drinking water!"[24]

At the center of the DAPL were two interns, Roberta Bowers and Hillel Liebert, both enrolled at the University of Michigan's School of Social Work, and they took the lead in building a steering committee as well as arranging initial meetings. The steering committee then came up with seven action projects, including picketing the Michigan Water Resources Commission's February meeting to demand stricter enforcement of water pollution law. "The giant industrial corporations must be stopped from dumping their filthy and dangerous wastes, especially in the heavily polluted Downriver Area," read one flier directed at union members and community residents. "Ford, Great Lakes Steel, Peerless Cement, Shell Oil and other companies, which have been pouring tremendous quantities of poisonous filth into our water for years must be made to pay for all costs of treatment and clean-up of their wastes." Likewise, the DAPL planned to raise the issue of Grosse Pointe, a wealthy suburb, for improperly managing its sewage wastes. "The unbelievably filthy and putrid sewage which they pour into Fox Creek," the flier explained, "is deposited on homes and in yards of Detroit residents," and even the popular Belle Isle Bathing Beach was affected.[25]

In April of the next year, Lincoln Park resident Joyce Vermillion led a group of DAPL women in marking the first Earth Day celebration as well. They staged protests at the Great Lakes Steel blast furnaces on Zug Island, in the Detroit River, where they met like-minded female protestors from Windsor, Canada, who joined them to make a party that was described by the *Detroit News* as "an irate band of women" from both sides of the border. Other, tamer, less defiant river clean-up efforts attracted more than a thousand people at a time, including children. Buoyed by all this activity, the DAPL soon had nearly 700 members, published a monthly newsletter, and held regular meetings at local union halls in the area.[26]

Later a group of self-described UAW wives met to form United Active Women, led by Winnie Fraser and Jessie Dillard, and assisted by Olga Madar and her assistant Charlene Knight. Their main purpose was to get involved in various consumer and environmental affairs—following what was by then very much a trend among civically engaged women—and they designated water-quality improvement as their particular concern. At first they worked on pollution from high-phosphate detergents, which the Detroit City Council banned in the early part of 1971. With that quick victory under their belt, the women's group arranged bus tours to give folks a close-up look at smoke and soot coming from area factory smokestacks as well as the industrial waste chemicals and sludge dumped into the Detroit River. "Be the first in your neighborhood," they wrote tongue-in-cheek in their newsletter, "to breathe Down River's famous hydrocarbons, sulfur dioxide, and carbon monoxide."[27]

The United Auto Worker's environmental activism was dealt a blow, however, by the unexpected loss of Walter Reuther's leadership. The UAW president had decided that the union needed a new labor education and vacation center, "a thing of beauty where man and nature can live in harmony," to replace the one at Port Huron. Against strong objections from the executive board, Reuther chose a spot among one thousand wooded acres in Onaway, an area quite remote from Detroit and often frequented by the city's elite. The week after speaking to University of Michigan students on the first Earth Day, in 1970, he flew out to see the nearly finished Black Lake Center with his wife, the architect, and a few others. Coming in for landing, their plane clipped a stand of trees, burst into a fireball, and crashed, killing everyone on board.

Despite the tragedy, the building was soon completed, and an environmental conference there went ahead as planned later that same year. Throughout the first half of the decade at least, Madar and the UAW executive board also continued to work at enacting more environmental legislation and strengthening existing regulatory laws as well as bringing labor unions, environmental organizations, and consumer groups together to develop a common agenda.[28] To institutionalize that alliance, in 1971 Senator Philip Hart of Michigan organized the Urban Environment Conference (UEC), which included the UAW, United

Steel Workers (USW), and Oil, Chemical and Atomic Workers (OCAW) as well as the Sierra Club and National Welfare Rights Organization. Later, in 1975, some of the same individuals and groups helped form Environmentalists for Full Employment (EFFE), which had close ties to the United Auto Workers.[29]

By 1976, though, there were noticeable fault lines and weak points. That spring, the UAW hosted another gathering at Black Lake, billed as Working for Environmental and Economic Justice and Jobs, cosponsored by the UEC, EFFE, and another organization called Environmental Action. Leonard Woodcock, the union's new president, opened the meeting with encouraging remarks, claiming an unprecedented level of "common cause between union members and environmentalists—between workers, poor people, minorities, and those seeking to protect our natural resources." Yet those words overstated the extent of cooperation somewhat, as poor union attendance and certain events at the conference suggested. Tom Donahue, an AFL-CIO executive assistant, even publicly scolded the Friends of the Earth leader David Brower, explaining that organized labor was primarily concerned with protecting workers' economic interests and could get involved in "social unionism … only so long as that primary function is fulfilled." This was a shaky foundation on which to build a movement that treated economic and environmental concerns as inextricably linked and foretold huge challenges in the future.[30]

The Eyes and Ears of the Community

Although the future of any labor-environmental alliance looked bleak in the late 1970s, the second Black Lake Conference had not been a complete failure, and, in fact, as Robert Gordon explains, it helped workers and environmentalists to continue building a collaborative relationship. First, the conference served as a public forum for making the case that there were ways to have more jobs with less harm to the environment, largely by substituting human labor for technology. Second, it helped strengthen the tentative links between labor unions and environmental groups and established EFFE as the main organization for mobilizing against job blackmail or otherwise resolving tensions between employment and environmental protection. And lastly, the conference encouraged many participants to set up local-level gatherings of labor, community, civil rights, and environmental activists, to discuss and resist corporate attempts to use divide-and-conquer strategies.[31]

One particular issue that drew a lot of attention at the time was nuclear power, which had been touted as a clean or pollution-free form of energy since the first reactors were sited in the 1950s. William Winpisinger, president of the International Association of Machinists (IAM), took the lead in galvanizing a campaign to expose that claim when he established the Citizen/Labor Energy Coalition (CLEC) in 1978. At its founding, CLEC included over 60 labor, consumer, environmental, religious, minority, and other organizations dedicated to shutting the nuclear industry down and filling the gap with renewable energy sources that would be safe for workers and the environment. The next year, there was a partial core meltdown at the Three Mile Island reactor, in Harrisburg, Pennsylvania, which forced the evacuation of 140,000 residents and dramatically demonstrated the risks of nuclear power. In the wake of the accident, activists held a national conference on safe energy and full employment, attended by 1,000 union workers from 55 different unions, and they staged a march in Harrisburg on the second anniversary. As a result of this and other organizing, public sentiment turned strongly against the nuclear industry, the Nuclear Regulatory Commission ceased granting permits for new plant construction, and some operational reactors were closed altogether.[32]

Sitting on the sidelines during this battle was the Oil Chemical and Atomic Workers, which hesitated to join a campaign that would literally wipe out the jobs of its 50,000 members in the nuclear industry. The union refrained from attacking environmental organizations and other unions rallying against nuclear power, however, a fact that was testament to its long and deep involvement with labor environmentalism as well as the not-too comfortable realization that radiation and other hazards to workers on the job suggested the possibility of threats to human health beyond plant gates.[33] Just as the United Auto Workers defied assumptions that its interest in protecting employees who produced exhaust-belching cars would necessarily hinder any chance that it could take the lead in fighting air and water pollution, the OCAW was among the pioneers of the modern environmental movement despite the fact it represented hundreds of thousands of workers in oil refining, chemical production, and nuclear energy.

Like the UAW, the OCAW's organizational prescience was due at least in some part to a key leader, Tony Mazzocchi, an Italian American from Brooklyn who was steeped in radical (communist) politics. Toward the end of the 1950s, when he was on the Oil Chemical and Atomic Workers executive board, Mazzocchi began working with another radical, a scientist named Barry Commoner, who established the Committee for Nuclear Information. By delving into the health problems associated with nuclear power, especially the dangers uranium miners faced, he started to connect the dots, so to speak, in terms of the dangerous conditions for workers. As his biographer Les Leopold notes, he came to see that the OCAW could evolve beyond a traditional labor union and become one of the largest and most formidable environmental organizations in the United States.[34]

As legislative director for the union in the 1960s, Mazzocchi was in a particularly good position to learn about, investigate, and respond to the abhorrent and declining working conditions in chemical production, which he soon realized companies not only tolerated but calculated into the cost of doing business. That is, the fog of smoke and dust that regularly plagued workers in many plants and the ill effects it caused them were a simple matter of accounting, with little in the way of government regulation or oversight to force their recognition as moral or social concerns. "In 1966," Mazzocchi remembered, "I started getting phone calls from locals on particular health and safety problems—because when people encounter a problem, they think there's a law to protect them. And I said, 'Yeah, there must be something'—and I started calling around. I couldn't find out anything. Gee, there's no law."[35] Despite the efforts of those in the field of industrial hygiene, by then many decades old, there was still a great deal to be done to move from an era of voluntary compliance (unreliable in a profit-driven economy) to legal obligation (essential to setting another standard besides the bottom line).

Acting on his new knowledge about the lack of regulatory tools, Mazzocchi began organizing within the OCAW to get the union engaged with a growing movement for federal occupational health and safety legislation. In a successful attempt to get a supporting resolution passed at the 1967 national convention, he invited Ralph Nader to speak, since the well-known consumer advocate was already familiar to delegates from his work on natural gas pipeline safety. Nader took the stage and explained the way occupational dangers had evolved, from simple injuries with immediate consequences to toxicity that posed a deadly long-term threat. Later, talking to hundreds of members in smaller meetings at union locals, often accompanied by medical doctors and scientists, Mazzocchi reiterated this key observation about latency, the possibility that effects of exposure might not show up until years later. As he well knew, that posed new challenges for determining cause, implementing remediation, and figuring compensation.[36]

Using his initial meetings with workers as a model, Mazzocchi developed a road show, called Hazards in the Industrial Environment, which debuted March 29, 1969, at a Holiday Inn in Kenilworth, New Jersey. This first run was attended by more than two hundred union leaders from the local OCAW district as well as workers from other chemical unions, and it began with a direct acknowledgement of chemical workers' particular plight. "Though we've talked about health and safety for a long time in the trade union movement," Mazzocchi noted in his opening remarks, "the emphasis had been on the safety aspect of it—whether a fellow gets his hand caught in a machine, or whether a gal gets her hair caught.... But the industry we work in had a danger that most people are unaware of, and it's insidious. It's the danger of a contaminated environment, the workplace, something we don't feel, see or smell, and of which most of us become contemptuous, simply because it doesn't affect us immediately. And then, when we do become ill, we attribute it to something other than the workplace."[37]

The initial road show, and the many that followed, gave workers a chance to speak for themselves, telling their stories, as Les Leopold puts it, revealing that they were "literally dying for a law." Bob Diehl, a Union Carbide employee, related how his company claimed that gasses from allyl alcohol were essentially harmless. He and other workers did their own research, however, at the Rutgers University chemistry library, and learned that the fumes were very harmful, not only potent enough to irritate eyes and mucous membranes but also, in high enough concentrations, liable to cause convulsions, coma, and death. Confronted with these possible effects, Diehl said, company officials acted surprised. On the other hand, many who attended came with only well-founded suspicions and hoped to get answers from the experts present. Steven Lawrence, an employee at American Cyanamid, came to the road show to find out about the range of pesticide products he and fellow workers handled, including malathion, parathion, thiamide, and xanathade. Everybody in the plant is exposed, he said, due to faulty equipment and management's overriding interest in production yield.[38]

In response to those testifying, Mazzocchi insisted that exposing dangers in the workplace was a critical step toward recognizing environmental problems in communities at large because those problems began in the workplace and spread. The point of organizing around health and safety issues, he noted, was not merely to defend the interests of the union's membership (or the interests of chemical workers) but rather to aid all the people affected by the toxic hazards of industrial production. "We're making the point that you can't be concerned about the general environment unless you're concerned about the industrial environment," Mazzocchi told audiences, "because the two are inseparable." And the rank-and-file seemed to understand this, just as many auto workers realized the role the UAW could and should play controlling and preventing pollution beyond plant gates. "Not only do we suffer from these fumes in the plant," Woodbridge Chemical employee Harold Smith acknowledged, "but the people in the community around our plant suffer. That means that somebody else's kid is inhaling these fumes when he wakes up in the morning."[39]

At the time, however, even workers in unionized chemical plants had few tools to address environmental dangers in the workplace. The guide companies followed on chemical exposure, *The Documentation of Threshold Values*, was written by committees affiliated with the American Conference of Governmental Industrial Hygienists (ACGIH), a group sponsored by private industry (despite the name). The committees included no representatives from labor or the general public, and ACGIH standards, already weak on exposure levels and limited to a small fraction of chemicals, were flexible according to the whim of plant management. The one law that did protect some workers, the Walsh-Healy Act, applied only to employees at companies with large federal government contracts, and under that law inspections were announced in advance and final results of the inspections were shown only to the company.[40]

To remedy the situation, the OCAW joined with several other unions to lobby for better regulatory legislation. They were helped along by dissident members of the United Mine Workers concerned about black lung (pneumoconiosis), who organized a wildcat strike and forced Congress to pass the Coal Mine Safety and Health Act. This act provided momentum for the movement for a broader law, enacted the following year. The Occupational Safety and Health Act (OSHA) required employers to provide a workplace "free from recognized hazards that are causing or likely to cause death or serious physical harm," gave organized labor and others the right to petition the secretary of labor for new or improved standards, and set up a protocol for record keeping, unannounced inspections, and federal enforcement. Additionally, OSHA created the National Institute of Occupational Safety and Health, to conduct research and education.[41]

In the wake of organized labor's achievement, Mazzocchi turned more of his attention to the oil industry, which, like chemical production, was plagued by a poor health and safety record. With bargaining for a national refinery contract looming, he managed to convince the rest of OCAW leadership to make the dismal record central to negotiations, seizing an opportunity to go beyond OSHA requirements. The union insisted on a joint Labor-Management Health and Safety Committee with the power to make binding recommendations, periodic company-paid plant inspections by independent and mutually agreed upon health experts, company-paid medical examinations for all employees by OCAW-approved doctors, and full disclosure of morbidity and mortality data. Although they initially balked, all but one of the nation's largest oil producers eventually accepted these demands by the end of 1972, leaving Shell Oil and the Oil Chemical and Atomic Workers in a stand-off.[42]

Shell officials claimed that the company alone was responsible for the health and safety of its employees, a concern that could "not be shared with the union," and it had some leverage to fight on that point. By the early part of the decade, much of its refining had been automated, meaning a traditional strike would not be very effective. OCAW leaders realized, however, that they were in a high-stakes battle. Caving to Shell on the health and safety clause "would endanger the integrity of the union in its dealings with other companies and would endanger the future of coordinated national bargaining with the industry." So, when 5,000 workers walked off the job the Oil Chemical and Atomic Workers adopted novel tactics. It won the endorsement of 11 main environmental organizations (which brought environmental activists to picket lines) and it began a nationwide boycott campaign (which led thousands of consumers to return their Shell credit cards).[43]

The labor-environmental alliance, one of the first of its kind during a strike, was built on the years of organizing and outreach that Mazzocchi and other progressive union leaders had done, convincing environmentalists that improving workplace health and safety was not only the right thing to do but also the logical first step in fighting pollution. "If toxic substances are present in oil refineries," the environmental allies announced, "they most assuredly are spreading outside the plant walls to neighboring communities." The struggle illustrated the "shared concerns of workers and environmentalists," they continued, and "we support the efforts of the OCAW in demanding a better environment, not just for its own workers, but for all Americans." Rather than dividing the union from environmental groups the fact that workers were involved in industrial production that made pollution was actually bringing them together.[44]

The potential for solidarity and collaboration could not be assumed at the outset, though, particularly in the case of the Sierra Club, an older organization. On the eve of the strike it was wrestling with a long-held aversion to mixing political and social issues with conservation. The club held two labor-environmental summits in 1972, both of which highlighted areas of disagreement, and the group hesitated in making an endorsement at the beginning of the Shell walkout. When other environmental groups and various labor unions finally convinced the Sierra Club's executive board to support the strike, the vote generated a considerable wave of internal criticism and opposition. "Have your Directors lost their minds?," asked one member in a letter to the leadership. "How can they be so foolish as to damage the credibility of the entire Sierra Organization by indulging in left wing social action?" Nevertheless, the club had officially joined the fray, and participation by many leaders and members in the fight was its own school for consciousness-raising.[45]

Faced with this mix of labor, environmental, and consumer opposition, Shell Oil struck back in tried-and-true fashion and eventually had its way. One plant manager in California told striking workers that they risked being permanently replaced. At another facility in Deer Park, Texas, where a segment of employees was growing disillusioned with the months-long walkout, the company opened up exclusive negotiations with the local, reaching a settlement that fell far short of initial demands. Shell agreed to a joint health and safety committee, for example, but its recommendations would not be binding. Likewise, it agreed to provide morbidity and mortality statistics but refused to pay for plant inspections by independent experts. Meanwhile, the OCAW strike fund was going broke, despite the very meager benefits striking workers were receiving. By mid-May, the union could no longer pay any benefits at all and the Oil Chemical and Atomic Workers was forced to settle for the contract bargained at the Deer Park plant.[46]

Despite what might be seen as a defeat, however, the strike was not a complete loss, and it did not interfere with industry-wide pattern bargaining as union leaders had expected. As Robert Gordon explains, the OCAW managed to keep the stronger health and safety clause in its other contracts when they were renewed. The union also helped to pressure OSHA for stricter standards on exposure to asbestos, radiation, mercury, benzene, and chemical pesticides. Just as importantly, the Shell battle brought the issue of worker health and safety to the attention of millions of Americans. Indicating how far environmentalists had come in a short period of time, Sierra Club president Mike McCloskey gave a rousing speech at the OCAW's 1973 biennial convention. "We have more in common than divides us," he declared. "We know that what is good for General Motors or Dow Chemical is not necessarily good for us all."[47]

A few years after the Shell strike, in 1977, Tony Mazzocchi won one of the OCAW's two vice president seats, and he was put in charge of health and safety as well as organizing, allowing him to continue his advocacy for engaging environmentalists and insisting on a broad definition of what counted as environmental issues. The impact he had in this respect was evident during the next decade, when the Oil Chemical and Atomic Workers waged a successful corporate campaign against MAPCO, an Oklahoma company that purchased a Memphis refinery and immediately demanded major concessions from the workforce. Rather than strike, the employees stayed on the job and reached out to local residents and national environmental organizations, emphasizing their common interests, including concerns about air quality, illegal lead sludge burial, and groundwater contamination. "You want the community to see the workers as important," Richard Leonard, the campaign coordinator explained.

"You want the community to visualize the union as a necessity to allow workers to be able to speak up concerning these environmental or health and safety questions and be the eyes and ears of the community, ideally."[48]

The OCAW used the same strategy in a fight with the chemical giant BASF, at a plant in Louisiana's so-called Cancer Alley. During the summer of 1984 the company offered workers a new contract that would have wiped out decades of gains, and when the union negotiators refused to accept it, management locked out all 370 production and maintenance employees. The Oil Chemical and Atomic Workers responded by sending Richard Miller, Mazzochi's young assistant, to build a broad coalition of local civic and community groups, national environmental organizations like the Sierra Club, and even the German Green Party. The goal was to pressure BASF back to the bargaining table by hammering away at the company's abysmal health and safety record as well as its long history as an environmental outlaw, and after five and a half years the alliance had success. On December 15, 1989, representatives from both sides reached an agreement that allowed all employees to return to the plant, established terms for improving working conditions, and spelled out plans for reducing the company's pollution.[49]

The BASF fight turned OCAW Local 4-620 into one of the most environmental-minded union locals in the country. Initially, many workers collaborated with community groups and environmental organizations simply as a means of increasing their leverage with the company. During and after the campaign, however, their attitudes changed, "and they began to see the value of raising environmental issues even when there was no labor dispute." "Five years ago," rank-and-file member Bobby Schneider explained, "I felt if you wanted your job and you wanted to live in this state, you were just going to have to put up with it. I certainly don't feel that way today. There are ways to make these plants safe—to cut down on wastes, to recycle wastes, and to find proper ways to get rid of the waste that's left." Others also explicitly rejected the notion that they had to sacrifice environmental quality and people's health for employment. "They keep threatening us with the loss of our jobs," noted John Diagle, "but we don't want those kinds of jobs anymore. We want clean jobs." Guided by such sentiments, Local 4-620 continued to nurture an alliance with environmentalists, primarily through their own separate organization, the Louisiana Labor-Neighbor Project and Louisiana Workers against Toxic Hazards.[50]

Yet despite taking a progressive approach on social and environmental issues, the Oil Chemical and Atomic Workers failed to become the leading environmental organization Tony Mazzocchi had once dreamed it might be. OCAW leaders had enough to do responding to layoffs and plant shutdowns, which caused a precipitous decline in membership. Between 1979 and 1994, the ranks shrunk by half, from 180,000 to 90,000.[51] This decline mirrored a broader, national decline in union density (the proportion of the labor force that belongs to unions), which reached a high of 35 percent in the middle 1950s, fell steadily thereafter, and recently dropped to 12.5 percent. As many observers have pointed out, the seemingly unstoppable contraction poses a huge challenge to any contemporary efforts within the American labor movement to form and sustain an alliance with environmentalists.

6

To Stir Up Dissent and Create Turmoil:
Inventing Environmental Justice

Although infamous for being ruled by coal interests since the end of the nineteenth century, central Appalachia has also seen many efforts to challenge that entrenched power. In the 1960s, one such effort consisted of a coalition of groups allied to end surface coal mining, or strip mining, which was devastating the regional economy and ruining the area landscape. Among the advocates for a ban were active and retired members of the United Mine Workers (UMW). These underground miners saw stripping as one of many efforts by coal operators to reduce labor costs through mechanization, and as residents of the mountain communities they experienced firsthand the damage that surface mining could do to homesteads, orchards, farmland, wells, and creeks. Yet their corrupt and undemocratic union was allied with the coal industry and unresponsive to these concerns, and national environmental organizations were preoccupied with protecting wilderness areas and defending endangered animal species. Consequently, the miners joined forces with other working people in the region, and because they had little faith in courts and legislatures to right glaring wrongs they formed local groups that tended to favor direct action, an approach which distinguished them from more conventional proponents of environmental reform.

One notable showdown between strip mining opponents and a coal operator took place in 1967, in Pike County, Kentucky, on land owned by farmer Jink Ray. Island Creek Coal had the mineral rights to this land and, by what was known as the "broad form deed," the company could destroy the surface to extract whatever was below, without getting permission or paying compensation. When workers moved in to start the operation, though, residents organized, establishing a chapter of the Appalachian Group to Save the Land and People (AGSLP). "We mean to stop them, one way or another," retired deep miner Bill Fields explained. "We'll use all the good means first. Then we'll use the bad ones." When reporters asked him if by "the bad ones" he meant violence, he elaborated: "If they try to run that bulldozer in here another foot, there'll be blood spilled on the mountain."[1] In the end there was no violence, but the company wasn't turned back until Ray's neighbors twice braved rolling boulders and stood in the way of bulldozers, making it clear they would not stop until they won. Then, seeing an opportunity to enhance his populist reputation, Governor Edward Breathitt finally intervened. He had Kentucky's Division of Reclamation cancel Island Creek's permit, on the grounds that adjacent property would be irremediably affected, something the agency never did in other cases.[2]

Strip coal operators in Pike County retaliated by utilizing their influence with police, judges, and various elected officials to (wrongly but tellingly) pin blame for the resistance on individuals affiliated with the federally funded Appalachian Volunteers (AVs) and the independently run Southern Conference Education Fund (SCEF). Like whites throughout the South who could not accept the possibility that poor African Americans could organize themselves to end segregation, the mountain region's elite did not believe that supposedly hillbillies would or could resist strip mining on their own. Following the confrontation on Ray's land, Commonwealth Attorney Thomas Ratliff (a past president of the Independent Coal Operators Association), along with several armed deputies, made nighttime raids on three antipoverty activists and charged them with sedition, specifically with attempting to overthrow the county government.[3] "From what I have seen of the evidence in this case," Ratliff said, "it is possible that Communist sympathizers may have infiltrated the antipoverty program not only in Pike County, but in other sections of the country as well." The objective of the radicals, he claimed, was "to stir up dissension and create turmoil among our poor."[4]

Of course, the fight against surface coal mining was not the only one to evidence a link between consolidated political power, economic inequality, and environmental ruin. Each of those elements was common in countless battles waged by ordinary Americans against social injustice over the course of the past 200 years, sometimes with and at other times despite the leadership and resources of organized labor. Yet opposition to stripping and similar struggles are largely absent from the traditional narrative about the origins and development of environmentalism. Even the prevailing history of the environmental justice movement—an alternative to the mainstream, reform-minded activism of most modern environmental groups and many labor unions—generally fails in this respect.

Scholarly and popular chronicles typically point to two events as marking the beginning of environmental justice activism. One was a drawn-out, heated controversy over buried chemicals at Love Canal, near Buffalo, New York, in the late 1970s. The other was a campaign to stop the construction of a landfill that would receive PCB-laden waste in Warren County, North Carolina, during the early 1980s. In both places, local residents organized themselves at the grass roots to deal with toxic waste, embraced a critical view of regulatory policy and political leaders, made community empowerment a central part of their fight, and often employed direct action, including nonviolent civil disobedience. The Warren County campaign also led to the "discovery" of "environmental racism," defined and statistically exposed in "Toxic Wastes and Race," a report published in 1987 by the United Church of Christ Commission for Racial Justice.

To be sure, two recent books have shown the way for more compelling revisionist interpretations of the decisive struggles by acknowledging the complex entanglement of class and race. In *Love Canal Revisited*, Elizabeth Blum expands the traditional scope of analysis beyond involvement of white working-class homemakers like Lois Gibbs. Many white working-class men, for example, were employed at nearby chemical plants and belonged to OCAW, UAW, and United Steelworkers (USW) locals with a solid record of concern for workplace dangers and industrial pollution. In 1979, as the reality of the toxic mess was becoming more apparent, these unions formed the West New York Council on Occupational Safety and Health and held a regional conference attended by more than 300 workers. They also donated thousands of dollars, office space, and members' time to the Love Canal Homeowners Association (LCHA). When frustrations mounted over the lack of an adequate response from state and federal officials, union men were among the main advocates of direct action, challenging voices of moderation among supporters in the middle-class Ecumenical Task Force (ETF). Just as important, it was Hooker Chemical employee Michael Bayliss who leaked a damning report to the press detailing the company's long history of dangerous chemical releases, knowledge of harmful effects, and attempts to withhold information about the accidents from the general public and plant workers.[5]

Blum draws attention to the role played by low-income black women as well, explaining how their concerns and activism diverged from whites' understanding of the situation and what to do about it. The women and their families made up a majority of the residents at Griffon Manor, a federal housing project across the street from Love Canal, and initially they were excluded by definition from the "homeowners'" association started by Gibbs. The guiding assumption seemed to be that renters could simply pick up and move, but in reality they also needed government aid to relocate. Even after the LCHA bylaws were changed to allow renter membership and the organization's goals were amended to incorporate aid for all those who needed to relocate, Griffon Manor residents still felt left out. Other welfare housing in the Buffalo area was already filled to capacity, and what was available could not accommodate large extended families. In response, the black women turned to the local branch of the National Association for the Advancement of Colored People (NAACP) and the ETF. With their help, they formed their own group, the Love Canal Renters Association, with a slightly different agenda.[6]

In a similar fashion, Eileen McGurty's *Transforming Environmentalism* shows the way for a reinterpretation of what happened in Warren County. While the case has been presented as "blacks fighting against the landfill in order to stop the racist siting," she points out, "the landfill controversy was much more complicated." Many of the county's black and white residents were poor, and there was a widespread notion that as poor rural dwellers distant from the center of power, they were fighting an uphill battle to keep toxic waste out of their community. It was only after the "standard approaches to challenging government decisions were exhausted" that folks moved into "contentious politics" and joined forces with civil rights leaders, who placed more emphasis on the issue of environmental racism. Even then, the underlying factor of social class kept whites committed to an interracial alliance. One elderly white woman who lived her whole life in Warren County participated in the protests, despite deep misgivings about doing anything that would empower blacks, "because they were putting [the landfill] in the poorest county and people were suffering enough." Yet the shifting rationale for resistance was just the beginning of a long-running and still unsettled dispute within the environmental justice movement, whether racial inequality or class inequity is more significant in determining exposure to environmental hazards.[7]

In fact, the debate within the movement about race and class is partly the product of historical amnesia, calling not only for better analysis of the familiar but also incorporation of events, people, and organizations that have not always been considered part of the standard narrative. Years before Love Canal and Warren County some labor unions actually incorporated a broad understanding of workers' complex economic and environmental concerns as well as clarity about unequal distribution of power in their confrontational strategies, tactics, and goals. In other instances, dissident rank and file demonstrated a sophisticated consciousness and tactical militancy, despite recalcitrant and corrupt union leadership, by joining local environmental struggles that exposed social inequities and emphasized community-based direct action. Whether labor-led or not, the cohesion and solidarity typical of these efforts tended to come at least partly from recognition of the ways in which economic exploitation and environmental degradation were inextricably linked to ethnic prejudice or racism. Basically, then, workers played the role of environmental justice pioneers.

Open Air Factories

Writing to the Environmental Defense Fund (EDF) in 1973, United Farm Workers (UFW) staff member Chris Meyers tried hard to check his frustration with the mainstream environmental movement. Although the union had been organizing Mexican and Mexican American migrant field hands in southern California for nearly a decade, making protection from exposure to pesticides central to their demands, recently established organizations like the EDF and older groups like the Sierra Club did not seem fully invested in supporting the workers' cause. "While there is much concern for those who will suffer the long term effects of indirect contact with pesticides on the consumer level," Meyers noted, "farm workers are dying every day from direct exposure in the fields." Rachel Carson had completely ignored field and orchard hands in her book *Silent Spring*, and environmental activists were perpetuating that oversight. One of the fixes for protecting consumers, switching from chlorinated hydrocarbons (which often left a chemical residue) to less persistent but acutely poisonous organophosphates, actually put workers at greater risk. To Meyers, however, that kind of approach was misguided and narrow-minded. "Surely," he complained at the end of his letter, "the fight for a balanced environment and the fight for social justice and dignity are not unrelated struggles."[8]

The UFW's efforts had begun several years earlier, in the mid-1960s, following on the heels of failed organizing campaigns by the National Farm Labor Union (NFLU) and the Agricultural Workers' Organizing Committee (AWOC). Despite those discouraging precedents, experienced (and radical) community organizer César Chávez felt there were good reasons to try once more and, perhaps, to expect at least some success. On the one hand, land-holding consolidation and crop specialization were concentrating workers in ever fewer places and making them easier to reach, while the demise of federal programs to bring temporary workers to orchards and fields stripped growers of one tool to overstock the labor pool and break strikes. On the other hand, there was an increasing proportion of Mexicans and Mexican Americans in the labor force, especially among less transient and moderately skilled orchard hands in the San Joaquin Valley, establishing the potential for a cohesive social movement that drew strength from cultural unity and a budding Chicano consciousness.[9]

Already by the early twentieth century the orchards and ranches of southern California were "factories in the field," as journalist Carey McWilliams famously put it in the 1930s, or "open air factories," as an anonymous auto worker later tagged them.[10] The operations, thousands of acres large, specialized in fruit, nut, and vegetable monocultures worked by migrants for low wages and involved the use of all manner of modern pesticides, herbicides, and synthetic fertilizers. "The crops produced were first and foremost commodities," I note in *Making a Living*, "little different from a car or steel rail, fashioned by alienated labor, and the land that grew them was an alien thing as well, doused with poisonous chemicals as if it were an inert adversary." Despite their frequent use of "free market" rhetoric, growers also relied heavily on state and federal governments, particularly for constructing and maintaining massive irrigation projects (essential for turning the desert into an Eden) as well as for securing and disciplining labor.[11]

Until the early 1940s, field and orchard hands were an ethnically mixed lot. Independence from the United States ended labor migration from the Philippines in 1934, however, and World War II siphoned off "Okies" and "Arkies" and other Anglos, first to work in manufacturing and then to join the military. In response, the federal government established the bracero program, which authorized the admission of a large number of Mexican migrant workers, supposedly on a temporary basis. After the wartime emergency had passed, the program was made permanent, providing a steady supply of cheap, vulnerable labor that helped growers drive down wages and undermine organizing efforts. Under pressure from the AFL-CIO, the liberal Kennedy administration began limiting the use of braceros, and in 1964, during Lyndon Johnson's presidency, Congress abolished the program entirely. In response, growers simply expanded their use of undocumented immigrants, who soon made up more than two-thirds of the region's agricultural labor force.[12]

Across the border, population growth and shrinking amounts of available village land pushed Mexican peasants to make repeated journeys north, allowing old and new households to survive with at least some degree of their independence and traditional way of life intact. "While the migrants are gone," social scientists Lucia Kaiser and Kathryn Dewey explain, "the women, children, and older people maintain the subsistence plots," small private holdings that had been carved out of dismantled *haciendas* after the 1910 Revolution. In fact, the *less* a particular community's farming was affected by modernization, the *more* likely it was that men and some women in that place were to seek out intermittent wage work in nearby towns or cities or to participate in seasonal migration to the United States. This suggests that recurrent mobility was, paradoxically, a form of resistance to larger economic forces.[13]

In southern California, however, working conditions were poor and getting worse. Federal and state laws setting wages and hours, providing unemployment insurance, and guaranteeing the right to organize excluded agricultural laborers, whether they were U.S. citizens, permanent residents, or undocumented migrants. Consequently, field and orchard hands might toil 60 hours a week or more for less than half the average factory wage and with high rents for shoddy camp housing deducted directly from paychecks. In addition, they received no government assistance when seasonal work ran out. Employment was contingent on obeying certain rules as well, some vague enough to be used in an arbitrary fashion, including an injunction against "refusal to carry out instructions" and a prohibition against "obscene or profane language."[14]

Another factor that contributed to objectionable working conditions was widespread and intense use of pesticides and herbicides. Specialized monoculture production created a perfect breeding ground for crop pests, prompting growers to adopt an arsenal of toxic weapons, but they killed off the natural enemies of increasingly resilient harmful insects, allowing their numbers to increase. Following the advice of agricultural extension agents, university scientists, and the chemical industry, growers doused fields and trees with still more chemical compounds. These were readily available after World War II, which had spurred considerable research to develop chemical and biological weapons that turned out to have parallel peacetime use as well. By the early 1960s, historian Linda Nash explains, "more than 16,000 pesticides had been registered in California, and farmers had become increasingly reliant upon applications of multiple chemicals."[15]

The impact pesticides and herbicides had on workers' well-being was already becoming clear by the early 1950s, when the California Department of Public Health (CDPH) began to investigate in the wake of an incident among pear workers using parathion. Despite chronic underreporting, it turned out, agriculture had a higher rate of occupational disease than any other sector of the state's economy. The greatest number of reported cases also happened to be in counties with the largest number of Mexican and Mexican American migrants, particularly Los Angeles, Fresno, Kern, and Tulare. And a large number of those incidents were associated with fruit and nut cultivation, which was mostly not mechanized and involved frequent encounters with treated foliage.[16] As CDPH investigators quickly realized, however, determining the exact cause of illness or death was very difficult, since fields and orchards were unlike controlled laboratory settings. A whole host of variables played into the disease etiology of chemical poisoning, including temperature and precipitation, soil and crop type, clothing worn or not worn, and frequency and recurrence of exposure.

In any case, morbidity and mortality seemed to be getting worse. This was especially true after growers responded to public concern about consumer health risks from pesticide residue by switching to organophosphate compounds that lingered less but were highly toxic during application and were rapidly absorbed through the skin. Year after year there were high-profile incidents where dozens of migrants were seriously poisoned and sometimes killed after coming into contact with these chemicals. Others were affected one or two or three at a time, sometimes seeking medical care but just as likely keeping their complaints to themselves and working in discomfort and pain.[17] Hilaro Garcia Jr. and some of his coworkers, for example, experienced extreme nausea and dizziness after they smelled a strange odor in the orange grove where they labored, prompting the foreman to send at least two men to the hospital for a couple of weeks. Joe Alejandro, however, regularly experienced skin blisters and irritated eyes from wet and dry sulfur compounds he sprayed on grapes yet never received any treatment. When the California Department of Public Health did a survey, 71 percent of 774 farmworkers questioned had some indication of illness, from stomach pains and headaches to chills and itching due to chemical exposure.[18]

Not surprisingly, field hands who came to the United States from Mexico were often in poorer health when they returned to their own subsistence farms, and they rightly attributed this to the pesticides they were required to use by growers. "These workers located disease not within their own bodies as germs or viruses," historian Linda Nash explains, "but in a landscape they found foreign and physically threatening and one over which they had little or no control." Workers even began to associate certain illnesses with specific crops. "My daughter gets swollen hands and feet, and welts, when picking tomatoes," Nash quotes one migrant laborer saying, and "my husband gets very sick at the stomach when picking the lemons and Valencia oranges." It was in this context, with the use of agricultural chemicals very much on people's minds, that a struggle for union representation at least temporarily thrived, and the contours of a new, alternative environmentalism were decisively formed.[19]

The renewed effort to organize migrant laborers was led by César Chávez and Dolores Huerta, Mexican Americans schooled in community organizing while on staff at the Community Service Organization (CSO), a grassroots initiative dedicated to Chicano civil rights. In 1962, Chávez moved to the fertile San Joaquin Valley, where Huerta had grown up and helped found the CSO's Stockton County chapter years before. Together, they cultivated local leadership and built the National Farm Workers' Association (NFWA). When the mostly Filipino AWOC declared a strike against table-grape growers in the fall of 1965, Chávez called a meeting of NFWA members and supporters at Our Lady of Guadalupe Church, in Delano, on Mexican Independence Day, to decide what to do. They quickly agreed to join the strike and the two organizations later merged to form the United Farm Workers Organizing Committee (UFWOC).

As the battle gathered momentum, several other unions came to the farmworkers' aid, rhetorically and financially. When Chávez led a march from Delano to Sacramento, UAW President Walter Reuther was by his side, having found a match for his own views on fighting racial inequality and improving the lot of workers. Just as important, he brought a check for $10,000 and promised $5,000 more every month. The International Longshoremen's and Warehousemen's Union also rose to the occasion, when dockworkers refused to handle struck Delano grapes. By leaving them to rot in port they declared the importance of labor solidarity. Later, the UAW bankrolled a documentary film, *Brothers and Sisters*, about "the timeless issue of poor people fighting [for] a decent way of life," and farmworker organizers used it to tour the country. "Strong unions have a responsibility to help the small struggling unions," Reuther contended, "to obtain recognition and win decent wages and working conditions."[20]

Midway through the strike, the UFWOC decided to focus heavily on pesticides, recognizing the serious threat they posed to orchard hands and realizing the issue's potential for broadening the campaign's appeal among consumers. Coordinated by volunteer nurse Marion Moses, the union established a health and safety commission to investigate workers' exposure, while California Rural Legal Assistance lawyer Ralph Abascal examined application records, lab analyses, and lawsuits. Once their knowledge reached a critical mass, "the union initiated an international boycott of table grapes, establishing boycott committees in major cities across the country and calling on labor, community, as well as environmental leaders to lend their personal support and organizational resources."[21]

Making the link between worker and consumer protection, however, was not always easy. When an otherwise radical environmental group from Berkeley decided to organize an "Ecology Walk" against "agri-chemical powers," for example, the officialdom attempted "to maintain a safe neutrality" regarding the strike, "so they could reach all the people they wanted to reach." But during the march, common participants, many of whom had worked on the grape boycott, decided to stay in Delano for Sunday mass, and a few addressed the workers present to let them know their feelings about supporting the strike. In response to one group member's account of their defiance, UFWOC staff argued that "the farm workers' struggle is a valid and important part of Ecology (not merely regarding the pesticides, but also in the important matter of preserving and respecting all our natural resources—including HUMAN)."[22]

The problem, it seemed, was that many middle-class environmental leaders were not entirely convinced that defending the natural world and human health demanded engagement with campaigns for social justice. In the minds of UFWOC leaders like Chávez, Huerta, and others, though, growers' intensive, reckless use of agricultural chemicals was inextricably linked to the balance of power between classes and the subordination of Mexicans and Mexican Americans as an ethnic group. To protect workers and consumers, as well as the land and other species, people had to reckon with economic exploitation and racism. "Motivated by profit," declared one UFWOC pamphlet, "[growers] continue to subject our people to systematic poisoning." The best means to change this situation was to build a vibrant, militant labor organization that could negotiate agreements with employers. "Only with Union contracts," the pamphlet concluded, "can our welfare be assured."[23]

Meanwhile, growers refused to give up their exclusive control over pesticide application. Much like employers in the oil industry who resisted ceding any ground to worker demands for changing production methods to insure health and safety, the lords of industrial agricultural were not about to give up their dominion over how fruits, nuts, and other crops were grown, even if that led to improved working conditions. Then, in August 1969, Senator Walter Mondale coordinated a series of congressional hearings titled Migrant and Seasonal Farmworker Powerlessness, with three full days devoted to pesticides. The UFWOC played the opportunity effectively, as Laura Pulido explains, with spokespeople "describing in detail how many chemicals were used in California, the extent of pesticide poisoning, what happened to injured workers, the degree to which the growers controlled the courts, the union's proposed solutions, and growers' refusal to negotiate."[24]

Following the hearings, in September, the union had its first breakthrough, signing a contract with Perrelli-Minetti and Sons that established a new baseline for protecting agricultural workers' health and safety. The contract included provisions establishing a joint health and safety committee, prohibiting the use of the pesticides DDT, aldrin, dieldrin, and endrin, restricting the use of other chlorinated hydrocarbons, and requiring a cholinesterase test whenever workers used other organophosphates. The UFWOC then signed an even more far-reaching contract with the Wonder Palms Ranch, and by the end of the next year, most table-grape growers, nearly 150 in all, had signed on to it as well. Like the Perrelli-Minetti contract, this version provided a modest wage increase, secured seniority rights, and set up a grievance process, but it also improved on the earlier health and safety clause. Now the union had the right to determine every member of health and safety committees, which effectively gave workers unrestricted power to make decisions about reentry after spraying as well as to refuse dangerous work.[25]

By pursuing a strategy that emphasized community mobilization and national outreach, as well as direct negotiations with employers, the UFWOC achieved gains that went well beyond the minimal pesticide oversight required under any regulatory law. Yet not coincidentally, in June 1971 the California Department of Agriculture developed standard reentry time intervals of its own. These rules regulated union and nonunion workers' return to orchards and vineyards sprayed with any one of a number of toxic chemicals. The agency also oversaw the phaseout of chlorinated hydrocarbons DDT and DDD, canceling most remaining uses.[26] As César Chávez had understood from the beginning, it was social unrest and the threat of contagious upheaval that moved an otherwise reluctant state to act.

It wasn't long, however, before the United Farm Workers (UFW), known by that shortened name after 1972, began losing ground. After their success in southern California vineyards, the union turned its focus on lettuce producers in the Salinas and Maria valleys. Anticipating the move, some of these growers signed sweetheart contracts with the International Brotherhood of Teamsters (IBT), which did little if anything to lift wages or improve working conditions. Just as the UFW grape contracts were set to expire, Teamster president Frank Fitzsimmons declared the IBT's intent to take those as well, an effort aided by union thugs, sympathetic local judges, and agricultural workers' continued exclusion from state and federal labor law governing union organizing.[27]

Besides their serious limitations when it came to boosting wages, IBT contracts fell far short in regulating pesticide application. The Coachella Valley Grape agreement, for example, which simply required the employer to follow existing state and federal law, skirted the need for an empowered health and safety committee. In practice, of course, new state regulatory rules were generally meaningless, since enforcement was shamefully inadequate. At the same time, efforts to pass federal pesticide legislation were undermined by compromise. Amendments required the Environmental Protection Agency to use cost-benefit analysis when imposing restrictions and to indemnify chemical companies, retailers, and farmers against losses they might incur under future restrictions, both of which requirements were economic disincentives to carrying out regulatory duties.[28] As a result, during the first half of the 1970s California's pesticide use and reports of occupational disease attributed to agricultural chemical exposure went up substantially, although the amount of harvested acreage changed little.[29]

Watching UFW power erode in the face of Teamster collusion with growers while the number of poisoned workers worsened, César Chávez sought help beyond the circles of organized labor, notably from mainstream environmental groups. Following the Earth Day celebration in 1973, he instructed Ramon Romero to write Environmental Action (the Earth Day coordinator) and request a list of like-minded organizations that were then supporting the Oil, Chemical, and Atomic Workers in their battle with Shell Oil. With that list, Chávez began writing letters to various leaders to make the farmworkers' case, mostly with disappointing results. "The unity which the union movement can have with the environmentalists is crucial to our survival," he explained to the Sierra Club's Brock Evans, "both in a spirit of justice and in the literal sense." The UFW's record of using contracts to restrict the use of pesticides, he also noted, was a basis on which unity could flourish. Evans replied with great sympathy for the farmworkers' cause and claimed that sentiment was shared by others in the Sierra Club, but the rhetorical support never translated into actual organizational assistance.[30]

The UFW also sought to equalize its contest with growers by getting legislation to protect agricultural laborers' right to organize. They achieved this goal in 1975, when the state of California passed the Agricultural Labor Relations Act. This law helped the union win a series of run-off elections with the Teamsters, enough to recover from a few of its earlier losses and convince the IBT to call off its own farmworker organizing. But California's Agricultural Labor Relations Board was overwhelmed with demands for its help and even shut down for a brief period for lack of operational funds. Then, in 1982, the state's Republican governor stacked the board with pro-grower members and cut its funding by a third, with the intended and expected results. By the middle of the decade, with only 10 percent of farmworkers counted as union members, most agricultural laborers were left without the protections from pesticides once provided by UFW contracts.[31]

Still, among the elements of organized labor that showed concern for environmental issues the United Farm Workers left an important legacy. The union's grapes and lettuce campaigns made explicit connections between class exploitation, racial discrimination, and environmental harm. Likewise, they put community organizing, sustained with militant rhetoric and confrontational tactics designed to alter the prevailing balance of power, front and center. In various environmental battles throughout the country during the next two decades, most of them waged by common people at the local level, these elements were quite evident.[32]

There Will Be a War

Much like their Mexican and Mexican American counterparts in southern California, many residents of southern Appalachia knew well how ethnic stereotypes and lack of power facilitated economic inequality. White mountaineers, in particular, had been branded for decades as backward hillbillies—inbred, inclined to feuding, and overly fond of moonshine—and that was no accident. From the mid-nineteenth century on, a host of observers had found cause for the region's poverty in both its people's values (or lack of values) and the supposed absence of "modernization," the industrial and urban transformation seen elsewhere in the United States. What was needed, these observers maintained, was cultural uplift and wage labor, changes that could only be imposed from the outside. In practice, this meant sending children off to public schools and private settlements that made every effort to shame them out of their mountain notions and habits and forcing independent semisubsistence farmers from their land to put them to work cutting timber and mining coal.

With the advance of extractive industry in Appalachia, mountaineers also acquired firsthand experience with the way unbridled capitalism engendered the ruin of natural landscapes. The first stage of development was bad enough in this respect, as logging and underground mining left clear-cuts, acid-laden streams, and other signs of "progress" in their wake. After World War II, however, the situation grew worse, as more and more coal operators began to employ surface mining methods. This manner of extracting coal required far fewer workers, significantly reducing labor costs and exacerbating Appalachia's chronic unemployment, and it caused serious environmental damage, from massive landslides to unprecedented flooding. That damage went mostly unchecked, since meaningful regulatory legislation was slow in coming, and even when there were laws on the books regulatory agencies were typically "captured" by the coal industry and hardly accountable to the public.

Local people affected by strip-mining, tried to do something, but unlike California migrant workers they initially had little reason to view organized labor as an ally. In the early 1960s, the United Mine Workers of America (UMW) was hopelessly corrupt and inept at representing its membership's interests. Tony Boyle ruled the union with an iron hand, forced locals to accept sweetheart contracts, and allied with mine operators on many issues, including opposition to even moderate environmental controls. At the UMW's constitutional convention in 1968, for example, union officers noted their agreement with the alarm expressed by coal trade groups over legislation recently introduced in Congress. "If permitted to stand, many of the pollution regulations and the theories underlying them would cause a severe disruption of the coal industry and widespread unemployment for the coal miners."[33]

Eventually, Boyle's authoritarian and inept leadership, as well as his involvement in murdering a candidate who challenged him for president, brought about his downfall. At the funeral for the assassinated opponent, Jock Yablonski, dissident UMW members organized Miners for Democracy (MFD), which successfully ran a reform slate in the 1972 elections. In the years following, the MFD's Arnold Miller, his officers, and dedicated local leaders opened the union to member participation and took a much stronger position in negotiating contracts with coal operators. At least during the next half decade, they also parted ways with industry trade groups in their opposition to environmental regulation. When the executive board was faced with endorsing a bill to establish the first federal controls on surface coal mining, Miller cast the favorable tie-breaking vote, demonstrating the union's new approach on a particularly controversial matter.

Years before his murder and the subsequent founding of MFD, Jock Yablonski had been president of the union's District 5, which covered much of the western Pennsylvania bituminous coalfields, where strip mining was steadily advancing on deep mining and causing widespread public concern. Although the state had passed one of the nation's first regulatory laws in 1945, that legislation proved generally inadequate, and sentiment developed for enacting stronger controls. Leading the way in this effort were the Pittsburgh-based Allegheny County Sportsmen's League (ACSL), a branch of the Pennsylvania Federation of Sportsmen's Clubs (PFSC), and the Allegheny County Labor Committee (ACLC), which included the USW, the International Brotherhood of Electrical Workers (IBEW), and the UMW. Actually, it's likely that there was some crossover between the organized sportsmen and organized labor, similar to the trend in Michigan. The working-class hunters and anglers were in a position to understand the link between strip operators' greed and their lack of concern for the environment, and they had resources at hand to mobilize and voice their concerns.

Supporters first introduced a stronger surface-mining control bill in the Pennsylvania assembly in June 1961, quickly winning passage but only over fierce objections meant to drive a wedge between workers and conservationists. "I don't see why we should give up a growing industry," argued Paige Varner, a Republican from Clarion, "for a few fish or a few trees." This was the same sort of argument used by opposition in the senate, guided by Democrat John Haluska, who represented a part of central Pennsylvania with numerous active strip mines and who happened to be the insurance agent and close friend of C.E. Powell, one of the state's largest strip mine operators. When House Bill 1438 and its anthracite companion came to the Local Government Committee, which Haluska led, he pledged "to go slow on this because it would hurt industry and make people lose their jobs."[34]

Despite the divisive rhetoric and calculated counter-charge, however, workers remained committed to improved controls. In the face of intransigence, the executive board of Westinghouse Local 601, a United Electrical Workers affiliate, unanimously passed a resolution calling on the senate to follow the assembly in quickly passing the regulatory bills. "The work of a greedy, small group of strip miners is designed to make Pennsylvania a desert wasteland," it read, and "obstruction to good legislation to control strip mining must be stopped." Once hearings began, the ACLC also announced its full support for the proposed laws. "We are unequivocally opposed," the organization declared, "to the selfish interests and to the legislators they appear to control who resist effective regulation of strip mining, [which] despoils our natural resources and endangers the health and lives of our citizens."[35]

Yet words were not the only weapons used in the battle. One night in July, someone or some group of people, probably deep miners with experience using explosives, dynamited a power shovel and bulldozer at a Fayette County strip site, causing $175,000 in damage. And when Senator Haluska continued to stall, he received a death threat from a like-minded ally. "I hate cheats and crooked politicians," a vigilante wrote. "Unless you act on the strip-mining bill within two weeks, by August 8, 1961, you might die rather suddenly." This was not a prank or a joke, the note assured, and the writer signed himself "an honest sportsman who is a good shot with a gun." The senator did take the threat seriously, in fact, and made the deadline by sending out watered-down versions of the bills with just two days to spare.[36]

Once the control bills were on the senate floor, the governor met with the parties involved and negotiated bills that were modest improvements on the ones Haluska's committee approved. Eight key members of the assembly continued to balk, though, seeking something more like the stronger original proposals. It was at this point, I explain in *To Save the Land and People*, that the UMW's Jock Yablonski and other union officials directly intervened. They brought the holdouts into the fold by convincing the governor to add strengthening provisions to his compromise package, which was later passed and signed into law. The union leaders' motivation to act as brokers at that moment was twofold: to achieve some kind of legislation that maintained habitats for wild game and protected fishing streams and to defend their members' economic interests (95 percent were underground miners) by equalizing the competitive advantages strip operators had over deep-mine operations.[37]

Not everyone was happy with the deal, however, particularly the Pennsylvania Federation of Sportsmen's Clubs, which declared its refusal to accept half a loaf. Yablonski claimed that the UMW had hoped for stricter regulations and vowed to bring his union back to the assembly for another round but he never did, and it was left to the PFSC to wage the battle alone. By the time they managed to get another bill passed, in 1963, the mine workers' union was seemingly irredeemably corrupt and, at least at the national level, hardly a leading advocate for labor environmentalism.[38] The only good reason Tony Boyle and other UMW leaders could see for passing control legislation was to quiet public clamor, the social upheaval spreading across the coalfields as state regulatory laws miserably failed, encouraging opponents to adopt radical tactics and provoking demands for complete abolition.

The heart of the growing militancy was eastern Kentucky, in part because state courts there had ruled that broad form deeds, which separated surface and mineral rights, allowed operators to destroy people's homes, farms, woodlots, and orchards in the process of extracting coal and to do so without getting permission to mine or paying compensation for damages. Floyd County deep miner Lewis Burke, among others, detested stripping not only for the job loss it caused but also for the real threat it posed to his own property, since Island Creek Coal Company owned the mineral rights and it could come in any time. That prospect had him ready to fight. "[I]f they come here to strip mine," he declared, "there will be a war, and I mean a war, because I have no intentions of getting off *my* land."[39]

When coal operator Bill Sturgill attempted to strip some property in Knott County, in 1965, he finally lit the fuse. The land was owned by Dan Gibson's stepson, who had been sent to Vietnam, and Gibson—perched on the top of a ridge with a shotgun in hand, daring the bulldozers to cross—made a stand. State police took him to jail, but he was quickly released and Sturgill agreed not to mine the property. Several weeks later, in June, local residents met in Hindman, the country seat, and formed the Appalachian Group to Save the Land and People (AGSLP), to ready themselves for more confrontations and, ultimately, to abolish surface coal mining altogether. Their rhetoric placed Gibson's action and their own radicalism squarely within a long American tradition of justified protest, dating back at least as far as the Declaration of Independence. "We feel we have been forsaken," they explained, "that we have no rights when a county sheriff can order a man off his own property and tell him he is trespassing; that he will be jailed if he doesn't readily comply."[40]

Although at times they used lawful, peaceful tactics—petitions, letters to newspapers, meetings and strip-mine tours—AGSLP members were inclined to employ a mix of violence, threatened violence, and nonviolent civil disobedience as well. When the Caperton Coal Company brought bulldozers onto Ollie Combs's homestead in the fall, for instance, a group of armed men ran them off. When they returned, Combs sat down in front of the bulldozers with two of her sons by her side, at which point they were carried away by police and jailed. After a picture of Combs eating Thanksgiving dinner behind bars made the *Courier Journal*, the state's main newspaper, Governor Breathitt declared his support for her, noting that "history has sometimes shown that unyielding insistence upon the enforcement of legal rights by the rich and powerful against the humble people of a community is not always the quickest course of action." He then instructed the public safety commissioner that state police were not to be used for the enforcement of civil processes in the courts without permission from the governor and he revoked Caperton's permit to mine the Combs's land.[41]

Deep miners played an even more important role in the struggle through industrial sabotage, or they were most probably among those involved in a series of explosions at strip sites. One of the first times this happened was in April 1967, when a diesel-powered shovel belonging to Kentucky River Coal was dynamited in Knott County. In June, another diesel shovel was blown up at a Kentucky Oak operation nearby. That same month strip-mining opponents exchanged gunfire with workers and dynamited a grader at the Tarr Heel Coal Company mine on Lost Creek, in Perry County. "They ran my men off," said Harold Sigmon, the head of the company, but "there was some shooting on both sides after that." Perhaps feeling provoked, in early August saboteurs used carbon nitrate to destroy a $90,000 auger, a D-9 bulldozer valued at $84,000, two trucks, two drills, and a welder at the same site.[42]

Of course, direct action could be effective to stop strip-mining in particular places but AGSLP activists knew that the only real solution to their problems was a legislative ban. Toward that end, they continued to pressure political leaders, holding up the possibility of continued ferment in the coalfields as the alternative to government redress. At a symposium on reclamation in Owensboro, Kentucky, just before the effort to protect Jink Ray's land, more than 200 people protested outside, finally securing a spot on the day's agenda. To explain their case, they distributed a written statement as well. "We must point out to you that a bulldozer moves much faster than courts and legislatures," it read, "so, while we wait for action by the state, we are prepared to protect our land by whatever means are necessary."[43]

The closest any Appalachian strip-mining opponents came to banning surface-extraction methods at the state level, however, was in West Virginia. That campaign had the advantage of tapping into organized insurgent sentiment among coal miners who were frustrated with their union's resistance to supporting strong legislation on black lung (coal miners' pneumoconiosis). To push the issue, UMW rank and file established the Black Lung Association (BLA) and called a statewide wildcat (unsanctioned) strike. This finally forced Congress to pass the 1969 Coal Mine Health and Safety Act, the model for the Occupational Safety and Health Act passed the next year and something like a culmination in the decades-long effort by reformers and scientists associated with industrial hygiene. Following these victories, BLA president and Boone County deep miner Arnold Miller took the lead in voicing dissident mine workers' support for banning surface mining, framing it as a threat to jobs and the environment.

When West Virginia's main opposition group Citizens to Abolish Strip Mining (CASM) held an informational meeting during the early part of 1971, the highlight of the evening was a panel discussion that included Arnold Miller and Ivan White, another Boone County coal miner and black lung activist as well as a House of Delegates member. They called on everyone present, many of them mine workers, to join a demonstration at the capitol to demand legislation prohibiting stripping.[44] The large gatherings and spirited marches were ultimately no match, though, for the coal industry's political power. Legislators seriously considered an abolition bill and then passed a measure permitting stripping where the heaviest mining was already taking place, allowing it on a limited basis and with no new permits for one year in others, and banning it for one year in areas where there were no current surface operations.

With the failure to outlaw surface coal mining in West Virginia, opponents throughout the coalfields turned more of their attention to the federal level.

West Virginia Congressman Ken Hechler, who had introduced the Coal Mine Health and Safety Act, first put forward a bill to ban stripping in 1970. After he reintroduced it in 1971, activists helped him secure additional cosponsors. One part of that work was an April briefing, in Washington, DC, centered on a panel that included Arnold Miller, Ivan White, and retired coal miner Clarence Pauley.[45] At the same time, UMW leaders acted in lockstep with the coal industry, characterizing the bill as "sheer nonsense," "so much political grandstanding," "a preservationist pipe-dream," and a threat to "badly needed jobs and electric power."[46]

Once Miller and other Miners for Democracy supporters began to campaign for a change in the union's leadership, however, they backed away from advocating an outright ban and promoted strong, well-enforced federal regulations instead. This was a pragmatic calculation, bowing to the influence exerted by a growing number of surface miners within the UMW, and it probably made the difference between victory and defeat in the very close 1972 elections. In the long run, it was a huge mistake, giving up on the one option that could effectively protect the Appalachian landscape and peoples' homesteads and, just as importantly, throwing aside the last chance to prevent the union's slow demise through technological unemployment. Without the mine workers acting in concert with environmentalists members of the House and Senate were no longer under the same pressure to appease mountain radicals, and so they also backed off.[47]

Yet organized labor was not entirely responsible for the battle's disappointing denouement. Mainstream environmental organizations were as much or more at fault for undermining the gathering momentum in support of a strip-mining ban. Although various environmental groups came to the aid of OCAW during the Shell strike and reached out to build an environmental-labor alliance in other cases, their response to farmworkers and mine workers was certainly wanting. In the case of coal miners and other ordinary mountain coalfield residents, in fact, the problem was not simple disinterest or neglect but actual betrayal. Through the first half of the 1970s, the Sierra Club's Peter Borelli and the Environmental Policy Center's Louise Dunlap, in particular, actively colluded (at first secretly and later openly) to use the threat of abolition as a foil to win a regulatory law. This was despite the fact that they claimed to represent common people at the grassroots, most of whom still remained steadfast in support for outlawing stripping.[48]

By mid-decade, the movement's imminent collapse was evident, suffusing the frustration Representative Ken Hechler expressed in a letter to activists. "My people in West Virginia and people throughout the nation," he wrote, "are getting more and more cynical about compromising politicians, Washington environmental groups who settle for the lowest common denominator, and those who enjoy the transient glory of winning a few commas or semi-colons while the people and the land continue to be exploited and destroyed." The Sierra Club and Environmental Policy Center leadership had repeatedly succumbed "to the temptation to move farther and farther away from abolition, to compromise and weaken their position long before it was strategically necessary, and to enable the coal exploiters to move the whole focus of the debate progressively and inexorably over toward greater freedom to exploit." In his statement, however, Hechler showed signs of wavering himself. While he encouraged support for his own recently introduced abolition bill, he implicitly acknowledged that this was now impossible and noted the importance of defining "the minimum standards you would accept in a regulatory bill."[49]

That April, the coal industry flexed its muscles as well, sponsoring a caravan of 600 to 700 independent coal haulers to Washington, DC, where they drove around town, set up pickets, and lobbied members of Congress and the White House staff. Their main goal was to stop *any* control law from being enacted, which they claimed would be the ruin of surface mining. "Protest H.R. 25—We Don't Need Another 25000 Unemployed," one banner read, and President Ford got the message, shortly after vetoing the regulatory bills Congress sent to him. Likewise, coal industry trade group spokesmen made it clear they no longer favored a federal law, which they had previously come around to support when they feared that opposing strong controls would lead to a ban. "All major coal producing states have their own functioning programs that regulate surface mining and require sound reclamation," American Mining Congress chair and Peabody Coal president Edwin Phelps argued. "The national debate that has raged over this issue," he insisted, "has outlived the need for Federal legislation."[50]

In the end, the result of all the compromise and the subsequent backlash was the Surface Mining Control and Reclamation Act (SMCRA), passed in 1977. Representatives from the Appalachian Coalition announced their opposition to the bill shortly before President Carter signed it into law, but folks like the EPC's Louise Dunlap were on hand for the Rose Garden ceremony, somewhat disappointed that the legislation wasn't stronger yet sure it represented a victory rather than a loss. Twenty years later, Dunlap acknowledged SMCRA's poor enforcement, for which she blamed the Interior Department and White House while insisting that the law itself was "fundamentally sound." Interestingly, in another venue, American Mining Congress representative Ben E. Lusk had called SMCRA's standards "demanding, inflexible, often counterproductive and always costly" but also described the law as fundamentally sound.[51]

Meanwhile, throughout the 1980s and 1990s, the United Mine Workers saw a steady decline in membership with the expansion of stripping by nonunion coal companies and energy conglomerates. West Virginia alone once had more than 100,000 union coal miners, yet by the end of the twentieth century there were only 19,000 miners in the state, and only half of those belonged to the UMW. Coal production soared to record levels, however, suggesting that it was improved efficiency achieved through new mining methods and technology rather than regulatory constraints causing the job loss. Still, the union leadership simplistically framed their predicament as a conspiracy engineered by environmentalists. At a 1999 rally to protest a judge's recent decision against Arch Coal for violating the Clean Water Act, which led the company to (unnecessarily) layoff thirty employees, UMW president Cecil Roberts declared that mine workers had been "kicked in the teeth again by the environmental community." Backed into a corner partly of the union's own making, Roberts and others refused to entertain a different vision, one that saw labor and environmental problems as inextricably linked in cause, effect, and solution.[52]

Conclusion: Rethinking Environmentalism, Past, and Present

As the first part of this book already briefly explained, industrial capitalism generated sharp criticism even in its earliest incarnation. When young "daughters of freemen" ventured beyond familiar hills and dales of New England farms to labor in the nation's first fully integrated cotton and woolen textile mills in the region they quickly grew disillusioned with conditions there and many did not hesitate to speak out. "The numerous class of females who are operatives," one worker wrote in *The Factory Girl's Album* of Exeter, New Hampshire, regularly put up with "thirteen hours of incessant toil." Confined to the "Prison walls of a factory," another mill girl noted, "we are continually inhaling cotton-dust, lamp smoke, and away from wholesome pure air."[1]

In fact, operatives also experienced profound disappointment with the way both migration and manufacturing upset their relationship with the natural world. They soon began to long for what was lost and to resent what had taken its place, and these feelings became part of their general indictment of the factory system. "The green hills of my childhood are again presented to my view," one worker wrote, under the pseudonym E.D. "I see my home amid its vines and flowers, the garden still blooming, and the orchard laden with its golden fruit … But ah! That sounding bell dispels the waking dream, and tells me that I am still a wanderer."[2]

Over the next few decades, the memory of Acadian rural homesteads seemed still more distant as residents of manufacturing cities confronted a dual, ever-worsening plague of industrial waste and untreated human sewage in local streams and rivers. In response, some concerned citizens, led by radicals fighting for the interests of common people, tried to address the problem through state intervention by extending the government's oversight to include public health. And they grounded this power in a long tradition of natural rights, the egalitarian philosophical principles enshrined in the Declaration of Independence. "Every person has a legitimate right to nature's gifts—pure water, air, and soil," the New Hampshire Board of Health observed in its first annual report, "a right belonging to every individual, and every community upon which no one should be allowed to trespass through carelessness, ignorance, or other cause."[3]

While less inclined to question the conditions they imposed on their workers and hesitant to accept constraints on industrial waste disposal, some early mill owners and managers also felt conflicted about the new materialism transforming popular culture as well as the factory production noticeably changing the natural landscape. Partly to resolve those feelings, they attempted to beautify mill yards, public thoroughfares, and other parcels scattered around industrial cities. "Managers and technical staff improved the look of company property, created green spaces and promenades, and provided public viewing points for natural or industrial vistas," write Pat Malone and Chuck Parrott. "They even developed entire systems of *greenways*, a modern term appropriate for describing linear parks or landscaped corridors from earlier periods." Although these endeavors were more common before the Civil War, they continued in the decades following.[4]

In Lowell, Massachusetts, the mill city at the geographic heart of America's Industrial Revolution, the most notable example of postbellum, elite-driven beautification was the creation of Rogers Fort Hill Park. Perched on the banks of the Concord River, the park was carved out of a 250-acre family farm owned by Emily and Elizabeth Rogers. Its main feature was a hill that once served as the site of a palisade fort built by Wannalancit, the last sachem (chief) of the Penacook Confederacy, who was then seeking protection for his tribe from Mohawk attacks. After purchasing the property in 1883, a developer's syndicate set aside a large parcel and commissioned landscape architect Ernest Bowditch to turn it into a pleasant, outdoor escape. His redesign included carriage drives and winding footpaths but retained the ground's natural character, leaving a few rocky outcrops and some of its rough terrain.

Interestingly, both Rogers Fort Hill Park and an adjacent garden cemetery (established in 1841) later figured in a public controversy over land use, a charged debate suggesting persistent discord between economic pursuits and environmental sensibility. It all started in the fall of 1909, after a multistory "beaming house" operated by the American Hide and Leather Company collapsed into a mess of warped timbers, green animal skins, and lime-water preparation vats, after which some of the wood caught on fire. "The women and children of the Polish colony nearby, whose husbands and fathers, in many cases, were employed in the tannery, poured into the streets screaming with terror," the *Lowell Sun* reported. Fortunately, only three workers were injured, none of them seriously. People in the area had foreseen the disaster, and when the men inside felt the "ramshackle affair" shaking, they quickly ran out of doors or jumped from windows.[5]

In the wake of the incident, American Hide and Leather Company officials proposed rebuilding the beaming house, where workers would continue to make hides ready for the rest of the tanning process by scraping them clean of dirt, blood, manure, fat, and hair. Some people balked at the prospect, however, fearing that it would perpetuate the awful stench that filled the air near the previous structure and mean more floating debris and accumulating muck in the Concord River. Landlords, in particular, complained that the smell and filth depressed property values and left them no choice but to rent to undesirable tenants. To bolster their case, they and others also voiced concerns about public health, still working with a concept of disease etiology that associated illness with inhaling miasmas, noxious gases from rotting waste. "The foul odors from this tannery," one petition declared, "are injurious to the people who reside in the vicinity." This and the impact on property values were more than adequate reasons, critics believed, to shut the business down.[6]

At a meeting before the board of health, however, Amalgamated Leather Workers president Dennis Halley communicated tannery employees' fears that prohibiting beaming work at Howe Street would lead American Hide and Leather to close altogether. This sentiment was echoed by the union's lawyer when he presented a petition, signed by nearly all 600 of the rank and file, asking the board for a continuance to save their jobs. Senior company managers and their lawyer echoed these sentiments and then made additional remarks. They claimed that the odors in question were not entirely the fault of the tannery, and to convince the board to allow a resumption of operations, they announced their intent to build a modern, odorless beaming house.[7]

Responding to union and company statements, board of health chair Dr. G. Forrest Martin explained that "the board is out for the best welfare of the city and has no desire to drive out any industry." He had no doubt the beaming house was a nuisance but, in an attempt to be "judicial" and "to treat the company as fair men," he also explained that there was a standing question about the proper way to deal with the problem and strongly recommended transferring all operations to another location within a reasonable period of time. Since American Hide and Leather already had another, larger set of buildings upstream in the more sparsely populated Perry Street area, with direct railroad access that could minimize the need for moving uncured hides around in open carts, this became the likely site for carrying out such a compromise.[8]

Lowell Sun editors took issue with the transfer proposal and called American Hide and Leather's bluff. If the tannery could not conduct its business in the city "without maintaining a nuisance injurious to public health, without infringing upon the rights of citizens in the surrounding district and without running counter to the public interest," they declared, "then the sooner it gets out of Lowell the better."[9] This opinion was reinforced in a cartoon the next day, showing a hand holding scales, with the beaming house on one side surrounded by clouds labeled "Disease" and "Foul Odors" and "Effluvia" and a group of people on the other labeled "People in the Vicinity of Howe St.," although the figures were elegantly dressed and hardly resembled mill workers or tannery hands.[10]

Throughout the summer and early fall, debate continued to center on landlord's property interests and general public health concerns but included a new element as well, the affect consolidated tannery operations at Perry Street would have on the nearby Fort Hill Park and Lowell Cemetery. Among various industries, tanning was perhaps the most incongruous with the romantic ideals enshrined there, and among the many steps in the tanning process beaming was the most objectionable to anyone seeking the clear air of a garden walk or wooded path. Additionally, and probably not inadvertently, midway through the final round of disagreement, local philanthropist Freeman B. Shedd donated 50 acres to the city, just next to Fort Hill, to be used for another public park. The grant was akin to giving money to a hospital, Judge John Pickman said, since "fresh air and the sunshine are the doctors there." The land was well suited for this purpose, *Lowell Sun* editors explained, "undulating as it does between hill and valley and including delightful wooded vales."[11]

In November, however, the city's board of health granted a permit to American Hide and Leather for a relocated beaming house. In announcing their decision, Dr. Martin reviewed the reasons for public opposition to the tannery consolidation. "The principal objections came from the park department," he explained, "because of the noxious odors which might interfere in the placing of a children's play grounds." Secondly, local residents feared the smells and sewage. But these and other concerns had been adequately addressed by the company, Martin insisted. The new plant would be constructed entirely of iron and cement, he noted, "a material that is impervious to the fluids used in the process of beaming." The company also pledged to build a new sewer connection to a municipal interceptor, at their own expense, "and thus do away with the practice of emptying into the Concord River."[12] These measures, he and the other board members felt, would suffice to remove all cause for complaint, and it would do right by the tannery. "By this step," they declared in their annual report, "an important industry has been saved to the city."[13]

Of course, the manner in which the beaming house controversy was resolved was not an entirely new approach. Many of the first industrial boosters often rationalized and defended the changes wrought by manufacturing on rivers, farms, and meadows as acceptable costs for the progress achieved. In this case, though, the explicitly stated question of jobs versus environment complicated the matter, with a segment of industrial interests as well as a group of workers promoting the former over the latter, revealing the influence and impact of industrial capitalism's development over time. Early on, the employing class did not frame their position and defend their interest by using the more modern terms, and workers did not necessarily think they were bound by them as a mutually exclusive choice.

As the twentieth century advanced, a range of factors led workers deeper and deeper into the pitfalls of the "classic dilemma." One among these was organized labor's own failure to put forward and follow a visionary long-term strategy that went beyond immediate concerns and narrow self-interest. The United Mine Workers' inadequate response to the challenge posed by the spread of surface mining is a case in point. In retrospect, reformers who took the UMW's leadership reins in the early 1970s should have continued to demand the abolition of stripping, which was first and foremost a coal industry effort at reducing labor costs by substituting technology. If Arnold Miller and others had somehow managed to find a way to stay in office while making the interests of deep miners the union's main if not exclusive priority, and if they had strengthened their collaborative relationship with the radicalized mountain activists pushing for a ban, the UMW would have better served more of its membership and greatly aided other residents of the Appalachian coalfields. Because the leaders did not do this, the union is presently, hastily and painfully, inching toward its demise, defending stripping against a growing chorus of critics and watching its numbers decline, while coal companies reach record levels of production.

To be sure, labor has never had a completely free hand to pick its way toward a truly viable plan for future survival and growth. Working people have faced numerous obstacles that were not of their own making, including resistance among mainstream environmental groups and individual activists to forming alliances, even on issues that seem to be ready-made for collaboration. When the head of the Sierra Club's Cumberland (Kentucky) chapter, Mike Flynn, refused to chair a state coalition dedicated to ending strip mining, for instance, it was because his group was "anxious to offend as few legislators as possible at his time in view of the Wild Rivers Bill in the legislative hopper." This frustrated longtime stripping foe and eastern Kentucky native Harry Caudill. Even setting aside the economic argument against surface mining, he believed, the group's position was misguided. "It is inconceivable to me that an organization like the Sierra Club, which was organized to preserve mountains for their beauty and majesty, can stand idly and silently by while the mountains in the state are destroyed," Caudill wrote, since "setting aside a small stretch of scenicly [sic] beautiful land is a trifling matter indeed compared to the rapidly advancing ruin of a whole mountain range."[14]

Likewise, the Environmental Defense Fund and similar groups failed to take the initiative in supporting the UFW's campaign to link farmworkers' and consumers' exposure to toxic pesticides, and when the union reached out they received a few kind words from broad-minded leaders but no real, tangible assistance. "It is important for us at this stage to make certain that policy positions that we take to support organized labor groups have a sound and strong environmental basis," Brock Evans wrote to César Chávez in 1973. "It is certainly my belief that your strong stand on pesticide control is such a basis, insofar as Sierra Club support and/or airing of your issues is concerned." Therefore, Brock continued, he was "sending this letter with my strong recommendations that we do what we can to help those in authority in San Francisco."[15] For whatever reason, though, nothing like the club's support for the OCAW's Shell boycott was ever forthcoming.

Workers' thinking and behavior also have been constrained or conditioned by larger economic, social, and political forces. High unemployment and rising inflation in the 1970s, along with deindustrialization and a so-called energy crisis, as well as a stepped-up effort by corporate capital to throw out the New Deal social contract (labor peace for good wages and benefits), all made visionary strategy difficult. In addition, the gathering storm of economic troubles hindered the ability of many working people (especially white men) to accept the major social changes that followed in the wake of the tumultuous 1960s. This helped nurture a conservative political and cultural backlash, temporarily moderated a bit by the collapse of President Richard Nixon's administration during Watergate but significant enough to erode anything like a consensus on the legitimacy of liberal, progressive values.

During the 1980s, with Ronald Reagan in to the White House, the New Right political agenda of "unfettered enterprise" was greatly advanced, leading to deep cuts in government spending (except the military), tax relief for the rich, deregulation and lax regulatory enforcement, as well as an assault on unions (begun when the president fired thousands of striking federal air-traffic controllers and continued with business-friendly appointments to the National Labor Relations Board). It was class war, plain and simple, though it was the ruling class that was winning. Some if not many working people went along with all or part of this, for a whole host of reasons, despite the obvious mismatch with their own economic interests. Perhaps most significant was the way the New Right wielded cultural wedge issues that, at the very least, created a contextual terrain that was challenging for any opposition to navigate.

Employers took advantage of the political and cultural rightward swing by emphasizing the common interest workers supposedly had with them in fighting against regulatory controls, including legislation to prevent water and air pollution. "It is the structure of the capitalist economy that creates the conditions for conflict between private economic interests and the protection of public goods," social scientist Brian Obach notes, "but it is the structure of American democracy that determines how such tensions are translated into political disputes." Using all the advantages at hand (inordinate influence on political campaigns, corporate control of the media, etc.), business skillfully played the "jobs versus environment" card. They warned of layoffs or complete shutdowns if they could not maintain maximum profitability, even though there was usually little or no evidence that protecting the environment (or attending to worker health and safety) posed a serious threat to a company's bottom line, and, usually, such efforts were more likely to lead to a net increase in jobs.[16]

There have been cases where environmental activism did demonstrably lead to job loss, most often in extractive industries, but there was always a back story illuminating what was really going on. Close to 10,000 loggers were put out of work as a consequence of measures to protect spotted-owl habitat in the Pacific Northwest, viewed by many as the quintessential example where "tree-huggers" (really, tree-sitters and spikers) took bread off someone's table. One study has since demonstrated, however, that timber industry employment had long been in decline and the few periods when job loss slowed corresponded to passage of environmental legislation and implementation of new rules and regulations. That suggests rapid depletion of resources, not conservation, was the main culprit, and there are several other likely factors, including automation, increased timber imports from Canada, and a shift in logging to the low-wage southeastern United States.[17]

Looking at the whole history of workers' changing attitudes about the environment over the course of industrialization, in fact, it's very clear that most of our common assumptions are widely off base. Just as importantly, the prevailing popular and academic interpretations of environmentalism are greatly at odds with what actually happened in the past. As *A People's History of Environmentalism* demonstrates, working people and their families were, more often than not, very much concerned with the impact industry had on the natural world and human health, and they played a leading role in organizing to stop abuses and correct problems, to conserve resources and prevent pollution. Sometimes they did this individually or in small groups, filing a lawsuit or breaking a dam, and other times they mobilized through their unions or formed dissident groups within those unions, lobbying state legislators or walking "wildcat" picket lines. All of these actions, I would argue, are part of a valuable historical inheritance, one that we should lucidly recognize in the present to help determine our struggle in the future.

Bibliographic Essay: A Few Books and Articles That Changed the Way We Think about Class and the History of Environmentalism in the United States

For the most part, every historian makes his or her own unique way to a particular perspective about the past. My path started at the University of Louisville, where I attended college, meandered through Ohio State University, where I was in graduate school, and continues at the University of Massachusetts Lowell, where I am now a professor in the history department. Although there were many formative experiences that shaped my thinking during this time (including things we don't normally talk about as academics, such as hiking in the woods, visiting museums, and doing community organizing), reading was among the most critical. In many cases, I can remember the actual moment when I started on a book for a course that I was taking or teaching through the latest issue of an academic journal and found something that at least slightly and sometimes grandly rearranged everything to follow. A few of those books and articles deserve specific mention here, to acknowledge their role in establishing a foundation for crafting *A People's History of Environmentalism in the United States*.

As some will recognize from the title alone, the literature dealing with a Marxist critique of capitalism is very important for theoretically grounding the narrative. This literature is a mix of original writings by Karl Marx, Frederick Engels, and others, as well as a vast mountain of scholarly meditations (and polemical diatribes) by philosophers, historians, economists, and the like about what the classics actually mean. Trying to understand any of it can often be hard-going, a bewildering encounter with dense, jargon-laden observations. There's even a joke about a young nineteenth-century German political economist who struggles to save volume after volume of a masterly manuscript from a fire in his flat, putting each one on the curb outside the burning building, finally held back by a worried crowd, bemoaning the fact that he still hadn't managed to grab a verb. Nevertheless, being persistent with what is sometimes called "historical materialism" is certainly worthwhile in the end.

One specific text that offers several fundamental, guiding principles is *The German Ideology*, which Marx and Engels wrote between the fall of 1845 and the summer of 1846. "The first premise of all human history," they stated at one point, "is, of course, the existence of living human individuals." The "of course" might seem gratuitous, but it mattered a great deal then and still does. It was an insistence against Hegel and other contemporary philosophers that human history has a "material" base, the very fact of peoples' own existence and the satisfaction of needs this "living" existence entailed. That then demands examination of "the physical organization of these individuals and their consequent relation to the rest of nature." In a mere couple of sentences, essentially, the pair advanced what is the central focus of social environmental history today—the interconnected and changing relationship of human beings to one another and to the natural world—as the quintessential concern of all historical investigation.[1]

Among the more contentious elements of Marx and Engel's point of view, however, were their notions about people's "physical organization," the social arrangement that evolved over time as part of efforts to appropriate the means of subsistence from nature. They believed, and I think it's a valid argument, that the development and expansion of "productive forces" to satisfy evolving needs entailed the rise of various stages in ownership of those forces, not only the land and its resources or the tools used to work the land and manufacture goods but also people themselves. Different classes had different claims, circumstances, and interests in this sense, which caused social conflict (struggle) and thereby played a key part in driving history.

At the heart of this social conflict was alienation, or estrangement, a concept most elaborately defined in the *Economic and Philosophic Manuscripts of 1844*. Under capitalism, Marx wrote, the free creative activity that is the distinctive essence of being human is reduced to a mere means of meeting animal needs—eating, drinking, and procreating—which workers do by selling their labor power for a wage and giving up any claim to the products of their labor. Workers then confront their labor and its products as alien things, over and above them, opposed to them, denying them. Because workers "can create nothing without nature," they are likewise estranged in a similar manner from nature, a thing owned by someone else and acted on for mere survival rather than the medium for self-expression and self-realization. And all of this happens because another class makes it so, through their unyielding "dominion," though that dominion and the exploitation and alienation it sustains does not go unchallenged. Workers can and do respond through individual and collective acts of resistance.[2]

Yet as promising as all this might seem for setting a course of study, scholars working in the field of environmental history (established in the mid-1970s) initially missed or dismissed most of these ideas. For one thing, when they talked about "materialism," they meant the way nature itself was a force in human history, not as a matter of people manipulating it to meet evolving needs but as a historical agent in its own right (think climate, soil type, microbe, etc.). For another thing, the first generation tended to ignore class divisions or other manifestations of social inequality as key elements of environmental experience. In that respect, they regarded "alienation" from nature as a mostly uncomplicated broadly held attitude, citing it as an explanation for why an undifferentiated mass of humanity hunted animals into extinction, caused epidemic soil erosion, and polluted air and waterways. Everyone, it seemed, was equally culpable for creating the problems necessitating resource conservation, wilderness protection, and environmental movements, which (however) supposedly originated from the genius of a few enlightened (usually elite) individuals.

The beginning of a corrective to this myopia began with the essay "Modes of Prophecy and Production," published in the *Journal of American History* in 1990. "If I were to point to the greatest weakness of environmental history as it has developed thus far," William Cronon wrote, "I would criticize its failure to probe below the level of the group to explore the implications of social divisions for environmental change." The field was plagued by "holism," he contended, which aided in examining our evolving relationship with nature over time but overlooked "the conflict and difference within groups of people," a critical element of that relationship. There were numerous studies about the productivity and sustainability of antebellum southern plantation staple crop cultivation, for example, but none "that adequately explores the different roles of slaves and masters and poor whites in reshaping the regional landscape."[3]

Similarly, in a 1996 *Environmental History* article, Alan Taylor took the field to task again for its practitioners' tendency to be "lumpers," embracing "a holism that washes out the human diversity of experience and identity." Preoccupied with understanding "the complicated and volatile relationships of humans to their ecosystems," he explained, environmental historians "often are tempted to depict societies and cultures as homogenous wholes," muting the "subdivisions and conflicts that so interest social historians." Cronon's popular study of colonial New England, *Changes in the Land*, one particular case in point, framed the era as a "stark" dichotomous clash between two cultures: subsistence-oriented natives and capitalist Europeans. As a remedy, Taylor recommended moving toward a "hybrid" approach, engaging the past as social environmental historians attentive to social stratification and conflict as well as to people's evolving relationship with nature. There were already some models for this, he pointed out, including John Mack Faragher's *Sugar Creek*, Ted Steinberg's *Nature Incorporated*, and Arthur McEvoy's *The Fisherman's Problem*.[4]

McEvoy's book was also an early example of environmental history that actually paid attention to work, the subject of another important theoretical-minded essay, "Are You an Environmentalist or Do You Work for a Living?" by Richard White. Like Taylor's article, it was published in 1996. This piece bemoaned the failure by historians and environmentalists alike to thoughtfully incorporate the connection people have to the environment through labor, a glaring omission considering its importance for the way humankind experiences the natural world. When they did acknowledge work, White argued, they either branded it as unredeemable destruction of the environment or talked only about a romanticized (and long-past) pastoral farming. "Coming to terms with modern work and machines," he noted, "involves both more complicated histories and an examination of how all work, and not just the work of loggers, farmers, fishers, and ranchers, intersects with nature."[5]

In fact, the 1990s saw a number of efforts by environmental historians that attempted, more or less, to follow these admonitions. One general account, Robert Gottlieb's *Forcing the Spring*, approached the American environmental movement as deeply rooted in twentieth-century campaigns to wrestle with the consequences of urbanization and industrialization, which necessarily meant recovering the experience of those most affected by those changes, past to present. "The problem with the story historians have told us," Gottlieb noted, "is whom it leaves out and what it fails to explain." In a sweeping, sometimes scattered chronicle intended to fill the gaps, he highlighted the efforts of several individuals, including settlement house reformers Alice Hamilton and Mary McDowell, United Farm Worker leader Cesar Chavez, and common steelworker Larry Davis.[6] Similarly, in *Deeper Shades of Green*, Jim Schwab moved through a number of case studies that highlighted the role played by ordinary people, including "blue-collar" workers, in (mostly) contemporary struggles to address and reign in the toxic hazards and other environmental dangers of the modern age.[7]

The first scholarly investigation to fully realize the promise of interpreting environmental activism through the revisionist lens of social environmental history, however, was Andrew Hurley's *Environmental Inequalities*. This book put "social differentiation" and "social equity" front and center to recount events in Gary, Indiana, during the 1960s and 1970s. Hurley examined swelling environmental activism among middle-class whites, working-class whites, and African Americans but paid particular attention to the links steelworkers made between workplace hazards and pollution beyond mill gates. When union leaders failed to fully engage both issues, he explained, rank-and-file activists organized for change. They established Workers for Democracy to push for more aggressive enforcement of occupational health and safety standards on the job and also helped found the Calumet Community Congress, which "orchestrated community groups to forge blue-collar front against polluting industries." Subsequently, these efforts helped fashion the foundation for a "multi-racial and multiclass environmental coalition," guided by Mayor Richard Hatcher, one that was cohesive enough to mount "the most sustained assault on corporate power for the entire postwar period."[8]

Following publication of Hurley's book, a number of comparable books and articles appeared, fleshing out other instances and aspects of "labor environmentalism." In *Environmentalism and Economic Justice*, Laura Pulido examined both the United Farm Workers' 1960s campaign to protect Mexican and Mexican American field hands from pesticides and a grazing conflict that involved "Hispano" sheep ranchers. These "subaltern" struggles reflected "larger existing inequalities and uneven power relations," conditions that required conflict-ridden challenges "to the dominant orders and practices." In both cases, a combination of racism and economic exploitation mediated people's experience with the environment, and the means for achieving redress included community organizing and militant protest, sometimes outside the law.[9]

Robert Gordon also examined the UFW campaign as an example of working-class environmentalism in a *Pacific Historical Review* article, but his most singular contribution to the scholarly literature was an assessment of the 1973 strike of the Oil, Chemical, and Atomic Workers (OCAW) against Shell Oil, in a piece published by *Environmental History*. Gordon explained how refinery workers' health and safety demands compelled major, mainstream environmental organizations, including the Sierra Club, to rally in their support, with members joining a boycott and even walking picket lines. Although the strike did not succeed in getting everything the OCAW had wanted at the bargaining table, it was "crucial" to "development of cooperative efforts between workers and environmentalists" throughout the rest of the decade. That is, until a "corporate and political counter-attack," aided by persistent differences over "core values" among the two groups, undermined the evolving alliance that had once seemed so promising.[10]

A more wide-ranging study of labor environmentalism, yet another *Environmental History* article, came from Scott Dewey. This was the first general survey of its kind, looking at the labor movement as a whole and examining unions' support for controlling pollution as far back as the 1940s. "Often exhibiting a sophisticated understanding of environmental issues," Dewey noted, "unions adopted relatively radical positions that were strikingly at odds with the views of the employers with whom they were supposedly allied against environmentalism." Like Gordon, however, he recognized how this "precocious" advocacy and cooperation between workers and environmentalists began to falter. "[T]he Oil Embargo of 1973, the growing energy crisis of the 1970s, the onset of chronic stagflation, the pressure of foreign competition, and other economic and social stresses," Dewey explained, "increasingly put both sides of this budding alliance on the defensive and drove a wedge between them." Subsequently, "worried workers moved closer to management's anti-environmental views, and both unions and environmentalists largely abandoned the earlier vision of a common front for social, economic, and environmental reform."[11]

I then made the narrative a little more complicated with an article assessing the UMW's shifting position on efforts to abolish surface coal mining in Appalachia, also published in *Environmental History*. Throughout most of the 1960s, my account related, the UMW was under corrupt, autocratic leadership and moved in lockstep with coal operators on most issues, including stripping. Initially, they claimed that any regulatory law would be the end of the coal industry, but eventually, when strip mining opponents seemed close to winning complete prohibition, they came around to accept the possibility of weak state (and later federal) controls. At the same time, many rank-and-file deep miners saw stripping as a threat to their jobs, in addition to the way it wreaked havoc on the land and poisoned streams, and they joined the campaign for a ban. In fact, this was one of several concerns that galvanized Miners for Democracy, a dissident movement that succeeded in taking power in 1972. Unfortunately, I concluded, the union's surface mining membership managed to force the new leadership to back away from abolition and, by the middle of the decade, the UMW had readopted its old position, supporting meager state controls.[12]

Meanwhile, several environmental historians brought class to the interpretation of resource conservation. In his 1997 book, *Common Lands, Common People*, Richard Judd located the origins of conservation in the communitarian ethics and actual experience of northern New England small farmers, suggesting that ideas about improving soil fertility, maintaining woodlots, and propagating fish arose from below rather than trickled down. So when George Perkins Marsh delivered an address on forest conservation before the Agricultural Society of Rutland County, Vermont, in 1847, he did not offer wholly original ideas, and the audience was receptive to what he had to say because his notions easily fit with their own thinking. Only later did elites take control of conservation, styling it according to their own distinct concerns and imposing it in a manner that often slighted or ignored the interests of common people.

The "hijacking" described by Judd explains the popular resistance to conservation that Louis Warren uncovered in *The Hunter's Game* and that Karl Jacoby related in *Crimes against Nature*. "Through conservation," Warren maintained, "local timber became property of the U.S. Forest Service, local water was diverted into federal irrigation projects, local land came under the aegis of the Bureau of Land Management, and state and federal agents stood between hunters and local game." New restrictions in Pennsylvania and other places he noted, effectively transformed hunting to supplement farm income or meager wages into "poaching." Yet common people persisted in doing this and, in a number of cases, threatened, attacked, and even killed game wardens who tried to stop them.[13] Likewise, in three different case studies, the Adirondacks, Yellowstone, and the Grand Canyon, Jacoby described various forms of "environmental banditry" local residents used to thwart and resist conservation and so-called wilderness protection. Although he also pointed out that their use of natural resources was rarely unchecked or rapacious. It followed a traditional "moral ecology," informal norms and conventions enforced through community sanction, "everything from ostracization and ridicule—acts that in the region's small, tight-knit villages could have serious consequences—to wrecked boats, killed dogs, and physical assaults."[14]

Benjamin Heber Johnson provided another example of the dynamic, where elite-driven environmental intervention faced popular opposition, in "Conservation, Subsistence, and Class at the Birth of Superior National Forest." Creation of this northern Minnesota forest, he argued, mostly benefited the "merchant elite" of nearby Ely at the expense of less privileged residents, many of whom made part of their living by hunting, trapping, and fishing there, especially during difficult economic times and strikes. "The result was a deepening of the gap between the way these two groups perceived the natural world around them and the bureaucracies that were increasingly regulating it." That gap, in turn, generated "widespread local opposition to the management of the forest, an opposition that lasts to this day."[15]

Clearly, by the eve of the new millennium, we were moving steadily toward a compelling revisionist account of environmental consciousness, policy, and protest, one with work and class in mind, and the surge of books and articles doing this did not stop. In *Hazards on the Job*, Christopher Sellers explored the development of an "industrial hygiene" movement, from the Progressive Era to the 1970s, showing how early concerns with occupational health and safety morphed into more general investigation of environmental health. There was a direct line, the book demonstrated, connecting John R. Commons and Alice Hamilton with Barry Commoner and Rachel Carson. "In their confrontation with the microenvironment of the factory," Sellers wrote of the industrial hygiene pioneers, "they concocted what are arguably our most important means for regulating the environment as a whole."[16]

In *Reasonable Use*, published in 2001, John Cumbler also took stock of the environmental implications of industrialization, chronicling the differential impact nineteenth-century manufacturing had on common people and precedent-setting efforts to protect them. Focusing on New England, where industry first made its mark, this account described the decline of migratory fish blocked by mill dams (undermining an important food source), the year-round flooding of grass meadows by those same dams (impeding small farmers' traditional use of the grass to feed livestock and produce manure), and the ever-increasing amount of noxious filth dumped into rivers by manufacturers and growing cities (creating the conditions for wave after wave of epidemics). It then went on to explain how a few voices began to speak out, defending the interests of farmers and workers, calling on the state to take responsibility for "the common good," and doing all this "in a fashion that makes them pioneers of modern environmentalism."[17]

Published two years later, my own book, *To Save the Land and People*, built on the earlier mine worker article to examine past opposition to strip mining in Appalachia. Here I contended that mountain activists' protest during the 1960s and 1970s differed significantly from the focus and approach of national, mainstream environmental groups, a contrast explained largely by divergent class interests. Farmers, miners, and other local residents knew firsthand that strip mining caused environmental and economic damage, and they were well aware of the way regulations failed to remedy the situation. Consequently, their organizing efforts were marked by distinct tactics, including nonviolent civil disobedience and industrial sabotage, as well as distinct demands, namely the complete abolition of surface coal mining. Ultimately, these grassroots opponents failed, undermined in part by environmental reformers who opportunistically presented Appalachian militancy as a foil, a reason for Congress to enact arguably weak regulatory legislation, but their efforts show the key role played by common people in the rise and evolution of a modern movement.[18]

Another critical case study, Lawrence Lipin's *Workers and the Wild*, charted the shift Oregon workers made in the early twentieth century from opposing anything that hindered "productive" use of natural resources—which they saw as primarily benefiting wealthy sportsmen—to supporting and encouraging fish and game laws and other conservation measures as well as articulating an aesthetic appreciation of nature. This transformation, Lipin noted, was facilitated in part by widespread ownership of automobiles (as mass production lowered the price), greater leisure time (granted by employers as part of "welfare capitalism" schemes and won by workers as part of union contracts), and the increased importance of industrial manufacturing to the state's economy (which put less emphasis on extractive industry in rural areas).[19]

In a somewhat different vein, Les Leopold made a significant contribution to understanding working-class environmentalism with his biography of Tony Mazzocchi, *The Man Who Hated Work and Loved Labor*, published in 2007. Influenced by a radical Brooklyn upbringing, Mazzocchi went on to become one of the most progressive-minded officials of the Oil, Chemical, and Atomic Workers. By the end of the end of the 1960s, he had made the union a central part of organized labor's efforts to win federal occupational health and safety legislation, and he framed the issue in a manner that won support from environmental activists. "Mazzocchi's conceptual breakthrough," Leopold maintained, "was that *pollution always starts in the workplace*, and then moves into the community and the natural environment. Workplace pollution, therefore, was the *source* of environmental degradation, and only strict workplace controls on pollutants and toxic substances could adequately protect us from hazards." In the decades to follow, this became the basis for nurturing a strategic alliance with the environmental movement, demonstrated most dramatically perhaps during the 1973 strike against Shell and, later in the mid-1980s, during workers' years-long battle with the BASF corporation in Louisiana.[20]

My book *Making a Living*, which came out in 2008, touched on many of the same themes covered by Lipin and Leopold, although it had a much wider scope, looking more generally at work as a central part of peoples' evolving relationship with nature during the rise and advance of industrial capitalism in the United States. It did this through six chronologically arranged case studies, from antebellum mill girls in Lowell, Massachusetts, to twentieth-century Mexican and Mexican American farm workers in southern California. Together, the various chapters showed that while workers' economic exploitation intensified, their sense of separation from the natural world also became more acute, and yet they did not simply allow this to just happen to them. Resisting loss of control over their labor as well as hoping to improve their meager wages and long hours, they practiced all kinds of informal individual and social protest, and they organized themselves into unions and political parties to assert their collective power. At the same time, I argued, working people relied on a mix of responses to deal with their estrangement from nature, from literary romanticism to hunting and fishing. These responses were not unrelated to their resistance to economic exploitation, and they often evolved into forms of environmental activism.[21]

Two other works appeared in 2008 that were equally important for charting new waters. One was Neil Maher's *Nature's New Deal*, a comprehensive account of the New Deal's Civilian Conservation Corps that—considering the fact environmental history as a field was founded in the 1970s—was long overdue. With three million working-class enrollees laboring to restore forests, farms, and beaches, as well as countless numbers of ordinary local residents affected by the program, besides heavy (largely favorable) national media coverage, the CCC's long-term impact on American environmental consciousness cannot be underestimated. In that respect, Maher maintained, it was a bridge between elite-led Progressive Era conservation, wilderness protection, and urban sanitation campaigns and a popular ("democratized") postwar environmental movement.[22]

The other book, to round out this bibliographic essay, was Elizabeth Blum's *Love Canal Revisited*, which focused on the familiar (almost mythological) events in a Niagara Falls suburb but reinterpreted them by paying special attention to class and race, aspects of the fight that had been largely ignored. When toxic waste was discovered buried underneath a local school, Blum noted, there was already a long history of area workers' involvement with health and safety issues as well as environmentalism, primarily through their unions, the OCAW, UAW, and others, and this consciousness and organizational infrastructure was marshaled to deal with the new problem. In addition, black women living with their families in public housing near the canal were also involved in the battle to protect their children's health and to win government assistance for relocation, though they often encountered resistance from white activists. "Marginalized by their race, class, and gender," Blum wrote, "these black women fought to be heard as they defined their environmental activism as an ongoing part of the civil rights struggle against racism and classism inherent in American society."[23]

To be sure, each of these articles and books is more nuanced than my descriptions here, so I encourage readers to explore the complexities of the works that seem interesting to them by going to the actual source. No doubt as they do this, still more publications will appear, defining and filling out the contours of an interpretation of American environmentalism that adequately recognizes the dimension of class. I can only hope that *A People's History of Environmentalism* will be useful to that endeavor as well.

Notes

Notes to Introduction

1 Ella, "A Weaver's Reverie," *Lowell Offering* I (1841), 188–89.

2 V.C.N., "A Morning Walk," *Operatives Magazine* (June 1841), 47; "J.R.," *Voice of Industry*, October 23, 1846, 4.

3 June 24, 1805, Tryphena Ely White, in *Tryphena Ely White's Journal* (New York: Grafton Press, 1904), 18–19.

4 Carl Hubert, "Bluntly Speaking," *The Bowhunter* (September 1953), Folder 3, "Occasional Issues of Out-of-Print Periodicals Devoted to Michigan Sports and Conservation, 1933–1965," State Archives of Michigan, Lansing, Michigan (hereafter cited as SCP Collection).

5 Harriet Arnow Simpson, *The Dollmaker* (New York: Harper Collins, 1972 [1954]), 274.

6 *Genesee Sportsman*, 1, Folder 4, Box 1, SCP Collection.

7 Walter Reuther Address, Folder 3, "Speeches; Clear Water Conference, November 6, 1965," Box 555, United Auto Workers, President's Office Collection, Archives of Labor and Urban Affairs, Wayne State University, Detroit, Michigan (hereafter cited as UAW President's Office Collection).

8 Olga Madar and August Scholle to All Recording Secretaries of UAW-CIO Local Union in Michigan, May 14, 1947, Folder "Camps, Children's Camp, 1948," Box 1, United Auto Workers Recreation Department Collection, Archives of Labor and Urban Affairs, Wayne State University, Detroit, Michigan (hereafter cited as UAW Recreation Collection).

9 Chad Montrie, "Class," in *A Companion to American Environmental History*, Douglas Sackman, ed. (Malden: Wiley-Blackwell, 2010).

10 Samuel P. Hays, *Beauty, Health, and Permanence: Environmental Politics in the United States, 1955–1985* (New York: Cambridge University Press, 1987), 34; Ted Steinberg, *Down to Earth: Nature's Role in American History* (New York: Oxford University Press, 2002), 249–50.

11 "Timeline: 70 Years of Environmental Change," www.nytimes.com/interactive/2010/04/22/science/earth/20100422_environment_timeline.html?ref=energy-environment (accessed May 3, 2010).

Notes to Chapter 1: Puritan to Yankee Redux: Farming, Fishing, and Our Very Own Dark, Satanic Mills

1 Henry David Thoreau, *A Week on the Concord and Merrimack Rivers* (New York: Library of America, 1985), 51.

2 Ibid., 28–29.

3 Amos Blanchard, *Consecration of the Lowell Cemetery* (Lowell: Leonard Huntress, 1841), 8–9.

4 Tamara Plakins Thornton, *Cultivating Gentlemen: The Meaning of Country Life among the Boston Elite, 1785–1860* (New Haven, CT: Yale University Press, 1989), 166.

5 Philip S. Foner, ed., *The Factory Girls* (Urbana: University of Illinois Press, 1977), 6–9.

6 John T. Cumbler, *Reasonable Use: The People, the Environment, and the State, New England 1790–1930* (New York: Oxford University Press, 2001), 117.

7 "Inaugural Address, George Runnels, January 2, 1882," 12, *Annual Report of the Board of Health of the City of Lowell for 1883*, 6; *Annual Report of the City Physician for the City of Lowell for 1889*, 6.

8 Brian Donohue, *The Great Meadow: Farmers and the Land in Colonial New England* (New Haven, CT: Yale University Press, 2004), 210, xv, 57, 60.

9 Ibid., xv.

10 Thoreau, *A Week on the Concord and Merrimack Rivers*, 7, 28–29, 32.

11 Cumbler, *Reasonable Use*, 23.

12 Brian Donohue, *The Great Meadow*, 187.

13 Cumbler, *Reasonable Use*, 26–27.

14 Theodore Steinberg, *Nature Incorporated: Industrialization and the Waters of New England* (Amherst: University of Massachusetts Press, 1991), 30–31.

15 David Daggett, "A Brief Account of a Trial at Law, in Which the Influence of Water Raised by a Mill-dam, on the Health of the Inhabitants in the Neighborhood Was Considered," *Memoirs of the Connecticut Academy of Arts and Sciences* (New Haven, 1813), vol. 1, pt. 1, no 12, 131–32, 134.

16 Cumbler, *Reasonable Use*, 26.

17 Ibid., 34.

18 Steinberg, *Nature Incorporated*, 64, 79.

19 Cumbler, *Reasonable Use*, 36.

20 Steinberg, *Nature Incorporated*, 38, 65.

21 Ibid., 141, 143, 146.

22 Ibid., 114–15, 161–62.

23 Cumbler, *Reasonable Use*, 67.

24 Ibid., 31–32, 16.

25 Thomas Dublin, *Women at Work: The Transformation of Work and Community in Lowell, Massachusetts, 1826–1860* (New York: Columbia University Press, 1979), 5–6.

26 Chad Montrie, *Making a Living: Work and Environment in the United States* (Chapel Hill: University of North Carolina Press, 2008), 14.

27 Hannah Josephson, *The Golden Threads: New England's Mill Girls and Magnates* (New York: Duell, Sloan and Pearce, 1949), 188.

28 *Voice of Industry*, October 9, 1846, quoted in Philip S. Foner, ed., *The Factory Girls* (Urbana: University of Illinois Press, 1977), 124.

29 Montrie, *Making a Living*, 14.

30 *Voice of Industry*, June 12, 1846, 3.

31 T*******, "Factory Girls' Reverie," *Lowell Offering* V (1845), 140. The page numbers listed here and in other notes for the *Offering* refer to the bound volumes published in Westport, Connecticut, by the Greenwood Reprint Corporation, 1970.

32 Montrie, *Making a Living*, 15–16.

33 June 26, 1821, Anna Blackwood Howell, "Diaries, 1819–1839," Octavo Volume "H," American Antiquarian Society, Worcester, Massachusetts.

34 July 3, 1805, Tryphena Ely White, in *Tryphena Ely White's Journal*, 20–21.

35 July 22, 23, and 26 and September 17, 1832, Sally Brown, in *The Diaries of Sally and Pamela Brown, 1832–38*, Blanche Brown Bryant and Gertrude Elaine Baker, eds. (Springfield, VT: William S. Bryant Foundation, 1970), 17, 21; Lydia Maria Child, *The American Frugal Housewife* (Mineola, NY: Dover, 1999), 25, 28; Montrie, *Making a Living*, 19.

36 July 7 and July 19, 1805, Tryphena Ely White, in *Tryphena Ely White's Journal*, 22, 25.

37 Alice Morse Earle, *Home Life in Colonial Days* (Stockbridge, MA: Berkshire Traveller Press, 1974 [1898]), 37–39.

38 Montrie, *Making a Living*, 17.

39 Ibid.; Earle, *Home Life*, 166–74, 193–202; Child, *The American Frugal Housewife*, 38–40; Rolla Milton Tryon, *Household Manufactures in the United States, 1640–1860* (New York: August M. Kelley, 1966), 191–212.

40 Mary H. Blewett, ed., *Caught between Two Worlds: The Diary of a Lowell Mill Girl, Susan Brown of Epsom, New Hampshire* (Lowell, MA: Lowell Museum, 1984), 14.

41 Nell Kull, ed., "'I Can Never Be So Happy There among All Those Mountains': The Letters of Sally Rice," *Vermont History* 38 (1970), 52.

42 Olive Sawyer to Sarah Bennett, May 15, 1839, in Thomas Dublin, ed., *Farm to Factory: Women's Letters, 1830–1860* (New York: Columbia University Press, 1981), 65.

43 Permielia Dame to George Dame, January 25, 1835, Dame Family Papers, New Hampshire Historical Society, Concord, New Hampshire.

44 *Voice of Industry*, December 11, 1846, 4.

45 *Factory Girl's Album*, September 12, 1846, quoted in Foner, ed., *The Factory Girls*, 221.

46 Adelaide [*sic*], "Alone with Nature," *Operatives Magazine* 3 (June 1841), 37.

47 Patrick Malone and Chuck Parrott, "Greenways in the Industrial City: Parks and Promenades along the Lowell Canals," *Journal of the Society for Industrial Archeology* 24 (1998), 19–24, 27; Alan S. Emmet, "Open Space in Lowell, 1826–1886," Research Paper

(1975), Center for Lowell History, 8–9; Maria Currier, "Shade Trees," *Lowell Offering* I (1841), 233.

48 Lydia Sarah Hall, "Lowell Cemetery," *Lowell Offering* I (1841), 186.

49 Foner, ed., *The Factory Girls*, 79–80.

50 V.C.N., "A Morning Walk," *Operatives Magazine* 3 (June 1841), 47.

51 Sarah Bagley, "Letter from Mount Washington House," *New England Offering* (November 1848), 171.

52 E.C.T., "Journey to Lebanon Springs," *Lowell Offering* II (1842), 191.

53 Clementine [*sic*], "The Scenes of Nature," *Operatives Magazine* 2 (May 1841), 29.

54 E.D., "Thoughts on Home," *Lowell Offering* III (1842–1843), 280.

55 Betsey Chamberlain, "Recollections of My Childhood," *Lowell Offering* I (1841), 78–79.

56 *Voice of Industry*, May 8, 1846, 3.

57 *Voice of Industry*, October 23, 1846, 4.

58 *Voice of Industry*, December 3, 1847, in Foner, ed., *The Factory Girls*, 92–93.

59 An Operative [Amelia Sargent], *Factory Life As It Is* (Lowell, MA: Lowell Publishing, 1982 [1845]), n.p.

60 Dublin, *Women at Work*, 140.

61 Cumbler, *Reasonable Use*, 54.

62 Massachusetts State Board of Health, *First Annual Report of the State Board of Health of Massachusetts* (January 1870), 15.

63 Cumbler, *Reasonable Use*, 3, 111.

64 *Annual Report of the Board of Health of the City of Lowell for 1883*, 6.

65 Massachusetts State Board of Health, *Eighth Annual Report of the State Board of Health of Massachusetts* (January 1877), 43.

66 Cumbler, *Reasonable Use*, 52, 109–10.

67 Josiah Curtis, *Brief Remarks on the Hygiene of Massachusetts, but More Particularly on the Cities of Boston and Lowell* (Philadelphia: T.K. and P.G. Collins, 1849), 20, 36.

68 *Annual Report of the Board of Health of the City of Lowell for 1889*, 6.

69 Cumbler, *Reasonable Use*, 110.

70 Ibid., 49, 62.

71 Steinberg, *Nature Incorporated*, 229–30; Cumbler, *Reasonable Use*, 117.

72 Ibid., 118, 121.

73 Ibid., 123, 124–25.

74 Richard Judd, *Common Lands, Common People: The Origins of Conservation in Northern New England* (Cambridge, MA: Harvard University Press, 1997), 151; Steinberg, *Nature Incorporated*, 193; Cumbler, *Reasonable Use*, 9, 93.

75 Judd, *Common Lands, Common People*, 170, 178.

76 Cumbler, *Reasonable Use*, 170.

77 Judd, *Common Lands, Common People*, 176.

Notes to Chapter 2: Why "Game Wardens" Carry Guns and Interpretive Rangers Dress like Soldiers: Class Conflict in Forests and Parks

1 Henry Chase, *Powers, Duties and Work of Game Wardens: A Handbook of Practical Information for Officers and Others Interested in the Enforcement of Fish and Game Laws* (Rutland, VT: Tuttle, 1910), 3, 110–11.

2 Ibid., 40, 119.

3 H. Duane Hampton, *How the U.S. Cavalry Saved Our National Parks* (Bloomington: Indiana University Press, 1971), 146, 148–49.

4 Karl Jacoby, *Crimes against Nature: Squatters, Poachers, Thieves, and the Hidden History of American Conservation* (Berkeley: University of California Press, 2001), 2–3, 5–6.

5 Judd, *Common Lands, Common People*, 123–24.

6 "Foreword" by Henry Fairfield Osborn in William T. Hornaday, *Our Vanishing Wild Life: Its Extermination and Preservation* (New York: Scribner, 1913), vii.

7 "The Alien Hunter," *Forest and Stream*, Vol. LXVIII, No. 2 (January 12, 1907), 47.

8 Hornaday, *Our Vanishing Wild Life*, x.

9 Ethelbert Stewart, quoted in Paul S. Sutter, *Driven Wild: How the Fight against Automobiles Launched the Modern Wilderness Movement* (Seattle: University of Washington Press, 2002), 44–45.

10 Jacoby, *Crimes against Nature*, 15–16.

11 Ibid., 17–18.

12 Ibid. 23–24, 53.

13 Ibid., 30, 36, 63.

14 Ibid., 50, 63.

15 Ibid., 41–42, 45–46.

16 Ibid., 62.

17 Hornaday, *Our Vanishing Wild Life*, 71.

18 Joseph Kalbfus, *Dr. Kalbfus' Book: A Sportsman's Experiences and Impressions of East and West* (Altoona, PA: Times Scribner, 1926), 290.

19 Louis Warren, *The Hunter's Game: Poachers and Conservationists in Twentieth-Century America* (New Haven, CT: Yale University Press, 1997), 23–24, 47.

20 Ibid., 28–30.

21 Hornaday, *Our Vanishing Wild Life*, 54; Adam Rome, "Nature Wars, Culture Wars: Immigration and Environmental Reform in the Progressive Era," *Environmental History* 13 (July 2008), 434.

22 "The Alien Hunter," *Forest and Stream*, Vol. LXVIII, No. 2 (January 12, 1907), 47.

23 Hornaday, *Our Vanishing Wild Life*, 100.

24 Ibid., 102–03; Kalbfus, *Dr. Kalbfus' Book*, 289.

25 Warren, *The Hunter's Game*, 22, 31.

26 Rome, "Nature Wars," 435; Kalbfus, *Dr. Kalbfus' Book*, 290–91; "Pennsylvania Alien Law Constitutional," *Forest and Stream*, Vol. LXXV, No. 27 (December 31, 1910), 1055.

27 Warren, *The Hunter's Game*, 45, 47.

28 Hornaday, *Our Vanishing Wild Life*, x, 94.

29 Steven Hahn, "Hunting, Fishing, and Foraging: Common Rights and Class Relations in the Postbellum South," *Radical History Review* 26 (1982), 38–40.

30 Charlie Davenport, 5, *Born in Slavery: Slave Narratives from the Federal Writers' Project, 1936–1938*, Library of Congress, Manuscript Division, <http:/memory.loc.government/ammem/snhtml/snack.htm> (hereafter cited as *Born in Slavery*).

31 James Bolton, in Ira Berlin et al., eds., *Remembering Slavery: African Americans Talk about Their Personal Experience of Slavery* (New York: New Press, 1998), 186; Henry Cheatem, 2, *Born in Slavery*.

32 Hahn, "Hunting, Fishing, and Foraging," 39–40.

33 Report by George W. Corliss, Pascagoula, Mississippi, August 31, 1867, 1, Roll 30, "Narrative Reports from Subordinate Officers, August 1865–October 1867," Records of the Assistant Commissioner for the State of Mississippi, Bureau of Refugee, Freedmen, and Abandoned Lands, 1865–1869, Record Group 105, National Archives, Washington, DC.

34 Hahn, "Hunting, Fishing, and Foraging," 44.

35 Ibid., 45; Hornaday, *Our Vanishing Wild Life*, 110.

36 Hahn, "Hunting, Fishing, and Foraging," 45, 49.

37 Ibid., 49, 51; Edward L. Ayers, *The Promise of the New South: Life after Reconstruction* (New York: Oxford University Press,1992), 189.

38 Hahn, "Hunting, Fishing, and Foraging," 56.

39 Charles Askins, "The South's Problem in Game Protection," *Recreation* (May 1909), quoted in Hornaday, *Our Vanishing Wild* Life, x, 110.

40 Theodore Roosevelt and George Bird Grinnell, eds., *Hunting in Many Lands: The Book of the Boone and Crockett Club* (New York: Forest and Stream, 1895), 362.

41 John Muir, *Our National Parks* (Boston: Houghton Mifflin, 1901), 12.

42 H. Duane Hampton, *How the U.S. Cavalry Saved Our National Parks* (Bloomington: Indiana University Press, 1971), 137–38.

43 William Cronon, "The Trouble with Wilderness; or, Getting Back to the Wrong Nature," in William Cronon, ed., *Uncommon Ground: Rethinking the Human Place in Nature* (New York: Norton, 1996), 69, 72, 76.

44 Ibid., 78.

45 Ibid., 85.

46 Hampton, *How the U.S. Cavalry Saved Our National Parks*, 133.

47 Joel Janetski, *The Indians of Yellowstone Park* (Salt Lake City: University of Utah Press, 1987), 43, 53.

48 Jacoby, *Crimes against Nature*, 84; Colonel P.W. Norris, quoted in Janetski, *The Indians of Yellowstone Park*, 77.

49 Janetski, *The Indians of Yellowstone Park*, 54.

50 Jacoby, *Crimes against Nature*, 90–91.

51 Ibid., 97–98; Richard A. Bartlett, *Yellowstone: A Wilderness Besieged* (Tucson: University of Arizona Press, 1985), 264.

52 Jacoby, *Crimes against Nature*, 92–93.

53 Bartlett, *Yellowstone*, 321; Jacoby, *Crimes against Nature*, 126.

54 Jacoby, *Crimes against Nature*, 102–05, 124–25; Hampton, *How the U.S. Cavalry Saved Our National Parks*, 149.

55 Jacoby, *Crimes against Nature*, 107–11.

56 Ibid., 86, 118–19.

57 Ibid., 132.

58 Lawrence Lipin, *Workers and the Wild: Conservation, Consumerism, and Labor in Oregon, 1910–1930* (Urbana: University of Illinois Press, 2007), 15.

59 Ibid., 67.

60 Ibid., 68.

61 Ibid., 69–70.

62 Ibid., 2–3.

63 Ibid., 102–03.

64 Jesse Steiner, quoted in Sutter, *Driven Wild*, 23–24, 19.

65 Daniel T. Rodgers, *The Work Ethic in Industrial America, 1850–1920* (Chicago: University of Chicago Press, 1979), 106.

66 Lipin, *Workers and the Wild*, 103–04.

67 "The Director's Corner," Folder "Recreation Reports, 1945–1948," Box 2, UAW Recreation Collection. See also Olga Madar, "What the UAW Is Doing about Recreation" (1959), Folder "History of the Department and Program Guides, ca. 1958–Mar. 1960," Box 2, UAW Recreation Collection.

Notes to Chapter 3: Missionaries Find the Urban Jungle: Sanitation and Worker Health and Safety

1 Upton Sinclair, *The Jungle* (New York: Bantam Books, 1981 [1906]), 24–25.

2 Robert A. Slayton, *Back of the Yards: The Making of a Local Democracy* (Chicago: University of Chicago Press, 1986), 26.

3 Dominic Pacyga, *Polish Immigrants and Industrial Chicago: Workers on the South Side, 1880–1922* (Columbus: Ohio State University Press, 1991), 73.

4 Jane Addams, *Twenty Years at Hull House* (New York: Signet, 1981 [1910]), 49, 81.

5 Ellen Richards, *The Cost of Cleanliness* (New York: John Wiley, 1911), 53.

6 David Ward, *Poverty, Ethnicity, and the American City, 1840–1925: Changing Conceptions of the Slum and the Ghetto* (Cambridge, UK: Cambridge University Press, 1989), 63.

7 Elizabeth D. Blum, "Women, Environmental Rationale, and Activism during the Progressive Era," in Glave, Dianne D., and Mark Stoll, eds., *"To Love the Wind and*

the Rain": *African Americans and Environmental History* (Pittsburgh: University of Pittsburgh Press, 2006), 90–91.

8 Daniel Eli Burnstein, *Next to Godliness: Confronting Dirt and Despair in Progressive Era New York City* (Urbana: University of Illinois Press, 2006), 3.

9 Alessandro Mastro-Valerio, "Remarks upon the Italian Colony in Chicago," in *Hull House Maps and Papers: A Presentation of Nationalities and Wages in a Congested District of Chicago* (New York: Thomas Y. Cromwell, 1895), 138–39.

10 Pacyga, *Polish Immigrants and Industrial Chicago*, 70.

11 "An Address before the League of American Municipalities," August 3, 1898, Samuel Milton Jones Papers, Toledo-Lucas County Public Library, Toledo, Ohio.

12 Hoyt Landon Warner, *Progressivism in Ohio, 1897–1917* (Columbus: Ohio State University Press, 1964), 33; Brand Whitlock, "'Golden Rule' Jones," *The World's Work* VIII (September 1904), 5308–11.

13 David Rosner and Gerald Markowitz, *Deadly Dust: Silicosis and the Politics of Occupational Disease in Twentieth-Century America* (Princeton, NJ: Princeton University Press, 1991), 4, 7.

14 Christopher Sellers, *Hazards of the Job: From Industrial Disease to Environmental Science* (Chapel Hill: University of North Carolina Press, 1997), 111, 144.

15 Department of Health (Chicago), "Annals of Health and Sanitation," in *Report for 1911–1918* (Chicago, 1919), 1485, 1497–99; Gavin F. Davenport, "The Sanitation Revolution in Illinois, 1870–1900," *Journal of the Illinois State Historical Society* LXVI (Autumn 1973), 316; Isaac D, Rawlings et al., *The Rise and Fall of Disease in Illinois* (State Department of Public Health, 1927), 338, 351.

16 Addams, *Twenty Years*, 49, 72; See also Mina Carson, *Settlement Folk: Social Thought and the American Settlement Movement, 1885–1930* (Chicago: University of Chicago Press, 1990) and Rivka Shpak Lissak, *Pluralism and Progressives: Hull House and the New Immigrants, 1890–1919* (Chicago: University of Chicago Press, 1989).

17 Thomas Lee Philpott, *The Slum and the Ghetto: Neighborhood Deterioration and Middle-Class Reform, Chicago, 1880–1930* (New York: Oxford University Press, 1978), 113; Addams, *Twenty Years*, 202.

18 *Chicago Tribune*, March 21, 1895 and March 15, 1895; Addams, *Twenty Years*, 203; *Journal* [Indianapolis, Indiana], July 20,1895; *Leader* [Bellevue, Iowa], June 27, 1895; *Star* [Kansas City, Missouri], March 29, 1896.

19 *News* [Indianapolis, Indiana], February 28, 1896; Addams, *Twenty Years*, 204.

20 Florence Kelley, "Hull House," *New England Magazine* 18 (June 1898), 565.

21 Ray Stannard Baker, "Hull House and the Ward Boss," *Outlook* 58 (March 26, 1898), 769–71; Addams, *Twenty Years*, 205; *Chicago Tribune*, March 7, 1898.

22 *Evening Journal* [Albany, New York], February 16, 1898.

23 *Chicago Daily News*, March 11, 1898; *Picayune* [New Orleans], March 17, 1898.

24 Kelley was explaining why settlement residents had established a "Practical Housekeeping Center" in the neighborhood. Alice Hamilton, a medical doctor, also

advised immigrant mothers visiting the Hull House well-baby clinic not to feed their babies bananas. Florence Kelley, "Unskilled Mothers," *Century Magazine* 73 (February 1907), 640–42.

25 Slayton, *Back of the Yards*, 173.

26 Sylvia Hood Washington, *Packing Them In: An Archaeology of Environmental Racism in Chicago, 1865–1954*. Lanham, MD: Lexington Books, 2004, 76, 79, 81, 85.

27 Ibid., 82–83; Slayton, *Back of the Yards*, 15, 27.

28 Ibid., 89–90.

29 Washington, *Packing Them In*, 88.

30 Howard Wilson, *Mary McDowell: Neighbor* (Chicago: University of Chicago Press, 1928), 146, 148–49, 151.

31 *Chicago Tribune*, July 22, 1913.

32 Judith Walzer Leavitt, *The Healthiest City: Milwaukee and the Politics of Health Reform* (Princeton, NJ: Princeton University Press, 1982), 123.

33 Ibid., 124–25.

34 Ibid., 127–28, 131–33.

35 Ibid., 133, 135, 138–39, 141.

36 Ibid., 141–44, 146.

37 Sally L. Miller, "Milwaukee: Of Ethnicity and Labor," in Bruce M. Stave, ed., *Socialism and the Cities* (Port Washington, NY: Kennikat Press, 1975), 48.

38 Leavitt, *The Healthiest City*, 154.

39 Gerd Korman, *Industrialization, Immigrants, and Americanizers: The View from Milwaukee, 1866–1921* (Madison: State Historical Society of Wisconsin, 1967), 116–17.

40 Barbara Sicherman, ed., *Alice Hamilton: A Life in Letters* (Cambridge, MA: Harvard University Press, 1984), 154.

41 Ibid., 155; Sellers, *Hazards of the Job*, 66.

42 Sicherman, ed., *Alice Hamilton*, 3–4, 154, 157–58.

43 Ibid., 181, 3.

44 Ibid., 6, 156–57.

45 Ibid., 158.

46 Ibid., 166.

47 Sellers, *Hazards of the Job*, 70, 104–05.

48 Ibid., 111, 146; Sicherman, ed., *Alice Hamilton*, 239.

49 Sellers, *Hazards of the Job*, 144, 154, 167.

50 Sicherman, ed., *Alice Hamilton*, 238.

51 Sellers, *Hazards of the Job*, 2–3, 222–23.

52 Lynn Page Snyder, "'The Death-Dealing Smog over Donora, Pennsylvania': Industrial Air Pollution, Public Health Policy, and the Politics of Expertise, 1948–1949," *Environmental History Review* 18, no. 1, (Spring, 1994), 117–20.

53 Ibid., 122–23.

Notes to Chapter 4: Green Relief and Recovery: By Which Working People and Nature Get a New Deal

1 *Andover Townsman*, June 1, 1934.

2 *Lawrence Eagle Tribune*, June 16, 1937.

3 Sherwood Anderson, quoted in Joseph Speakman, *At Work in Penn's Woods: The Civilian Conservation Corps in Pennsylvania* (University Park: Pennsylvania State University Press, 2006), 2.

4 Neil Maher, *Nature's New Deal: The Civilian Conservation Corps and the Roots of the American Environmental Movement* (New York: Oxford University Press, 2008), 3–4, 66.

5 Ibid., 67–73.

6 Paul Sutter, "New Deal Conservation: A View from the Wilderness," in Henry L. Henderson and David B. Woolner, eds., *FDR and the Environment* (New York: Palgrave Macmillan, 2005), 93.

7 Maher, *Nature's New Deal*, 12, 37.

8 Ibid., 39–40.

9 Ibid., 79–82, 116.

10 Speakman, *At Work in Penn's Woods*, 2, 4–5, 25, 33.

11 Ibid., ix, 25.

12 Alfred E. Cornebise, *The CCC Chronicles: Camp Newspapers of the Civilian Conservation Corps, 1933–1942* (Jefferson, NC: McFarland, 2004), 85.

13 Wayne Hinton and Elizabeth Green, *With Picks, Shovels, and Hope: The CCC and Its Legacy on the Colorado Plateau* (Missoula, MT: Mountain Press, 2008), 20–21.

14 David Draves, *Builder of Men: Life in C.C.C. Camps of New Hampshire* (Portsmouth, NH: Peter E. Randall, 1992), 1.

15 J.C. Ryan, *The CCC and Me* (Duluth, MN: J.C. Ryan, 1987), 30.

16 Cornebise, *The CCC Chronicles*, 99.

17 Thomas W. Patton, "'A Forest Camp Disgrace': The Rebellion of the Civilian Conservation Corps Workers at Preston, New York, July 7, 1933," *New York History* 82 (Summer 2001), 240.

18 Olen Cole Jr., *The African American Experience in the Civilian Conservation Corps* (Gainesville: University Press of Florida, 1999), 21.

19 Renee Corona Kolvet and Victoria Ford, *The Civilian Conservation Corps in Nevada, The Civilian Conservation Corps in Nevada: From Boys to Men* (Reno and Las Vegas: University of Nevada Press, 2006), 59.

20 Hinton and Green, *With Picks, Shovels, and Hope*, 15, 36–37.

21 Maher, *Nature's New Deal*, 84.

22 Kay E. Kiefer and Paul E. Fellows, *Hobnail Boots and Khaki Suits: A Brief Look at the Great Depression and the Civilian Conservation Corps As Seen through the Eyes of Those Who Were There* (Chicago: Adams Press, 1983), 75.

23 Robert Moore, *The Civilian Conservation Corps in Arizona's Rim Country: Working in the Woods* (Reno and Las Vegas: University of Nevada Press, 2006), 111.

24 Speakman, *At Work in Penn's Woods*, 104–05.

25 Maher, *Nature's New Deal*, 102.

26 Draves, *Builder of Men*, 352.

27 Ibid., 123–27.

28 Kiefer and Fellows, *Hobnail Boots and Khaki Suits*, 143.

29 Maher, *Nature's New Deal*, 87–91.

30 Speakman, *At Work in Penn's Woods*, 103.

31 Cornebise, *The CCC Chronicles*, 219.

32 Ibid., 219–21.

33 Speakman, *At Work in Penn's Woods*, 114

34 Hinton and Green, *With Picks, Shovels, and Hope*, 64.

35 Moore, *The Civilian Conservation Corps in Arizona's Rim Country*, 81.

36 Kiefer and Fellows, *Hobnail Boots and Khaki Suits*, 143.

37 Ryan, *The CCC and Me*, 31.

38 Maher, *Nature's New Deal*, 10–11.

39 Ibid., 130.

40 Ibid., 163–64.

41 "CCC Realizes Dream of Col. Parker of Chain of Forest Playgrounds Here: 'Road Builder' Deeded 1,000 Acres to State—This Tract Has Been More Than Doubled—Wilderness Being Reclaimed," newspaper article with no date or name of paper, in "Harold Parker Forest" Folder, Andover Historical Society, Andover, Massachusetts; *The Andover Townsman*, 6/1/1934.

42 Maher, *Nature's New Deal*, 168, 173; Sutter, *Driven Wild*, 239.

43 Sutter, *Driven Wild*, 256.

44 S.E. Sangster, "Fish and Game Laws" (May 27, 1941), 12, in Michigan Writers' Project, Department of Natural Resources, 89–55, Box 1, 1940–1943, State Archives of Michigan, Lansing, Michigan.

45 Lipin, *Workers and the Wild*, 105.

46 Sutter, *Driven Wild*, 23.

47 Michael B. Smith, "'The Ego Ideal of the Good Camper' and the Nature of Summer Camp," *Environmental History* 11 (January 2006), 74–75, 76, 79.

48 Leslie Paris, *Children's Nature: The Rise of the American Summer Camp* (New York: New York University Press, 2008), 42–45, 49.

49 *Saginaw Valley Sportsman* (November 1949), Folder 15, Box 1, SCP Collection.

50 Olga Madar and August Scholle [President, Michigan CIO Council] to All Recording Secretaries of UAW-CIO Local Unions in Michigan, May 14, 1947, Folder "Camps, Children's Camp, 1948," Box 1, UAW Recreation Collection; "The FDR-CIO Labor Center Camp for Children," 1947, Folder "Camps, Children's Camp, 1950," Box 1, UAW Recreation Collection.

51 Walter Reuther to Olga Madar, February 25, 1948, Folder "Camps, Children's Camp, 1948," Box 1, UAW Recreation Collection; "Michigan Department of Conservation—Division of Parks and Recreation—Seasonal Group Camp Application and Permit," Folder "Camps, Children's Camp, 1948," Box 1, UAW Recreation Collection; "Children's Camp" Press Release, June 14, 1948, Folder "Camps, Children's Camp, 1948," Box 1, UAW Recreation Collection.

52 "Report of F.D.R. C.I.O. Camp for Children," n.d., Folder "Camps, Children's Camp, 1948," Box 1, UAW Recreation Collection.

53 Brochure for FDR-AFL-CIO Children's Camp (1962), Folder "Camp Folders; 1958, 1960–1962," Box 2, UAW Recreation Collection.

54 Montrie, *Making a Living*, 105–06.

Notes to Chapter 5: A Popular Crusade: Organized Labor Takes the Lead against Pollution

1 Walter Reuther, untitled speech, Folder 4, "Speeches, Mar. 1963," Box 552, UAW President's Office Collection; Thomas Kimball [NWF executive director] to Walter Reuther, February 7, 1963, Folder 4, "Speeches, Mar. 1963," Box 552, UAW President's Office Collection; *Detroit News*, March 1, 1963, Folder 4, "Speeches, Mar. 1963," Box 552, UAW President's Office Collection.

2 Walter Reuther, untitled speech, Folder 6, "Speeches; Water Pollution Control Federation, September 25, 1968," Box 559, UAW President's Office Collection.

3 Ibid.

4 Ibid.

5 Scott Dewey, "Working for the Environment: Organized Labor and the Origins of Environmentalism in the United States, 1948–1970," *Environmental History* 3 (January 1998), 45–46.

6 Maher, *Nature's New Deal*, 67.

7 Ken Morris, Chairman, Oakland County UAW-CAP Council, Statement to the Michigan Waterways Commission, Department of Natural Resources, Hearing on Public Access Site Program, November 24, 1970, Folder "Public Access to Lakes in MI, Legislation, 1971," Box 11, United Auto Workers, Conservation and Recreation Departments Collection, Archives of Labor and Urban Affairs, Wayne State University, Detroit Michigan (hereafter cited as UAW Conservation and Recreation Collection); Paul Massaron, International Representative, UAW Region I-B, Statement at the Water Management Needs Conference, February 27, 1971, Folder "Public Access to Lakes in MI, Legislation, 1971," Box 11, UAW Conservation and Recreation Collection.

8 Joyce Shaw Peterson, *American Automobile Workers, 1900–1933* (Albany: State University of New York Press, 1987), 31, 36–42, 50; Kevin Boyle, *The UAW and the Heyday of American Liberalism, 1945–1968* (Ithaca, NY: Cornell University Press, 1995), 12.

9 S.E. Sangster, "Fish and Game Laws" (1941), 4, 6–8, Folder 8, Box 1, Michigan Writers' Project, Department of Natural Resources Collection, State Archives of Michigan, Lansing, Michigan (hereafter cited MWP-DNR Collection); Richard Bailey, "Outline of Fur and Game History," 6–7, Folder 3, Box 1, MWP-DNR Collection; See also John Reiger, *American Sportsmen and the Origins of Conservation* (Norman: University of Oklahoma Press, 1975).

10 "Southern Michigan State Game Areas and Recreation Areas, 1949–1950," Folder 3, Box 6, RG-68–66, State Archives of Michigan, Lansing, Michigan; *Kent League Sportsman* (October 1949), 9, Folder 6, Box 1, SCP Collection.

11 *Genesee Sportsman* (December 1949), 4, Folder 4, Box 1, SCP Collection; Montrie, *Making a Living*, 97.

12 *Genesee Sportsman* (September 1950), Folder 4, Box 1, SCP Collection; *Kent League Sportsman* (June 1949), Folder 6, Box 1, SCP Collection.

13 *Macomb County Sportsman* (October 1949), Folder 7, Box 1, SCP Collection; *Genesee Sportsman* (January 1949) and (September 1950), Folder 4, Box 1, SCP Collection; Montrie, *Making a Living*, 98.

14 *Barry County Sportsman*, June 1949, Folder 2, Box 1, SCP Collection.

15 *Kent League Sportsman* (January 1949), Folder 6, Box 1, SCP Collection.

16 *Genesee Sportsman* (October 1949 and June 1951), Folder 4, Box 1, SCP Collection; *Kent League Sportsman* (January 1949 and February 1949), Folder 6, Box 1, SCP Collection; *Macomb County Sportsman* (September 1949), Folder 7, Box 1, SCP Collection; *Afield and Afloat in Jackson County* (February 1947), Folder 1, Box 1, SCP Collection; *Saginaw Valley Sportsman* (January 1949), Folder 15, Box 1, SCP Collection; Montrie, *Making a Living*, 101.

17 *Saginaw Valley Sportsman* (July 1949), Folder 15, Box 1, SCP Collection; Montrie, *Making a Living*, 102.

18 Nelson Lichtenstein, *Walter Reuther: The Most Dangerous Man in Detroit* (Urbana: University of Illinois Press, 1995), 300–08; Kevin Boyle, "Little More Than Ashes: The UAW and American Reform in the 1960s," in Kevin Boyle, ed., *Organized Labor and American Politics, 1894–1994* (Albany: State University of New York Press, 1998), 217–21, 230–31; Boyle, *The UAW and the Heyday of American Liberalism*, 11, 34–36.

19 Draft of article for "The Director's Corner," n.d., Folder "Recreation Reports, 1945–1948," Box 2, UAW Recreation Collection.

20 Montrie, *Making a Living*, 108; Adam Rome, "'Give Earth a Chance': The Environmental Movement and the Sixties," *Journal of American History* 90 (September 2003), 528–32; Dewey, "Working for the Environment," 51–52.

21 Ibid., 53.

22 "Recreation Department Collection Guide" and "Brief History of UAW Environmental Leadership," Folder "Conservation & Recreation Depts. History, Policies & Operations, 1930s–1970s," Box 11, UAW Conservation and Recreation Collection.

23 Montrie, *Making a Living*, 108; Dewey, "Working for the Environment," 52.

24 Bard Young [Director, Region 1A UAW], Phillip Terrana [President Local Union #174], and Olga Madar to "UAW Member and Spouse," November 25, 1969, Folder "Down River Anti-Pollution League; Corres & Reports, 1969," Box 2, UAW Conservation and Recreation Collection; Montrie, *Making a Living*, 109.

25 "Join Citizens from Downriver, Fox Creek, and Center City in Picketline," Folder "DAPL Flyers, 1970–71," Box 2, UAW Recreation and Conservation Collection.

26 Montrie, *Making a Living*, 110.

27 Ibid., 111.

28 Lichtenstein, *Walter Reuther*, 436–37.

29 Robert Gordon, "Environmental Blues: Working-Class Environmentalism and the Labor-Environmental Alliance" (Wayne State University, Ph.D. diss., 2004), 91–92.

30 Robert Gottlieb, *Forcing the Spring: The Transformation of the American Environmental Movement* (Washington, DC: Island Press, 1993), 291; Gordon, "Environmental Blues," 214–17.

31 Ibid., 224.

32 Ibid., 291, 296.

33 Ibid., 293.

34 Les Leopold, *The Man Who Hated Work and Loved Labor: The Life and Times of Tony Mazzocchi* (White River Junction, VT: Chelsea Green, 2007), 229.

35 Ibid., 230.

36 Ibid., 235, 245–46.

37 Ibid., 247–48.

38 Ibid., 248–51.

39 Ibid., 246, 253, 272.

40 Ibid., 247.

41 Gordon, "Environmental Blues," 55; Leopold, *The Man Who Hated Work and Loved Labor*, 281.

42 Robert Gordon, "'Shell No!': OCAW and the Labor-Environmental Alliance," *Environmental History* 3 (October 1998), 468.

43 Ibid., 469.

44 Ibid., 470.

45 Ibid, 472–73.

46 Ibid., 474; Les Leopold, *The Man Who Hated Work and Loved Labor*, 306.

47 Gordon, "'Shell No!'" 475.

48 Timothy Minchin, *Forging a Common Bond: Labor Activism during the BASF Lockout* (Gainesville: University Press of Florida, 2003), 59–60.

49 Ibid., 1–3; Gordon, "Environmental Blues," 336.

50 Jim Schwab, *Deeper Shades of Green: The Rise of Blue-Collar and Minority Environmentalism in America* (San Francisco: Sierra Club Books, 1994), 240; Minchin, *Forging a Common Bond*, 2, 154–55, 158.

51 Ibid., 175.

Notes to Chapter 6: To Stir Up Dissension and Create Turmoil: Inventing Environmental Justice

1 *Courier Journal*, July 9, 1967; July 11, 1967; *Mountain Eagle*, July 20, 1967.

2 *Courier Journal*, July 19, 1967; *New York Times*, July 18, 1967; July 19, 1967.

3 Gene L. Mason, "The Subversive Poor," *Nation*, December 30, 1968, quoted in Caudill, *My Land Is Dying* (New York: Dutton, 1973), 88–89; Joe Mulloy and Karen Mulloy, The War on Poverty in Appalachian Kentucky Oral History Project, Special Collections, University of Kentucky (hereafter cited as War on Poverty Project).

4 *New York Times*, August 27, 1967; *Courier Journal*, September 27, 1967; Paul Good, "Kentucky's Coal Beds of Sedition," *Nation*, September 4, 1967, in David S. Walls and John B.Stephenson eds., *Appalachia in the Sixties: Decade of Reawakening* (Lexington: University Press of Kentucky, 1972), 192; Joe Mulloy, War on Poverty Project.

5 Elizabeth D. Blum, *Love Canal Revisited: Race, Class, and Gender in Environmental Activism* (Lawrence: University Press of Kansas, 2008), 57–60.

6 Ibid., 63, 69–70, 73.

7 Eileen McGurty, *Transforming Environmentalism: Warren County, PCBs, and the Origins of Environmental Justice* (New Brunswick, NJ: Rutgers University Press, 2007), 73, 80, 110.

8 Chris Meyer to Victoria A. Hays, August 24, 1973, Folder 21, "Environmental Action," Box 3, United Farm Workers: Work Department Collection, Archives of Labor and Urban Affairs, Wayne State University, Detroit, Michigan (hereafter cited as UFW Work Department Collection).

9 Montrie, *Making a Living*, 123.

10 Carey McWilliams, *Factories in the Field: The Story of Migratory Farm Labor in California* (Santa Barbara, CA: Peregrine Publishers, 1971 [1935]); Speech to introduce "Brothers and Sisters," n.d., Folder 8, "Speech File, n.d." Box 46, United Farm Workers Information and Research Department Collection, Archives of Labor and Urban Affairs, Wayne State University, Detroit, Michigan (hereafter cited as UFW Information and Research Collection).

11 Montrie, *Making a Living*, 116–17.

12 Craig J. Jenkins, *The Politics of Insurgency: The Farm Worker Movement in the 1960s* (New York: Columbia University Press, 1985), 80–82.

13 Lucia L. Kaiser and Kathryn G. Dewey, "Migration, Cash Cropping and Subsistence Agriculture: Relationships to Household Food Expenditures in Rural Mexico," *Social Science and Medicine* 33 (1991), 1115–16.

14 Ellen Casper, "A Social History of Farm Labor in California, with Special Emphasis on the United Farm Workers Union and California Rural Legal Assistance" (Ph.D. diss., New School for Social Research, 1984), 77; "Di Giorgio Fruit Corporation, Ranch and Packing House Rules," Folder 18, "Workers Statements, 1967," Box 14, United Farm Workers: Central Administration Files Collection, Archives of Labor and Urban

Affairs, Wayne State University, Detroit, Michigan (hereafter cited as UFW Central Administration Files Collection).

15 Linda Nash, "The Fruits of Ill-Health: Pesticides and Workers' Bodies in Post–World War II California," *Osiris* 19 (2004), 205.

16 Ibid., 205, 207; Laura Pulido, *Environmentalism and Economic Justice: Two Chicano Struggles in the Southwest* (Tucson: University of Arizona Press, 1998 [1996]), 77, 81; "Domestic Agricultural Migrants in the United States (1965)," Public Health Service Publication No. 540, Folder 1, "Farm Labor Migration Patterns, 1965–69," Box 13, UFW Information and Research Collection.

17 Affidavit of Dr. Irma West, n.d., Folder 18, "Pesticides, 1968–73," Box 21, UFW Administration Files Collection.

18 Affidavit of Hilario Garcia Jr., 1968, Folder 1, "Pesticides 1964–1970," Box 24, UFW Information and Research Collection; Affidavit of Joe Alejandro, n.d., Folder 18, "Pesticides, 1968–73," Box 21, UFW Central Administration Files Collection; Affidavit of Francisco Mendoza, n.d., Folder 18, "Pesticides, 1968–73," Box 21, UFW Administration Files Collection; Robert Gordon, "Poisons in the Fields: The United Farm Workers, Pesticides, and Environmental Politics," *Pacific Historical Review* 68 (February 1999), 58; Montrie, *Making a Living*, 120.

19 Linda Nash, "The Fruits of Ill-Health," 213; Montrie, *Making a Living*, 114–15.

20 Speech to introduce "Brothers and Sisters," n.d., Folder 8, "Speech File, n.d." Box 46, UFW Information and Research Collection; Walter Reuther and Ken Morris [Region 1B Director] to Local Presidents, Recording Secretaries, Financial Secretaries, CAP and Education Committee Chairmen, April 22, 1969, Folder 13, "United Automobile Workers (UAW), 1969–1970," Box 75, United Farm Workers Office of the President Collection, Archives of Labor and Urban Affairs, Wayne State University, Detroit, Michigan (hereafter cited as UFW President Collection).

21 Pulido, *Environmentalism and Economic Justice*, 85–86, 105; Montrie, *Making a Living*, 124.

22 James Maguire to United Farm Workers Organization, December 2, 1969, Folder 15, "Ecology Walk, 1969–1970," Box 6, UFW Administration Files Collection; Jim Drake to César Chávez, April 16, 1970, Internal Memorandum, Folder 15, "Ecology Walk, 1969–1970," Box 6, UFW Administration Files Collection.

23 Pulido, *Environmentalism and Economic Justice*, 58–9; "Pesticides: The Poisons We Eat," Folder 20, "Pesticides, Leaflets, n.d.," Box 21, UFW Administration Files Collection.

24 Pulido, *Environmentalism and Economic Justice*, 114–15.

25 Ibid., 114–17; Gordon, "Poisons in the Fields," 51, 62–63.

26 California Department of Public Health, Bureau of Occupational Health and Environmental Epidemiology, *Occupational Disease in California Attributed to Pesticides and Other Agricultural Chemicals, 1970* (n.p., 1971), 5.

27 Gordon, "Poisons in the Fields," 65; Maralyn Edid, *Farm Labor Organizing: Trends and Prospects* (Ithaca, NY: ILR Press, 1994), 38–39; Montrie, *Making a Living*, 125–26.

28 "Coachella Valley Grape Crop Agreement," April 16, 1973, "Grape Contracts, 1970–1973," Box 15, UFW Information and Research Collection; Gordon, "Poisons in the Fields," 52, 65.

29 California Department of Public Health, Bureau of Occupational Health and Environmental Epidemiology, *Occupational Disease in California Attributed to Pesticides and Other Agricultural Chemicals, 1971–1973* (n.p., 1974), 2.

30 Cathy Lerza to Ramon Romero, April 30, 1973, Folder 21, "Environmental Action," Box 3, UFW Work Department Collection; César Chávez to Brock Evans, May 9, 1973, Folder 21, "Environmental Action," Box 3, UFW Work Department Collection; Brock Evans to César Chávez, June 5, 1973, Folder 21, "Environmental Action," Box 3, UFW, Work Department Collection; Montrie, *Making a Living*, 126.

31 Gordon, "Poisons in the Fields," 73–74; Edid, *Farm Labor Organizing*, 12, 42–43.

32 Montrie, *Making a Living*, 128.

33 United Mine Workers of America, *Proceedings of the 45th Constitutional Convention* (1968), 111, 162–63.

34 *Pittsburgh Press*, June 21, 1961, June 25, 1961, and June 30, 1961; Richard H.K. Vietor, *Environmental Politics and the Coal Coalition* (College Station: Texas A&M University Press, 1980), 63.

35 *Pittsburgh Press*, June 29, 1961 and July 10, 1961.

36 Ibid., July 12, 1961, and July 26, 1961.

37 Ibid., August 23, 1961; Chad Montrie, *To Save the Land and People: A History of Opposition to Surface Coal Mining in Appalachia* (Chapel Hill: University of North Carolina Press, 2003), 52–53.

38 Ibid., August 28, 1961, 1, 7; August 29, 1961, 1, 2; Pa. Laws 1961, 1210.

39 Montrie, *To Save the Land and People*, 57–58; Lewis Burke, in Laurel Shackelford and Bill Weinberg, eds, *Our Appalachia* (New York: Hill and Wang, 1977), 353–54.

40 *Mountain Eagle*, June 3, 1965.

41 Harry Caudill, *My Land Is Dying* (New York: Dutton, 1973), 80–81; Montrie, *To Save the Land and People*, 79.

42 *New York Times*, July 30, 1967, 29; Caudill, *My Land Is Dying*, 87; *Courier Journal*, August 10, 1967, 1; At the end of the summer of 1968, saboteurs also destroyed $750,000 worth of equipment at a Round Mountain Coal Company operation in Leslie County. Later, in December, someone blew up $1,000,000 worth of equipment, including one shovel and six bulldozers, at a Blue Diamond Coal strip operation in Campbell County, Tennessee, near the state border. T.N. Bethell, "Hot Time Ahead," *Mountain Life and Work* (April 1969), in David S. Walls and John B. Stephenson, eds., *Appalachia in the Sixties: Decade of Reawakening*, (Lexington: University Press of Kentucky, 1972), 116–19; See also Montrie, *To Save the Land and People*, 87–88.

43 Program from Strip Mining Symposium, July 13, 1967 (Owensboro: AV Information Office), Folder 6, Box 5, Gordon Ebersole/The Congress for Appalachian Development Manuscript Collection, East Tennessee State University (hereafter cited as Ebersole

Papers); "Why We Come to Owensboro: A Report to Governor Breathitt, July 13, 1967," Folder 6, Box 5, Ebersole Papers.

44 *Charleston Gazette*, February 5, 1971; February 10, 1971, and February 11, 1971.

45 Ken Hechler, press releases, April 22, 1971, May 21, 1971, copies in author's possession; Announcement, April 22, 1971, Folder 6, "Strip Mining," Box 170, Ken Hechler Manuscript Collection, Morrow Library, Marshall University (hereafter cited as Ken Hechler Papers).

46 *United Mine Workers Journal [UMWJ]* 82 (January 1971), 4, 6; *UMWJ* 82 (February 1971), 3; *UMWJ* 82, (March 1971), 9.

47 Montrie, *To Save the Land and People*, 151–53, 172.

48 Ibid., 163.

49 Ken Hechler to "Friends of the Coalition against Strip Mining," January 18, 1975, Folder 8, "Strip Mining," Box 170, Ken Hechler Papers; Montrie, *To Save the Land and People*, 168.

50 World-News [Roanoke, Virginia], April 9, 1975, April 14, 1975; House Subcommittee on Energy and the Environment, Hearings before the Subcommittee on Energy and the Environment of the Committee on Interior and Insular Affairs on H.R. 2, Surface Mining Control and Reclamation Act of 1977, 95th Cong., 1st sess., (1977), 37–38, 185 (Part I).

51 *Reporter* [Citizens Coal Council], Special Issue, August 3, 1997, 7, 13; House Subcommittee on Energy and the Environment, Committee on Interior and Insular Affairs, *Tenth Anniversary of the Surface Mining Control and Reclamation Act of 1977*, 100th Cong., 1st sess., (1987), 1, 65–66.

52 *Charleston Gazette*, June 6, 1999.

Notes to Conclusion

1 "The Operatives' Life," from the *Factory Girls' Album* [Exeter, NH], June 20, 1846, in Philip S. Foner, ed., *The Factory Girls* (Urbana: University of Illinois Press, 1977), 79-80; E.M., in *Factory Girl's Album*, September 12, 1846, in Foner, ed., *The Factory Girls*, 221.

2 E.D., "Thoughts on Home," *Lowell Offering*, III (1842–1843), 280.

3 Cumbler, *Reasonable Use*, 3.

4 Patrick Malone and Chuck Parrott, "Greenways in the Industrial City: Parks and Promenades along the Lowell Canals," *Journal of the Society for Industrial Archeology* 24, no. 1 (1998), 19.

5 *Lowell Sun*, September 15, 1909.

6 *Lowell Sun*, September 15 and 16, 1909.

7 *Lowell Sun*, September 20, 1909.

8 Ibid.

9 *Lowell Sun*, September 22, 1909.

10 *Lowell Sun*, September 23, 1909.

11 *Lowell Sun*, July 16, 1910.

12 *Lowell Courier Citizen*, November 8, 1910.

13 Ibid.; *Annual Report of the Board of Health of the City of Lowell for 1909*, 9; *Annual Report of the Board of Health of the City of Lowell for 1910*, 10–11.

14 Mike Flynn to Jim Butler, December 18, 1969, and Harry Caudill to Jim Butler, December 18, 1969, Folder 1, "Kentucky Conservation Council and ad hoc Committee on Strip-Mining, January 3, 1969–December 31, 1969," Box 24, Harry Caudill Papers.

15 Brock Evans to Cesar Chavez, June 5, 1973, Folder 21, "Environmental Action," Box 3, UFW Work Department Collection.

16 Brian Obach, *Labor and the Environmental Movement: The Quest for Common Ground* (Cambridge, MA: MIT Press, 2004), 11, 33–36.

17 Ibid., 37–38.

Notes to Bibliographic Essay

1 Karl Marx and Frederick Engels, *The German Ideology* (New York: International Publishers, 2001 [1970]), 42, 48.

2 Karl Marx, *Economic and Philosophic Manuscripts of 1844* (New York: International Publishers, 2001 [1964]), 109–14.

3 William Cronon, "Modes of Prophecy and Production: Placing Nature in History," *Journal of American History* 76 (March 1990), 1129; It actually took some time for a book of that sort to appear, and we are only just now starting to witness other scholars following up with additional studies. See Mart A. Stewart, *"What Nature Suffers to Groe": Life, Labor, and Landscape on the Georgia Coast, 1680–1920* (Athens: University of Georgia Press, 2002 [1996]).

4 Alan Taylor, "Unnatural Inequalities: Social and Environmental Histories," *Environmental History* 1 (October 1996), 7, 9–11; See William Cronon, *Changes in the Land: Indians, Colonists, and the Ecology of New England* (New York: Hill and Wang, 1983), John Mack Faragher, *Sugar Creek: Life on the Illinois Prairie* (New Haven, CT: Yale University Press, 1986), Theodore Steinberg, *Nature Incorporated: Industrialization and the Waters of New England* (New York: Cambridge University Press, 1991), Arthur McEvoy, *The Fisherman's Problem: Ecology and Law in the California Fisheries, 1850–1980* (New York: Cambridge University Press, 1986).

5 Richard White, "'Are You an Environmentalist or Do You Work for a Living?': Work and Nature," in William Cronon, ed., *Uncommon Ground: Rethinking the Human Place in Nature* (New York: Norton, 1996), 182.

6 Gottlieb, *Forcing the Spring*, 7.

7 Schwab, *Deeper Shades of Green*.

8 Andrew Hurley, *Environmental Inequalities: Class, Race, and Industrial Pollution in Gary, Indiana, 1945–1980* (Chapel Hill: University of North Carolina Press, 1995), xiv, 104, 137.

9 Pulido, *Environmentalism and Economic Justice*, xv, xviii.

10 Gordon, "Poisons in the Fields, 51–77; Gordon, "'Shell No!'" 461, 478–79.

11 Scott Dewey, "Working for the Environment, 46–47.

12 Chad Montrie, "Expedient Environmentalism: Opposition to Coal Surface Mining in Appalachia and the United Mine Workers of America, 1945–1977," *Environmental History* 5 (January 2000), 75–98.

13 Louis Warren, *The Hunter's Game: Poachers and Conservationists in Twentieth-Century America* (New Haven, CT: Yale University Press, 1997), 11.

14 Jacoby, *Crimes Against Nature*, 24.

15 Benjamin Heber Johnson, "Conservation, Subsistence, and Class at the Birth of Superior National Forest," *Environmental History* 4 (January 1999), 81.

16 Christopher Sellers, *Hazards of the Job: From Industrial Disease to Environmental Science* (Chapel Hill: University of North Carolina Press, 1997), 2.

17 Cumbler, *Reasonable Use*, 185.

18 Montrie, *To Save the Land and People*.

19 Lawrence Lipin, *Workers and the Wild: Conservation, Consumerism, and Labor in Oregon, 1910–1930* (Urbana: University of Illinois Press, 2007).

20 Les Leopold, *The Man Who Hated Work and Loved Labor: The Life and Times of Tony Mazzocchi* (White River Junction, Vermont: Chelsea Green, 2007), 246.

21 Montrie, *Making a Living*.

22 Maher, *Nature's New Deal*, 10.

23 Blum, *Love Canal Revisited*, 4.

Select Bibliography

Blum, Elizabeth D. *Love Canal Revisited: Race, Class, and Gender in Environmental Activism*. Lawrence: University Press of Kansas, 2008.

Boyle, Kevin. *The UAW and the Heyday of American Liberalism, 1945–1968*. Ithaca, NY: Cornell University Press, 1995.

Cohen, G.A. *Karl Marx's Theory of History: A Defence*. Princeton, NJ: Princeton University Press, 2000.

Cole, Olen, Jr. *The African American Experience in the Civilian Conservation Corps*. Gainesville: University Press of Florida, 1999.

Cornebise, Alfred E. *The CCC Chronicles: Camp Newspapers of the Civilian Conservation Corps, 1933–1942*. Jefferson, NC: McFarland, 2004.

Cumbler, John. *Reasonable Use: The People, Environment, and the State, New England 1790–1930*. New York: Oxford University Press, 2001.

Cutler, Jonathan. *Labor's Time: Shorter Hours, the UAW, and the Struggle for American Unionism*. Philadelphia, PA: Temple University Press, 2004.

Derickson, Alan. *Black Lung: Anatomy of a Public Health Disaster*. Ithaca, NY: Cornell University Press, 1998.

Dewey, Scott. *Don't Breathe the Air: Air Pollution and U.S. Environmental Politics, 1945–1970*. College Station: Texas A&M University Press, 2000.

Donohue, Brian. *The Great Meadow: Farmers and the Land in Colonial New England*. New Haven, CT: Yale University Press, 2004.

Draves, David. *Builder of Men: Life in C.C.C. Camps of New Hampshire*. Portsmouth, NH: Peter E. Randall, 1992.

Dublin, Thomas, ed. *Farm to Factory: Women's Letters, 1830–1860*. New York: Columbia University Press, 1981.

Dublin, Thomas, *Women at Work: The Transformation of Work and Community in Lowell, Massachusetts, 1826–1860*. New York: Columbia University Press, 1979.

Edid, Maralyn. *Farm Labor Organizing: Trends & Prospects*. Ithaca, NY: ILR Press, 1994.

Estabrook, Thomas. *Labor-Environmental Coalitions: Lessons from a Louisiana Petrochemical Region.* Amityville, NY: Baywood, 2007.

Gottlieb, Robert. *Forcing the Spring: The Transformation of the American Environmental Movement.* Washington, DC: Island Press, 1993.

Hinton, Wayne, and Elizabeth Green. *With Picks, Shovels, and Hope: The CCC and Its Legacy on the Colorado Plateau.* Missoula, MT: Mountain Press, 2008.

Hurley, Andrew. *Environmental Inequalities: Class, Race, and Industrial Pollution in* Gary, Indiana, 1945–1980. Chapel Hill: University of North Carolina Press, 1995.

Jacoby, Karl. *Crimes against Nature: Squatters, Poachers, Thieves, and the Hidden History of American Conservation.* Berkeley: University of California Press, 2001.

Jenkins, J., Craig. *The Politics of Insurgency: The Farm Worker Movement in the 1960s.* New York: Columbia University Press, 1985.

Judd, Richard. *Common Lands, Common People: The Origins of Conservation in Northern New England.* Cambridge, MA: Harvard University Press, 1997.

Kiefer, E., Kay, and Paul E. Fellows. *Hobnail Boots and Khaki Suits: A Brief Look at the Great Depression and the Civilian Conservation Corps as Seen through the Eyes of Those Who Were There.* Chicago: Adams Press, 1983.

Kolvet, Renee Corona, and Victoria Ford. *The Civilian Conservation Corps in Nevada: From Boys to Men.* Reno and Las Vegas: University of Nevada Press, 2006.

Leavitt, Judith Walzer. *The Healthiest City: Milwaukee and the Politics of Health Reform.* Princeton, NJ: Princeton University Press, 1982.

Leopold, Les. *The Man Who Hated Work and Loved Labor.* White River Junction, VT: Chelsea Green, 2007.

Lichtenstein, Nelson. *Walter Reuther: The Most Dangerous Man in Detroit.* Urbana: University of Illinois Press, 1995.

Lipin, Lawrence. *Workers and the Wild: Conservation, Consumerism, and Labor in Oregon, 1910–1930.* Urbana: University of Illinois Press, 2007.

Maher, Neil. *Nature's New Deal: The Civilian Conservation Corps and the Roots of the American Environmental Movement.* New York: Oxford University Press, 2008.

Marks, Stuart A. *Southern Hunting in Black and White: Nature, History, and Ritual in a Carolina Community.* Princeton, NJ: Princeton University Press, 1991.

Marx, Karl. *Capital: A Critique of Political Economy, Vol. 1.* New York: International Publishers, 1967.

Marx, Karl. *A Contribution to the Critique of Political Economy*. New York: International Publishers, 1970.

Marx, Karl. *Pre-Capitalist Economic Formations*. New York: International Publishers, 2000.

Marx, Karl, and Frederick Engels. *The German Ideology*. New York: International Publishers, 2001.

McEvoy, Arthur. *The Fisherman's Problem: Ecology and Law in the California Fisheries, 1850–1980*. Cambridge, UK: Cambridge University Press, 1986.

McGurty, Eileen. *Transforming Environmentalism: Warren County, PCBs, and the Origins of the Environmental Justice Movement*. New Brunswick, NJ: Rutgers University Press, 2007.

McWilliams, Carey. *Factories in the Field: The Story of Migratory Farm Labor in California*. Santa Barbara, CA: Peregrine, 1971.

Meister, Dick, and Anne Loftis. *A Long Time Coming: The Struggle to Unionize America's Farm Workers*. New York: Macmillan, 1977.

Mercier, Laura. *Labor, Community, and Culture in Montana's Smelter City*. Urbana: University of Illinois Press, 2001.

Meyer, Stephen. *The Five Dollar Day: Labor Management and Social Control in the Ford Motor Company, 1908–1921*. Albany: State University of New York Press, 1981.

Minchin, Timothy. *Forging a Common Bond: Labor Activism during the BASF Lockout*. Gainesville: University Press of Florida, 2003.

Montrie, Chad. *Making a Living: Work and Environment in the United States*. Chapel Hill: University of North Carolina Press, 2008.

Montrie, Chad. *To Save the Land and People: A History of Opposition to Surface Coal Mining in Appalachia*. Chapel Hill: University of North Carolina Press, 2003.

Morse, Kathryn. *The Nature of Gold: An Environmental History of the Klondike Gold Rush*. Seattle: University of Washington Press, 2003.

Nolte, M., Chester, ed. *Civilian Conservation Corps: The Way We Remember It, 1933–1942: Personal Stories of Life in the CCC*. Paducah, KY: Turner, 1990.

Obach, Brian. *Labor and the Environmental Movement: The Quest for Common Ground*. Cambridge, MA: MIT Press, 2004.

Paris, Leslie. *Children's Nature: The Rise of the American Summer Camp*. New York: New York University Press, 2008.

Phillips, Sarah. *This Land, This Nation: Conservation, Rural America, and the New Deal*. New York: Cambridge University Press, 2007.

Proctor, Nicolas W. *Bathed in Bloood: Hunting and Mastery in the Old South*. Charlottesville: University Press of Virginia, 2002.

Pulido, Laura. *Environmentalism and Economic Justice.* Tucson: University of Arizona Press, 1996.

Rosner, David, and Gerald Markowitz. *Deadly Dust: Silicosis and the Politics of Occupational Disease in Twentieth-Century America.* Princeton, NJ: Princeton University Press, 1991.

Russell, Howard S. *A Long Deep Furrow: Three Centuries of Farming in New England.* Hanover, NH: University Press of New England, 1976.

Ryan, J.C. *The CCC and Me.* Duluth, MN: J.C. Ryan, 1987.

Sackman, Douglas Cazaux. *Orange Empire: California and the Fruits of Eden.* Berkeley: University of California Press, 2005.

Schwab, Jim. *Deeper Shades of Green: The Rise of Blue-Collar and Minority Environmentalism in America.* San Francisco: Sierra Club Books, 1994.

Sellers, Christopher. *Hazards of the Job: From Industrial Disease to Environmental Science.* Chapel Hill: University of North Carolina Press, 1997.

Slayton, Robert A. *Back of the Yards: The Making of a Local Democracy.* Chicago: University of Chicago Press, 1986.

Smith, Barbara Ellen. *Digging Our Own Graves: Coal Miners and the Struggle over Black Lung Disease.* Philadelphia, PA: Temple University Press, 1987.

Speakman, Joseph. *At Work in Penn's Woods: The Civilian Conservation Corps in Pennsylvania.* University Park: Pennsylvania State University Press, 2006.

Steinberg, Theodore. *Nature Incorporated: Industrialization and the Waters of New England.* Amherst: University of Massachusetts Press, 1991.

Sutter, Paul S. *Driven Wild: How the Fight against Automobiles Launched the Modern Wilderness Movement.* Seattle and London: University of Washington Press, 2002.

Thorton, Tamara Plakins. *Cultivating Gentlemen: The Meaning of Country Life among the Boston Elite, 1785–1860.* New Haven, CT: Yale University Press, 1989.

Wagner, Thomas E., and Phillip J. Obermiller. *African American Miners and Migrants: The Eastern Kentucky Social Club.* Chicago: University of Illinois Press, 2004.

Warren, Louis. *The Hunter's Game: Poachers and Conservationists in Twentieth-Century America.* New Haven, CT: Yale University Press, 1997.

Washington, Sylvia Hood. *Packing Them In: An Archaeology of Environmental Racism in Chicago, 1865–1954.* Lanham, MD: Lexington Books, 2004.

Wilson, Howard. *Mary McDowell: Neighbor.* Chicago: University of Chicago Press, 1928.

Index